W9-ATG-437

THE UNITED STATES
AND THE DEVELOPMENT
OF THE PUERTO RICAN
STATUS QUESTION
1936-1968

THE UNITED STATES AND THE DEVELOPMENT OF THE PUERTO RICAN STATUS QUESTION 1936-1968

by Surendra Bhana

THE UNIVERSITY PRESS OF KANSAS
Lawrence, Manhattan, Wichita

© Copyright 1975 by The University Press of Kansas
Printed in the United States of America

Library of Congress Cataloging in Publication Data

Bhana, Surendra, 1939–
    The United States and the development of the Puerto
Rican status question, 1936–1968.

    A revision of the author's thesis, University of
Kansas.
    Bibliography: p.
    1. Puerto Rico—Politics and government—1898–1952.
2. Puerto Rico—Politics and government—1952–
3. United States—Relations (general) with Puerto Rico.
4. Puerto Rico—Relations (general) with the United
States. I. Title.
F1975.B45   1975   320.9'7295'05   74–7077
ISBN 0–7006–0126–0

To

DON McCOY

friend and mentor

Acknowledgments

The question of Puerto Rican status has never ceased to be debated by the people of the Caribbean island since it was acquired by the United States in 1898. Why, then, begin the study in 1936? The date represents the beginnings of a significant departure in the debate. The murder of Col. E. Francis Riggs, the Tydings independence bill, and the split in the Liberal party created conditions for the birth of the *Partido Popular Democrático,* the party of Luis Muñoz Marín that was to deviate from the "either independence or statehood" approach and to implement the Commonwealth. The study traces the development of the new status up to 1968.

Puerto Rico achieved rapid progress in its political autonomy within the scope of the study. The major portion of the book is devoted to its discussion. The formulation and implementation of the Commonwealth status, however, is highlighted, for it is within this brilliant and unique experiment in federalism that the Puerto Ricans have attempted to accommodate their economic needs and wants and to satisfy their sense of *dignidad.* Its great merit, of course, is that it is not irrevocable. If in the future Puerto Ricans should decide upon some other form of status arrangement, they can draw upon the fruits of past debate on the question.

I enjoyed sharing in the debate, thanks to Donald R. McCoy, who originally suggested the study of the topic. My debt to Professor McCoy extends beyond that, however. He wisely guided me in the original research, and later advised in the revision and expansion of the work.

Thanks are expressed to the Harry S. Truman Library Institute for a grant-in-aid and to the Graduate School of the University of Kansas for travel grants for the original study.

The assistance rendered by the staff of the various libraries and archives is gratefully acknowledged: the Franklin D. Roosevelt Library, the Harry S. Truman Library (especially Messrs. Philip D. Lagerquist and Ervin Mueller), the Library of Congress, the National Archives, the Nebraska State Historical Society, the Washington National Records Center, and the Western Historical Manuscript Collection at Columbia, Missouri.

Mr. Oscar L. Chapman and Mr. Jasper C. Bell kindly gave me their consent for the use of their private papers.

I am deeply indebted to the following persons for their comments, criticism, and information on selected parts of the original manuscript: Dr. Antonio Fernós-Isern, who perused chapters 6, 7, 8, 9, and 11; Mr. Abe Fortas, who read chapter 4; Mr. Miguel García Méndez, who studied chapters 7, 8, 9, and 11; Mr. Vincente Geigel Polanco, who examined chapters 5, 7, 8, 9, and 11; and Mr. Muñoz Marín, who commented briefly on parts of the introduction. Their comments and criticisms have considerably improved the book's balance and perspective.

Dr. Frank K. Haszard kindly supplied me with statistics compiled by the Office of Economic and Financial Research in the Puerto Rican Department of Treasury. His comments on the Puerto Rican economy have been much appreciated.

Sincere thanks are expressed to Mr. Vic Comras of the United States Consulate in Durban and to Mr. Gavin Maasdorp of the University of Natal for kindly reading chapter 10 and offering useful suggestions.

Numerous persons have helped in the research and preparation of the manuscript, to whom I express gratitude. Among them are Carol Buehrens, John Dagené, Zubaida Jeewa, friends, and members of my family.

Finally, I owe to my wife, Kala, more gratitude than even she is willing to acknowledge. Her patience and forbearance I have frequently taxed to the limit.

viii

Contents

Setting the Scene

The twin issues of governmental structures and autonomy became prominent in insular politics long before Puerto Rico was acquired by the United States in the Spanish-American War of 1898. Puerto Rican liberals advanced plans for political and administrative reform on several occasions after 1815. The success and permanence of such plans rested upon the political fortunes of liberal elements in Spain. On at least three occasions when the liberals were in power in Spain, for instance, Spain promised to restore the Provincial Assembly and elective town councils. Again in 1868, the Puerto Ricans won the right to nominate local deputies to the national parliament in Spain. The concessions were not permanent because they were made by Madrid under one kind of pressure or another, and because the liberals by whom they were made lost political ground in Spain. Puerto Rico's greatest success came in November, 1897, when the liberal ministry in Madrid, fearing open rebellion such as the one then raging in Cuba, granted the island the Charter of Autonomy. The charter gave Puerto Rico a quasi-dominion status and retained insular representation in the Cortes. It provided for a bicameral insular legislature in which one of the Houses was partially elective and the other was completely elective.[1]

1

The question as to whether Puerto Rico's newly acquired quasi-dominion status would have become a lasting arrangement in the relationship between the island and Spain became academic as events interrupted its progress. The island's first assembly under the charter had barely started operating when some eight months later war broke out between Spain and the United States. American troops landed in Puerto Rico in August, 1898, and Spain ceded to the United States sovereign and proprietary rights over the island. The charter was of no practical consequence, as the United States consolidated its sovereignty by military rule in the next two years.[2]

Puerto Rico's status and autonomy assumed new dimensions under United States jurisdiction. The Colossus of the North was economically powerful and geographically close. Puerto Ricans by and large welcomed the opportunity to associate with a powerful neighbor and hoped to share in its prosperity. They were fully aware that their 3500-square-mile Caribbean island in the Greater Antilles lacked adequate natural resources, and whatever economic benefits that might accrue as a result of this new relationship would afford many the opportunity to escape grinding poverty. But they were also aware that the United States was culturally and politically Anglo-Saxon and that any kind of continued association with the mainland would require them to adjust to and accommodate the political and cultural traditions and values of the continental power. This, in short, has been the source of the unending debate on the issue of political status: how to strike a happy balance between Puerto Rico's economic needs, which could be filled through uninterrupted association with the United States, and the cultural divergence between the mainland and the island.[3]

Perhaps this question would never have been drawn out in the perennial debate that has wrought "spiritual anguish" among the Puerto Ricans, according to Luis Muñoz Marín, had the Congress of the United States been certain as to what Puerto Rico's eventual fate was going to be. But Congress was hesitant from the very beginning. This was manifested in the position it took that the territory of Puerto Rico was different from other United States territories that were intended for eventual statehood. Nor was it indicated whether Puerto Rico should some day be permitted to be an independent state. Congress' ambiguity was further reinforced by Supreme Court decisions in a series of insular cases. The Supreme Court differentiated in some fancy judicial double-talk between "incorporated territories" intended for eventual statehood and "unincorporated territories" not intended for such a status. Puerto Rico, it declared, was an "unincorporated territory." In effect, what the Supreme Court decision meant was that the eventual fate of Puerto Rico must be decided by Congress.[4]

It was in this state of mind that Congress proceeded to grant a measure of autonomy to Puerto Rico and to impose a unique constitutional arrangement upon the island. The Foraker Act of 1900 permitted the people of Puerto Rico to elect a House of Delegates, but the essential powers of administration were reserved in an appointed executive. The act also provided for a limited application of a tariff schedule. Seventeen years later, Congress acted once more on Puerto Rico. The Jones Act of 1917 (also known as the Organic Act of 1917) provided for a bicameral legislature, and the powers of the appointed governor were somewhat restricted as he was required to seek the advice and consent of the insular Senate in the appointment of the heads of some of the executive departments. But the president continued to fill posts such as the commissioner of education, the auditor, the attorney general, and judges of the Supreme Court of Puerto Rico. Besides, he retained veto power over all insular legislation. In some respects, the Spanish Charter of Autonomy of 1897 promised more. But the feature of the act that continued to treat the island in a unique constitutional arrangement was the provision that extended United States citizenship to the people of Puerto Rico without their having to pay federal taxes. While this aspect pleased the advocates of statehood in the island, it did not signify Congress' intentions as to what Puerto Rico's eventual fate was going to be.[5]

Congress' unwillingness to clarify the status issue turned it gradually into what Gordon K. Lewis has called a "magnificent obsession."[6] The platforms of the various political parties were either for statehood or independence. The degree of commitment to these goals, however, was diluted, for it was common for a party favoring one goal to switch its loyalties to another. Indeed, to the extent that the Puerto Ricans are responsible for this prolonged debate, there has never been a strong enough movement for independence in Puerto Rico to which Congress might react. The Nationalist party was so small in numbers that both the United States and other Puerto Rican parties could disregard it as being unrepresentative of majority will. The same was true of other thorough-going *independentista* groups.

A lack of clear preference of status position on the part of the Puerto Ricans added to their frustration and feeling of uncertainty and pervaded insular politics to the point of diverting the island's attention from the most pressing problem of Puerto Rico, namely, the low standard of living of most of its inhabitants. This fact has persuaded at least two historians to label the status debate as "sterile," "futile," and "needless frustration."[7] However useless this debate might seem in terms of desirable goals, its very prevalence represented a force of considerable importance in the lives of Puerto Ricans and denoted a need constantly nagging to be fulfilled.

This study emphasizes the attempts of Luis Muñoz Marín to define the needs of the Puerto Rican people and explains the way in which he set out to fulfill them. He gradually abandoned independence as a practical goal for Puerto Rico and embarked instead upon the road of autonomy. This approach harmonized well with Puerto Rico's economic needs, he argued. In effect, what he told his compatriots was that Puerto Rico could not afford to abandon the United States. They largely agreed, and he launched a bold and innovative economic program called "Operation Bootstrap." The program strengthened both the economy and the island's ties with the United States.

The approach suited the United States well. The United States recognized the island's strategic value both during and after World War II. Some members of Congress felt that Puerto Rico as a somewhat Americanized Latin American entity might serve a useful function in the dialogue necessary between the United States and Latin America. Others felt a patronizing concern for conditions on the island, believing that the United States should not abandon those responsibilities that it implicitly undertook to fulfill when it acquired Puerto Rico in 1898. Congress and the administration, always concerned as to what Puerto Ricans might do with self-government, precipitate or otherwise, decided to extend the island autonomy in progressive doses: the appointment of a native Puerto Rican as governor in 1946, the passage of the Elective Governor's Act in 1947, and the enactment of Public Law 600 in 1950 to permit the islanders to write their own constitution. By June, 1952, none of the posts in Puerto Rican internal government was appointive. The administration and Congress were considerably persuaded in their progressive attitude toward Puerto Rican self-government by the talents of the remarkable Puerto Rican Muñoz Marín.

Even though Muñoz Marín succeeded in winning for Puerto Rico a great amount of autonomy in 1952, the political agitation that surrounded the status issue continued. The Puerto Rican leader claimed the Commonwealth to be more than what it really was. To him it was voluntary association with the United States, with features that could be the basis of a permanent relationship between the island and the mainland. It was really, however, a unique constitutional arrangement growing from the earlier pattern established by the Foraker Act and the Jones Act, with one crucially important feature unchanged—namely, Congress had final say in matters concerning Puerto Rico. This is what he discovered in 1959 and thereafter when he attempted to get Congress to enhance the Commonwealth status. Muñoz Marín's failure in 1959 reopened the status controversy with much of its old fury. It will likely continue at least until Puerto Rico becomes either a state or an independent country, or finds a way to refine the Commonwealth status into a completely acceptable middle way.

Throughout this study, the word "autonomy" is used to mean political freedom for Puerto Ricans in their internal affairs. The United States can intervene if conditions warrant such a drastic step. For instance, should civil disturbances in Puerto Rico endanger its relations with its Caribbean neighbors or with the United States itself, Washington would possibly intervene in accordance with its constitutional responsibility over the island's foreign affairs and its defense. Or, as in legal matters involving mainland citizens, the United States Supreme Court has the power of final arbitrament.

The word "status" is a term of general description of the possible relationships between United States and Puerto Rico. The three likely solutions over which the debate has taken place are "independence," "statehood," and some dominion-like status. The Commonwealth concept has dominion-like but unique features, and is likely not the final solution. "Autonomy" overlaps all three terms of description. However, as it is used here, "autonomy" does not mean "independence," since its advocates, and indeed Puerto Ricans generally, have always understood that it implied limited political freedom.

The two terms "autonomy" and "status" were separated for

practical political purposes at the start of the Truman administration, when the issue of Puerto Rico's permanent relationship with the United States appeared to be an insolvable problem. It was decided then to grant "autonomy" first and to proceed to the settlement of the "status" question on a permanent basis later when conditions made it possible. "Autonomy" came to the Puerto Ricans in large, progressive doses. The Commonwealth arrangement gave considerable political freedom to the Puerto Ricans; but when in 1959 and thereafter attempts were made to define more clearly specific areas of authority as belonging to Puerto Rico or the United States, it was realized that "autonomy" was merely an inseparable part of the larger question of "status."

CHAPTER ONE

Politics in Puerto Rico
and the Tydings Bill of 1936

There were four political parties in Puerto Rico in 1936, the year in which Senator Millard E. Tydings of Maryland, Democratic chairman of the Senate Committee on Territories and Insular Affairs, introduced an independence bill in Congress. They were not separated by deep, divisive ideological differences, nor by differentiable programs and policies. This was generally true of all political parties, ever since the island became an American possession in 1898. Personalities and patronage proved to be more important factors in party organizations. Even the status question, the only issue over which the party leadership adopted definite positions, aroused "less than consistent zeal" among its supporters.[1]

In 1936 the parties that were in control of the island legislature and the important post of resident commissioner were the Union Republican and the Socialist. The two had fused in 1924 to form the Coalition, as the group was generally called. The Union Republicans by and large drew their leadership from the business and professional classes,[2] and their policies reflected the interests of these classes.[3] The party was organized in 1899, and commanded a majority in the legislature until 1904. It remained out of power for nearly three decades as dissidents left its ranks to join other political groups. In the 1920s, for instance, many

Union Republicans transferred their loyalties to the Union party. It was partly because of this that the party leadership combined its forces with the Socialist party in 1924, an arrangement largely born out of a desire to control the legislature of the island. The Coalition had to wait until 1932, when under the leadership of its Union Republican leader, Rafael Martínez Nadal, it secured a majority in the Puerto Rican legislature. The group hung on to the majority until 1940, when it was defeated by the newly formed *Partido Popular Democrático* (PPD).[4] The Union Republican party favored the continued presence of United States jurisdiction in Puerto Rico, but it was not firmly committed to statehood in 1936.[5]

The Socialist party was founded by Santiago Iglesias in 1915 as a political extension of his Free Federation of Labor. The party had little to do with Marxism. Its leader took his cue from Samuel Gompers, the head of the American Federation of Labor on the mainland, as to what its political role should be. Iglesias had suffered persecution at the hands of the Spanish authorities for his unionist activities and had zealously welcomed the United States in 1898 as a future guarantor of union rights. The Socialist leader continued to exercise powerful influence over party affairs until his death in 1940. Indeed, his expedient and undoctrinaire approach to politics left its imprint on the party's course. In 1924 he led his followers into a political merger with the Union Republicans, and was happy to allow Martínez Nadal to play the dominant role as chief of the Coalition. In 1932 when the Coalition won the elections, Iglesias was elected as resident commissioner in Washington for four years. The Coalition weathered mild and serious crises over issues such as labor strikes, largely due to the political finesse of Iglesias.[6] The Socialist party took no hard position on the question of the island's political status. Both statehood and independence were equally acceptable, although Iglesias personally leaned towards statehood because of his strong pro-United States sentiments.[7]

The third large political group formed the Liberal party. Its roots can be traced to the Union party, which was founded in 1904 by a highly respected fighter for the political freedom for the island, Luis Muñoz Rivera. He fairly dominated insular politics until his death in 1917, when Antonio Barceló, another seasoned politician, took over the leadership of the party. Barceló kept his group in power in the 1920s by a series of political combinations.

Shortly after the 1928 elections, however, the political alliance he had forged with dissident elements of the Union Republican party, known as the *Alianza,* began to come apart. The veteran politician attempted to smooth out differences within the *Alianza* without success. He tried to revive the Union party in the hope of reasserting his leadership, but was blocked in doing so by the maneuverings of his opponents. Forced to dissolve the *Alianza,* he organized the Liberal party in 1929.[8]

At the time the new party was organized Barceló stated that its goal was not independence but autonomy in local matters. The party's platform of March 13, 1932, however, suggests that his position had changed markedly. The plank dealing with status declared that the party's purpose was "to demand the immediate recognition of the sovereignty of Puerto Rico." In a letter to President-elect Franklin D. Roosevelt on December 21, 1932, Barceló reasoned that Puerto Rico's independence would help meet the island's "moral and material" needs.[9]

The party's position on status was elaborated by Muñoz Marín, son of Muñoz Rivera, who had been persuaded to run as senator-at-large in 1932. As editor of *La Democracia* (San Juan), Muñoz Marín examined the economic implications of the Liberal party's independence plank with special reference to sugar production and United States tariff laws. He pointed out in a series of three articles how the tariff laws of the United States had resulted in the abnormal growth of sugar production at the expense of a diversified agricultural economy. Independence, he asserted, would correct this imbalance. He insisted, however, that any independence program would of necessity have to include a period of transition. Any abrupt changes would seriously dislocate the Puerto Rican economy. The young editor offered no details except to say that the coffee industry might be revived, and that the transition period should be "under the sovereignty of Puerto Rico."[10]

In the 1932 elections the Liberal party polled 170,168 votes, which, however, were not sufficient to beat the combined votes of 208,232 polled by the Union Republican (110,794) and the Socialist (97,438) parties.[11] The Coalition secured the legislative majority and therefore looked forward to wielding political patronage in the next four years.

The Nationalist party, founded in 1920, constituted the fourth political group. Small in numbers, but fanatical in conviction, the party regulars single-mindedly pursued the goal of total and immediate independence. Their leader was Pedro Albizu Campos, trained at Harvard Law School as a lawyer, who because of his charisma and compelling eloquence quickly rose to leadership of the party in 1930, a few years after he had joined it. The dark-skinned Albizu Campos had encountered racial discrimination when he enlisted in the United States Army during World War I, an experience over which he harbored bitter thoughts and which allegedly expressed itself in the party's violently anti-United States stance.[12] Little is said about his views on government and economics in official documents and published material. He did maintain contact with other leftist groups in Latin America. Indeed, he married Laura Meneses, who was a member of Peru's anti-United States group, the *Alianza Popular Revolucionaria Americana* (APRA).[13]

Until 1932 the Nationalist party had made no serious attempt to participate in insular elections. The party relied heavily on sensational tactics. In 1930, for instance, the party attempted to sell bonds in order to turn the island into a republic. What success, if any, this and later attempts had is not known. The radical group had more success in another incident involving a letter written by a Dr. Cornelius Rhoads, who was connected with the Rockefeller Foundation. The physician, while practicing on the island, suggested a campaign to exterminate the islanders. The Nationalists capitalized on the letter and reaped considerable publicity.[14]

In yet another sensation-seeking action, Albizu Campos and a group of his followers disrupted a Liberal convention in March, 1932, and forced Barceló to share the floor with the fiery leader. The evening ended amicably enough with the two leaders promising each other cooperation on matters of mutual interest. Differences, however, dissipated whatever warmth there had been between the two groups in the next few months. At a huge Nationalist rally on July 9, 1932, the radical harangued his audience for two-and-a-half hours, denouncing Barceló and others as traitors and accusing Governor Blanton Winship of repression against Nationalist supporters. Then, in words which were going to haunt him four years later, he vowed that if any Nationalist lost his life at police hands, the chief of insular police would pay for it with his own.[15]

Under a Puerto Rican electoral law, new parties were required to prove that they had support of at least 10 percent of the total votes of the previous election. The Nationalists needed about 24,000 signatures to get on the ballots in 1932. The signatures, ironically, were secured by the Union Republican party, a political group that had little in common with the Nationalist party. The Union Republican party helped because it desired to split the votes of the Liberal party. As it turned out, the Nationalist party polled in 1932 a mere 5,257 votes (the vote for Albizu Campos personally was 11,634), which was less than 2 percent of the total votes polled.[16]

Their weak showing at the polls did not discourage many Nationalists from continuing with the politics of agitation. One such occasion before 1936 ended in violence and tragedy. In October, Albizu Campos directed a virulent attack upon university students for not being active in the independence movement. His reference to the boys as "sissies" and to the girls as "drunkards" stung the students into organizing a protest meeting on October 24, 1935. The police feared trouble and posted men outside the gates. In the altercations that followed, three of the Nationalists were shot dead, the fourth was seriously wounded, and a policeman was injured.[17] Albizu Campos delivered a long funeral oration for his three fallen compatriots, accused the governor of seeking to eliminate all Nationalists, and promised to trade the life of a continental for every Nationalist killed.[18]

Under the provisions of the Organic Act of 1917, the three major parties[19] of Puerto Rico could compete electorally for the bicameral legislature of nineteen Senate seats, and thirty-nine House seats, in addition to the important post of resident commissioner in Washington.[20] The political group that commanded a majority in the insular legislature and selected one of its own members to be resident commissioner had some leverage with the United States—appointed representative on the island, the governor. The governor was empowered to appoint the executive heads of the Interior, Agriculture and Labor, and Health departments. The president named persons to fill the remaining posts: attorney general, commissioner of education, the auditor, and the justices of the Puerto Rican Supreme Court, positions which were regarded as too important to be left to the governor. As a further check on the insular legislature, the president possessed the power of ultimate veto over insular legislation,[21] although this prerogative was seldom used.

This arrangement was clearly designed to insulate the executive branch from popular legislative supervision, as Gordon K. Lewis points out.[22] The governor had in effect assumed many of the powers of public policies normally exercised by the popularly elected segments of the government in a typically noncolonial situation.[23] Outside of creating confusion as to the precise roles of the executive and legislative branches in Puerto Rico, this arrangement placed great store on good understanding and relationship between the party controlling the legislature and the appointed governor. But should the governor cooperate too closely with the party in power, he was sure to invite charges of partiality by the political group or groups that did not control the insular legislature. This is what did happen, as it will be seen later in the chapter, when Governor Robert H. Gore insisted on offering posts to the Coalition in 1933, excluding Liberals from patronage because of their supposed anti-Americanism.[24] Then too, other federal officials in charge of Puerto Rican affairs did not always work through the governor because they felt that one or both were not in sympathy with the general administration policy. Congressional committees in charge of the island also desired to make their influence felt in the administration of the Caribbean possession. Under these conditions, a smooth coordination of the various governmental agencies was impossible.

The political system was severely tried in the 1930s when the island's economic and social problems reached new heights of severity. Puerto Rico had suffered two devastating hurricanes, in 1928 and 1932. These natural disasters helped to turn scholars' attention to the island's economic plight. Two studies that were to have considerable influence on administrators were the Brookings Institution study by Victor S. Clark, et al., *Puerto Rico and Its Problems*,[25] and Justine and Bailey Diffie's *Puerto Rico: A Broken Pledge*.[26] At the root of Puerto Rico's problems, the studies pointed out, was the dominance of its economy by the sugar industry, and its attendant evils of monocultural trends. Four absentee sugar corporations held thousands of acres of land in excess of the legal 500-acre limit; they yielded large profits for the corporations, but there was not the corresponding increase in real wages for their laborers. The scholars did not agree on all aspects, but they did spotlight the need for an urgent and determined effort to rehabilitate the lopsided economy of the over-populated island.

The Roosevelt administration recognized that programs of economic rehabilitation would require improved coordination and a close watch on Puerto Rican affairs. This concern translated itself into President Roosevelt's transfer of the island's administration from the Department of War to that of the Interior on March 8, 1934, by Executive Order No. 6726.[27] Two months later the president created in the Interior department the Division of Territories and Insular Possessions (DTIP). In October, 1934, Dr. Ernest Gruening of Maine, a liberal well versed in Latin American affairs, was appointed as its first director. He was responsible for the administration of Alaska, Hawaii, Puerto Rico, and the Virgin Islands.[28] On the occasion of naming Dr. Gruening as the director, Assistant Secretary of the Interior Oscar L. Chapman defined the agency's immediate goals. It was the administration's policy, Chapman declared, to encourage "political and economic autonomy" in the territories. He stressed, however, that the more compelling need was economic rehabilitation, especially in Puerto Rico and the Virgin Islands. "The people cannot be self-sufficient," he said, "in either living or government without the discovery of new methods and new resources." The sugar corporations, he charged, had made profits but had not benefited the island as a whole. Diversifying the territory's economy was an answer, and the way this could be done was by reviving the coffee industry and encouraging the growth of the citrus fruit industry. The assistant secretary left no doubt that political autonomy was not his overriding concern at the time.[29]

The administrative reorganization did not eliminate the friction in the working of the political system. If anything, the introduction of the new division and its director merely exacerbated the rivalry among the various political groups on the island. The circumstances surrounding the creation and functioning of the Puerto Rican Emergency Relief Administration (PRERA), superseded later by the Puerto Rican Reconstruction Administration (PRRA), will illustrate this.

Before discussing the PRERA and PRRA it is necessary, however, to point out that Governor Gore's brief but stormy term of office had helped the Liberal party to establish closer contact with the White House. Gore, appointed governor in 1933, mainly in payment for his party loyalty, decided that the island's important political posts should go to the Coalition. He passed over Liberals because as advocates of independence they were anti-American, so he maintained. In attempting to displace the commissioner of education, Dr. José Padín, from his cabinet for the commissioner's supposed Liberal sympathies, and in naming a Coalition member to the board of directors of the University of Puerto Rico, he incurred the wrath of the Liberals and the university students, and lost much public support. Worst of all, he lost the confidence of the Roosevelt administration and was forced to retire.[30]

If anybody came out on top in the whole affair it was Liberal Senator Muñoz Marín. As editor of *La Democracia,* he had used his political and literary gift to establish himself as a Liberal leader of considerable rank. More importantly, his association with Ruby Black, a Washington correspondent and a friend of Mrs. Eleanor Roosevelt's, gained him access to the confidence of the first lady and, through her, the president. On November 7, 1933, Muñoz Marín had tea with Mrs. Roosevelt and briefly chatted with the president. They no doubt conversed about economic conditions in Puerto Rico, and about Gore's open partiality. Ruby Black maintains, according to Mathews, that Mrs. Roosevelt was influential in increasing relief funds for the island.[31] Mrs. Roosevelt's own account bears out at least her concern for the island and her reminding the president of its needs.[32]

In the next few years two federal agencies were to show a pro-Liberal attitude. In August, 1933, James Bourne was named the director of the first agency, the PRERA. Bourne was a friend of the president's, and superintendent of canneries of Hill Brothers, Inc., in Puerto Rico.[33] The PRERA began its task with direct relief, but soon expanded it to work relief programs with a view towards future plans of reconstruction.[34] The director hired many Liberals to work on the staff of the PRERA because he felt that the Coalition members were generally opposed to the extension of the New Deal programs on the island, and their presence would hamper the agency's efficiency. In a meeting with Gore, when he was still governor, and Coalition leader Martínez Nadal, Bourne refused to drop Liberal members from his list of employees, a stand in which he received the support of Federal Emergency Relief Administration director Harry Hopkins. Soon thereafter, in November, 1933, the Coalition declared Bourne *persona non grata.*[35] When Blanton Winship became the governor, the Coalition tried through a legislative measure to control the agency. Governor Winship and Dr. Gruening, upon reconsideration, supported the measure. However, because of an administrative mixup in Washington, the governor was called upon to veto the bill.[36]

There had been much talk both on the island and in Washington about instituting a program of rehabilitation to correct many longstanding ills in Puerto Rico. On March 10, 1936, a "Round Table Conference" was organized towards this end. Its twenty-eight participants included the various insular interests and continental representatives. Notable among the continentals were Mrs. Roosevelt, then visiting the island, and Rexford G. Tugwell of the Department of Agriculture. The first lady's presence, the president had argued, would underscore the concern and sincerity of Assistant Secretary Tugwell.[37] The meeting's primary purpose was to air ideas and views concerning reconstruction. One of those to suggest a plan was Dr. Carlos Chardón, whose homestead scheme, later to be the essential features of the Chardón Plan, may have germinated in the minds of Tugwell and his fellow workers.[38]

Soon thereafter, Roosevelt appointed a three-man Puerto Rican Policy Commission under the chairmanship of Dr. Chardón, much to the discomfort of the Coalition. The Commission spent May and June of 1934 in Washington working on its report. The report, more commonly known as the Chardón Plan, envisaged acquiring a certain acreage of productive sugar land and marginal cane land, together with the mill facilities on these lands, to achieve the following: reduce sugar production; diversify agricultural production and grow more food crops; eliminate the land monopoly of sugar corporations; create about 10,000 homesteads with adequate housing and farming facilities; create employment on a permanent basis for about 17,000 men.[39] The plan was not to become public until about a year later.

In May, 1935, President Roosevelt created the Puerto Rican Reconstruction Administration (PRRA), which was to supersede the PRERA. Dr. Gruening was named the director.[40] He now held two posts: as director of PRRA he was responsible to the president; as director of DTIP he was responsible to Secretary of the Interior Harold L. Ickes. Ickes was unhappy that he had not been consulted on the appointment. Furthermore, he hoped that since he did not have supervisory power over PRRA the president would keep a close watch over its activities. The secretary feared a "blowout" in Puerto Rico, and if that should happen both he and the president would be blamed.[41] James Bourne, too, was unhappy because he had not been named PRRA's director. As director of PRERA, Bourne had taken steps to initiate a rehabilitation program in the hope that he would be placed in charge of the whole reconstruction program. The PRERA director was passed over and the agency discontinued about a year later, presumably because of his estrangement with the Coalition group, which had accused him of running the agency independently of the local government and of favoring the Liberals.[42]

Four groups in Puerto Rico, according to Mathews, vied for control of the entire reconstruction program. The first was the sugar *central* interests; the second was the Coalition; third, Governor Blanton Winship and Commissioner Menéndez Ramos; and fourth, the friends of the Chardón Plan and the New Deal, notably Senator Muñoz Marín and Jesús T. Piñero, president of the island's independent sugar growers.[43] The newly appointed Dr. Gruening appeared to favor working with the fourth group. Muñoz Marín had played his cards well when he had secured from the president in December of 1934 a message for the Puerto Rican people. The message had endorsed the Chardón Plan.[44]

The Coalition's worst fears were realized when Gruening appointed Dr. Chardón in June, 1935, as regional administrator of PRRA. When the complete list of appointments became known, the Coalition felt completely excluded. Of the thirteen appointees four were Liberals, two were anti-Coalition, four continental Americans, one Socialist, and two neutrals. Gruening had excluded Coalition members, presumably because of their opposition to the Chardón Plan.[45] Earl Parker Hanson was one of the continental Americans appointed as a planning consultant to the PRRA. He states in his book that Muñoz Marín had so strongly supported the PRRA that he had become very closely identified with the agency's efforts. Or as Hanson put it, "Muñoz *was* the PRRA, to be supported, or opposed as such according to individual orientations."[46]

The Coalition opposed the PRRA, as was to be expected. It was controlled by officials who were Liberal party supporters or sympathizers. Furthermore, the PRRA's policy was to break up the sugar monopoly, and the Interior department had already taken steps to enforce the 500-acre law.[47] The secretary himself had confirmed the administration's intention of breaking up big sugar estates when he visited the island in January, 1936.[48] In a conversation with Luis Ferré, then an industrialist and later the governor of Puerto Rico between 1968 and 1972, Ickes is reported as having said about the sugar industry, "No industry has the right to exist if it lives on the hunger and misery of the masses." Asked whether the economic distress of the island could not be relieved by taxing the industry, the secretary snapped back that a legislature controlled by the sugar men was not likely to impose such taxes.[49]

By 1936, then, the position briefly was as follows: the governor, Blanton Winship, a military man with a conservative background, managed as best he could with an insular legislature dominated by the Coalition group. The Liberals did not particularly like him, as Ickes reflected in his diary, and would just as soon be rid of him.[50] What is significant is that the governor, like the Coalition, had no control over the PRRA, whose director, in working closely with the Liberal party, merely widened the gap between the governor and the Liberals, and added to the confusion of the diffusion of federal power. Dr. Gruening believed that the Liberal party stood closer to the goals of the New Deal. It was generally believed that the party would win in 1936, and the secretary of the Interior seemed to accept the general sentiment.[51] In all this, Muñoz Marín emerged as the doyen of the Liberals, whose status as son of Muñoz Rivera, his good relations with the White House, and his considerable flair for politics and writing were placed at the party's disposal. The Nationalist party remained outside of the squabbles over patronage in deliberate contempt of insular politics, its goals being absolute severance of ties with a country for which it had no love.

The murder of a police chief was to change the political situation greatly. Those who had formerly enjoyed the administration's blessing were soon to fall out of favor, among them Muñoz Marín; the Liberal party suffered a split over the issue of independence, and was likely cheated out of an electoral victory in 1936; a new party was to emerge two years later, which fairly sealed the doom of the Liberal party, all to the great satisfaction of the Coalition. All this occurred because the administration thought the assassination an opportune moment to offer Puerto Rico political independence hastily, unexpectedly, and disingenuously.

On his way home from mass, the insular police chief, Col. E. Francis Riggs, was shot and killed on February 23, 1936, in a plot involving two Nationalist youths, Elías Beauchamp and Hiran Rosado. The two were taken to the police station, where, according to the police, they unexpectedly reached for a rack full of riot guns, and were killed by a fusillade of police bullets.[52] There was no death penalty in Puerto Rico, and to the crowd outside that heard the volley of fire, it appeared like instant retribution.

There were sharp but differing reactions on the island. Governor Winship looked upon it as a matter of law and order, and promised to get tough with those who broke the law.[53] He meant what he said, because about two weeks later he had the federal authorities arrest Albizu Campos and six other Nationalists on charges of conspiring to overthrow the insular government, and apparently had the backing of Secretary Ickes.[54] The earlier utterances of the Nationalist leader had come to haunt him.

The overwhelming majority of Puerto Ricans denounced the Nationalist violence but appeared to draw somewhat different conclusions from it. At least two Puerto Rican newspapers, as reported by the *New York Times,* believed that the events should be viewed from their political perspective and called for an investigation into the police action that resulted in the death of the two youths.[55] Martínez Nadal regarded both incidents as tragedies.[56] In Washington, Resident Commissioner Santiago Iglesias reassured Congress that the police chief's murder should in no way reflect upon the loyalty of the Puerto Rican people, but reminded Congress, with the aid of editorials in leading continental newspapers, of its duty in resolving the island's status question.[57] The Liberal party organ, *La Democracia,* while in no way condoning the murder of Colonel Riggs, believed the killing by the police was indefensible.[58]

Secretary Ickes appeared to be piqued by the islanders' criticism of the administration's handling of the whole affair, and its tardiness over resolving the status question. He threatened to stop further appropriations to the island,[59] with what serious intentions it is not clear. A day later, March 9, 1936, he issued the following statement:

> The people of Puerto Rico have a perfect right within the limits of the Constitution to seek whatever form of government they deem best for themselves. The administra-

tion will give careful and sympathetic consideration to any definite political demand which is demonstrably backed by a majority of the people of Puerto Rico.[60]

The statement foreshadowed the independence bill that was introduced on April 23, 1936, by Senator Tydings. There is no evidence to suggest, however, that the secretary had such a bill in mind when he made the statement. An examination into the background of the bill shows that it originated with Dr. Gruening.

On March 13, 1936, Dr. Gruening dispatched a memorandum to the secretary expressing his willingness to allow Puerto Ricans to decide in the November elections on independence. If the vote should be yes the United States should provide a period of transition to complete surrendering insular responsibility to the islanders. If, on the other hand, the vote was no, the matter should be considered settled "certainly for a generation." He recommended that the legal division in the Interior department be instructed to submit a draft of such a bill to the secretary, the president, and Senator Tydings.[61]

The matter was discussed at the March 18, 1936, cabinet meeting. Ickes reiterated his desire to see the island obtain independence if it should choose it. He doubted, however, whether the bill to be introduced in the present session had any chance of becoming law. That did not matter, he seemed to think, because it was intended to have a "quieting effect . . . on Puerto Rican public opinion."[62]

A day after the cabinet meeting Ickes instructed Gruening to give the Maryland senator a draft of the independence bill, clearly specifying that the senator not tag it as an administration measure. He did not read the bill, he went on to say, but approved it because a discussion with Gruening had satisfied him that it was in accordance with the administration's general policy.[63] Frederick Bernays Wiener, a department lawyer, was selected to draft the bill under Gruening's supervision. Two drafts of the bill emerged from this, the second of which contained tariff schedules.[64] The second draft was forwarded by Gruening to the Senate chairman of the Committee on Territories and Insular Affairs on March 27. Gruening believed that the bill was "generous" and would meet the possible charge that it did not offer a "fair alternative."[65] The bill that Senator Tydings introduced about a month later was essentially the same as the Gruening draft bill.

On April 23, 1936, Senator Tydings, who was a close friend of the late Colonel Riggs' and was co-sponsor of the Tydings-McDuffie Act of 1935, which started the Philippines on a ten-year road to independence, presented two bills. The first, S.4528, provided for regulating the conduct of elections in Puerto Rico. He cited instances of fraud and violence at the polls, and insisted that only federal supervision could ensure honest elections. The second bill, S.4529, called for a referendum in Puerto Rico on independence in November, 1937. If the Puerto Ricans should vote yes, a four-year transition period was to be provided for, with a graduated tariff scale of 25 percent yearly. At the end of the fourth year, Puerto Rico would pay duty on its commodities on the same basis as other sovereign states.[66] Contrary to the wishes of the president and the secretary, the senator said to the press that the bill had the administration's backing.[67]

The bill took Puerto Rican leaders by surprise. Muñoz Marín, who was in Washington at the time, said he had no prior knowledge of the bill. He seemed to appear certain, however, that it was not Tydings who had written the bill but someone else.[68] It is possible he had an inkling that Gruening was behind the independence offer, because he stated in an unusually candid memorandum to the secretary (see Appendix A for the complete text) some ten months later that the bill had been "the fruit of Dr. Gruening's twisted and unadmirable state of mind."[69] The bill did not deserve serious consideration, he told newsmen, because it totally neglected giving the island economic safeguards. "It would have to be a bill," he explained, "under which Puerto Rico could produce most of its food and clothing, establish industries for local consumption and export a reasonable quota of its cash crops, in exchange for which rights the United States would have insured in Puerto Rico a permanent market for its wheat, cotton, metals, machinery, coal, petroleum and other commodities that cannot be produced in Puerto Rico."[70]

Four days later the Liberal senator translated his objections into a series of five amendments. The memorandum containing the amendments, it should be noted, was submitted to Dr. Gruening. The first requested the omission of the four-year transition period. The second provided for a referendum in June, 1937. If the vote should be in the affirmative, a constitutional convention was to be elected around January, 1938. The third dealt with the framing and subsequent approving of the constitution;

this done, the convention delegates and United States representatives designated by the president would work out reciprocity treaties and whatever other treaties deemed necessary. The fourth referred to the signing and ratification of the treaties by the Puerto Rican convention and the United States Senate, respectively. Thereafter, provision for the election of the island's first sovereign government was to be made. The fifth amendment sought to continue the present status until the provisions under the preceding four amendments were completed.[71]

Muñoz Marín went on to point out by way of emphasis that the reciprocity treaties should include: reasonable quotas for the island's cash crops in the United States market; liberal tariff provisions in terms of Puerto Rican needs and the mainland's interests; permission to allow the island to negotiate treaties with certain other nations to sell certain products and to facilitate emigration schemes; huge loans from the United States, so that the new insular government could continue with the program of reconstruction.[72]

The suggested amendments were sweeping in nature, and in fact called for the rewriting of the Tydings bill. They were presumably intended to show up the bill's gross inadequacy. The Liberal advocate of independence, like others on the island, doubted the administration's sincerity in the offer.[73] He did not lose his enthusiasm for independence, but made clear under what conditions he was prepared to accept it.

Other Puerto Rican leaders were equally critical of the bill, many of them pointing to a conspicuous absence of economic safeguards. Martínez Nadal, president of the Puerto Rican Senate and leader of the Coalition, called the bill a "betrayal" by the United States of the advocates of independence and statehood alike because it spelled economic ruin for the island.[74] Leader of the Socialist party and Resident Commissioner Santiago Iglesias called the bill "unjust, arbitrary, and devastating for Puerto Rico."[75] Puerto Rican interest groups and the press voiced similar criticism. Only the Nationalist group welcomed the bill. Indeed, Nationalist leader Albizu Campos said that only the withdrawal of the United States armed forces remained to be discussed.[76]

Except for Governor Winship, who remained silent, other high United States officials outwardly remained enthusiastic about the bill and denied charges of insincerity. Ickes called the bill "good" and flatly rejected the idea that it was meant to coerce Puerto Rico into maintaining its present status.[77] Gruening termed the measure "admirable" and added somewhat sarcastically that "nothing could be any further from the spirit and purpose of this administration than to keep a people which was not consulted originally about its annexation under our flag if they do not desire to be there."[78]

Privately, however, the secretary, Senator Tydings, and Dr. Gruening must have felt differently. Secretary Ickes and Senator Tydings were both appalled by the conditions in Puerto Rico they found on visits to the island. They probably realized that Puerto Rico could not afford independence.[79] Dr. Gruening did not feel differently from the secretary or the senator. The director's role in the PRRA Planning Division report affair seems to suggest that he did not wish to hear what he already knew. The Planning Division, presumably unaware of its director's role in the Tydings bill, prepared a report on May 2, 1936. The report categorically stated that the bill did not provide adequate safeguards against economic disaster.[80] Hanson, one of those who prepared the report, explains more dramatically in his book, "From every conceivable vantage point, we dealt with Puerto Rican realities; from every conceivable vantage point it was clear that the terms of independence provided for in the Tydings bill would double and treble the island's prevailing starvation and could result in nothing short of chaos." The Planning staff dutifully submitted the report to their superior in Washington, only to be rapped for doing so. Gruening, so Hanson maintains, directed him by cable to burn all copies in San Juan.[81] It must be pointed out, however, that the DTIP chief instructed PRRA regional director Dr. Chardón to investigate the economic consequences of the bill.[82]

Two other instances dramatized the inadequacies of the bill. On May 7, 1936, an American Labor party Congressman from New York City, Vito Marcantonio, presented H.R.12611. The bill provided for the island's independence on unrealistically liberal terms: no tariff barriers whatever on Puerto Rican goods, no restrictions on insular emigration to the mainland, and a total withdrawal of the United States in all respects within ninety days, plus what he called "indemnity" without limitations.[83]

The second concerned a report in the *New York Times* of possible consequences to United States business interests on the island. Sugar and construction companies were reported as having held back temporarily contemplated expansions; credit arrangements were being rejected; the Puerto Rican government bonds suffered losses at first, but later recovered. Private bank deposits, however, were not affected.[84]

Insular and continental criticism of the serious weakness of the bill convinced Senator Tydings to withdraw the message, if that is not what he had intended to do from the very beginning. He introduced Senate Joint Resolution 270 on May 25, 1936, providing for the appointment of a joint Puerto Rican–United States committee of seventeen to study all aspects relevant to independence. The resolution passed seven days later, except that the committee membership was reduced to fifteen.[85]

The Tydings bill was introduced and withdrawn in the course of four to five weeks. In addition to causing bad and bruised feelings among friends, it brought out issues that had hitherto remained in the background. Dr. Gruening's relationship with the Liberals soured, particularly with Muñoz Marín, as he moved to cooperate with the Coalition. Subsequently, Muñoz Marín's relationship with the administration cooled somewhat. A serious consequence, however, was the splitting of the Liberal party, the major issue being the party's stand on independence in the 1936 elections. The rupture was to be permanent, and out of it was to emerge Muñoz Marín's new party, the *Partido Popular Democrático* (PPD).

CHAPTER TWO

The Organization and Triumph
of the *Partido Popular Democrático*

The Liberal party was made up broadly of two groups of followers. The first consisted of professional classes, which set independence for the island as their immediate goal. This group was in sympathy with Nationalist leader Albizu Campos' cause, but looked to Muñoz Marín as its leader. The second group was comprised of persons, who, while believing in independence, insisted that Puerto Rico's economic reconstruction would make it necessary to hold off political severance with the United States until sometime in the future. In the meanwhile, it was willing to settle for greater autonomy. The leader of this group was Barceló. The unity and well-being of the party depended heavily upon the harmonious relations of the two party leaders.[1]

The Tydings bill placed a severe strain on this unity, and was in part responsible for its undoing. Its introduction in Congress appeared to coincide with the struggle for leadership between Barceló and Muñoz Marín. Differences between the two were rumored in the press when Barceló visited Washington in May, 1936, to discuss with Muñoz Marín, who unofficially represented the Liberals in Washington, the party's position on the Tydings bill. Barceló's stand was that the party should settle for greater autonomy for the time being without abandoning the goal of independence. Muñoz Marín was keenly aware that the independence bill had already split the party and that the party was likely to suffer a defeat in the November elections.[2] He described the bill's effects to Secretary Ickes seven months later in a memorandum, which has been and will be discussed in detail elsewhere in this chapter: "It was obviously impossible for a political force to win an election when the chief political plank of its platform was apparently defined by the U.S. government, which has the deciding power, as ruin and starvation." An election held "under such clear-cut economic duress," he continued, could not be regarded as an expression of public opinion.[3]

Muñoz Marín feared that an electoral defeat for the Liberal party would undermine the goal of independence for the island. He therefore urged Barceló to direct the party not to participate in the elections. Barceló appeared to accept the argument, and called upon all political parties to seek suspension of the elections.[4] The Republican and Socialist parties, as Barceló probably knew, would have none of it. And the Liberal party itself, under Barceló's guidance, decided on July 27, 1936, to participate in the elections.[5]

Muñoz Marín's dilemma was understandable. He could not very well reject the Tydings bill without his radical supporters at least questioning the strength of his commitment to independence; still less could he accept it and hope to escape criticism about its shortcomings. The course of action he pursued, while not always easy to explain, reflected in part his pique about not having been consulted by Washington officials about the Tydings bill. He saw that lack of consultation as a slap in his face and felt that it was representative of the "forces that had been supporting the Administration against the vicious attacks of the sugar corporations and their representatives," as he argued in his January, 1937, memorandum to the secretary.[6]

On June 22, 1936, he announced the resignation of his Senate seat and made known his nonavailability for the post of resident commissioner. He explained his action to Secretary Ickes as "proof of the sincerity of [his] conviction."[7] His real reason appeared to be to have a free hand in maintaining the loyalty of his followers, some of whom threatened to bolt the Liberal party, and to be present on the island to exercise vigilant leadership.[8]

Barceló realized that a Liberal party ticket without Muñoz Marín's name would greatly handicap the party's election campaign. But the veteran politician was shrewd enough to perceive that if Muñoz Marín did not accept the resident commissioner's post, which he thought the ex-senator had a good chance of winning, it would leave Muñoz Marín hunting the same political grounds as he. He attempted, therefore, to pressure Muñoz Marín into running for the Washington post, first by submitting his own resignation from the party leadership, and second by getting the Liberal party convention to reject Muñoz Marín's *retraimiento*. For the moment he was able to prevent an open breach by permitting Muñoz Marín to write into the party platform a demand for independence with "economic justice," but he could not persuade him to run for the office of resident commissioner.[9]

Disagreements emerged, however, at the Liberal party's nominating convention of August 16–18, 1936. Muñoz Marín and some of his followers withdrew from the meeting in anger because, he claimed, Barceló had gone back on an informal agreement to prevent one Lastra Charriez from running for any public office. A day after the convention Barceló strengthened his control over the party's central committee by removing Muñoz Marín's supporters.[10]

Muñoz Marín and 236 of his supporters responded by calling a meeting at Coamo and demanding that they be given representation on the central committee. When this action failed, Muñoz Marín called a giant rally at Caguas on August 28, 1936, and formed a new political group, *Acción Social Independentista* (ASI), which, as it turned out, formed the nucleus of the PPD. Muñoz Marín's desire was to demonstrate his strength to Barceló.[11] The breach was to become absolute some ten months later.

In the meanwhile a divided Liberal party went to the polls; and although it failed to elect its own member as resident commissioner, it performed unexpectedly well. The party received 252,457 votes, compared to 297,033 polled by the Coalition.[12] The defeat of the Liberal forces, Muñoz Marín maintained in his memorandum to Ickes in January, 1937, was "through no fault of their own," implying that it was partly the administration's in supporting the Tydings bill.[13]

Before discussing the final breach between Baceló and Muñoz Marín in June, 1937, and the subsequent formation of the PPD, it is necessary to examine the administration's estrangement with the Liberal party following the assassination of Colonel Riggs.

The Liberal party lost the grace it formerly enjoyed from the administration. Gruening reversed his former policy of favoring Liberals and turned to Coalition members for cooperation. He desired to have little to do with known advocates of independence. In his dual capacity as director of PRRA (until 1937) and DTIP, Gruening exercised considerable influence on administration policies toward Puerto Rico, even though his relations with Secretary Ickes were not completely harmonious.

He ordered the investigation of the PRRA with the intention of purging it of the Liberal element, especially those employees who believed in independence for the island. The witch-hunt forced the resignation of Dr. Chardón, which killed all hopes of pursuing a reconstruction policy along the lines of the Chardón Plan. Furthermore, Gruening resigned as director of PRRA in July, 1937. Indeed, its new director, Miles Fairbanks, wrote Secretary Ickes in February, 1938, about the possibility of liquidating the agency. It would be true to say that in deserting the Liberal group the administration turned away from the group most willing to help in the island's economic reconstruction.[14]

In yet another matter, namely, the teaching of English on the island, the administration acted hastily on Gruening's advice. When Senator William H. King of Utah visited the island in August, 1936, he became overly sensitive about the inability of most Puerto Ricans to speak English. Soon thereafter, Gruening polled many continentals and a few Puerto Ricans on the subject of teaching English.[15] Whatever the result of this private poll, Gruening decided that greater emphasis should be placed on the teaching of English. He secured the resignation of Commissioner of Education José Padin in November, 1936, and urged the president, much to the annoyance of Secretary Ickes, who felt that Gruening was circumventing his authority,[16] to appoint Dr. José Gallardo as the new commissioner.[17]

When President Roosevelt appointed Dr. Gallardo the commissioner of education on April 17, 1937, he made clear the administration's attitude with regard to the teaching of English. The president said he was disappointed that thousands of Puerto Ricans had "little and often virtually no knowledge" of the language. "It is an indispensable part of American policy," he continued, "that the coming generation of American citizens in Puerto Rico grow up with complete facility in the English tongue. It is the language of our nation. Only through the acquisition of this language will Puerto Ricans secure a better understanding of American ideals and principles." He reassured Puerto Ricans that he did not mean that the Spanish language should be excluded, but meant that only by knowing the English language could the islanders take full advantage of the economic opportunities on the mainland.[18]

Apart from treating an essentially pedagogical question in political terms, the administration was also poorly advised as to the timing of the reversal. Emotions among the Puerto Ricans were high after the murder of Colonel Riggs and the subsequent trial and conviction of Albizu Campos and six other Nationalists. The Nationalists had secured a permit from the mayor of Ponce to conduct a peaceful parade on March 21, 1937. Governor Winship was fearful of what might happen, and he directed the insular police chief to cancel the permit. The cancellation arrived a few hours before the parade, but the Nationalists could not be dissuaded to call off the march. They argued that it was impossible to do so at such short notice and decided to go ahead as planned. The insular police chief decided to encircle the town square with a contingent of 150 police in case of trouble. A shot was fired by somebody, triggering off more shooting, which left nineteen persons dead, two of whom were policemen, and over a hundred persons injured. The tragedy was referred to in the insular press as the Ponce Massacre.[19] The islanders did not think that the authorities were blameless, and were wont to accept the findings of Arthur G. Hays, who investigated for the American Civil Liberties Union, instead of the one-sided report of Governor Winship, which appeared to exonerate the police action.[20]

Under these circumstances the appointment of Dr. Gallardo was interpreted by the Puerto Ricans as an administration attempt to impose a policy of Americanization upon the islanders. Muñoz Marín reminded the president sharply in a radiogram message that the president's sentiments, as expressed in his letter appointing Gallardo, constituted a reversal of the administration's position from one envisaging independence to that of "the permanency of United States jurisdiction over Puerto Rico." He continued, "We protest against the attempt to impose educational norms on our children, forcing us to adopt [a] new national language not our own, even though ours be incidentally respected."[21] Despite protests, the new commissioner of education promptly began to remove teachers who were opposed to intensifying the teaching of English, and who supported the independence of the island.[22]

Gruening's displeasure with the Liberals was in part the result of his personal disagreement with Muñoz Marín. His relationship with the former senator soured over a seemingly nonessential matter. At the time of the murder of Colonel Riggs, the director had asked Muñoz Marín to issue a public condemnation of the act. Muñoz Marín hedged, thinking that to condemn the murder would be politically inexpedient. He would make such a statement, he finally agreed, if Gruening at the same time issued a condemnation of the police action in the death of the two Nationalist youths accused of the murder of Colonel Riggs. Gruening refused to do so, and there the matter rested. It was only after the introduction of the Tydings bill that Muñoz Marín realized that his refusal had offended Gruening.[23] Gruening was a sensitive man who tended to interpret disagreements as a personal affront. However, the incident suggests that he did not make a clear distinction between an *independentista* like Muñoz Marín and Albizu Campos. Indeed, even Secretary Ickes suspected Muñoz Marín of being connected with the Nationalists.[24]

The effect of this was to deprive Muñoz Marín of access to official channels in Washington. Secretary Ickes directed Assistant Secretary Chapman to be "more sparing" in the interviews granted to the Puerto Rican leader. "I would also avoid," he continued, "at least for the time being any social overtures such as having him to luncheon or accepting luncheon engagements offered by him." Ickes' pique appeared to be justified, because Muñoz Marín was capitalizing politically on his relationship with the officers of the Interior department and with Mrs. Roosevelt.[25]

Muñoz Marín was convinced that the administration's reversal was the result of misinformation on the part of Gruening. In the memorandum to the secretary referred to earlier, he attributed the Tydings bill to Gruening's "twisted and unadmirable state of mind." Later in the same memorandum he spoke of the director in this way, "Even under the Roosevelt Administration, the state of mind of one individual, in a key position, has been enough to swamp the character of generosity of the Roosevelt–Puerto Rican policy, to place the island unnecessarily in the hands of the worst reactionary interests, poisoning the whole situation with the spirit of distrust and revenge."[26] Three months later, Muñoz Marín pointed out to the president that Gruening, among others, was responsible for "presenting a jaundiced picture of Puerto Rican realities."[27]

It was presumably with the intention of clearing some of the confusion and misinformation concerning his position on the status question that he dispatched to Secretary Ickes the lengthy memorandum already referred to several times in this study.[28] The January 5, 1937, document is notable for its detail and candor; and since its author was to assume a key position in the next decade in the formulation of the 1952 Commonwealth Constitution of Puerto Rico, it is appropriate to examine it thoroughly.

All were opposed to the present "colonial status" because the powers of the Puerto Rican government were "delegated and therefore revocable." Puerto Ricans had, therefore, two options before them, statehood and independence. He saw few advantages to the United States if the island became a state in the Union. Muñoz Marín saw difficulties for the United States if it were to incorporate a people "unassimilated and . . . [of] unassimilable nationality." Furthermore, the United States and Puerto Rico should be terrified by the "perpetual quality of statehood," for whatever inherent weaknesses that it may hold for both may be continued indefinitely.[29]

Muñoz Marín saw few, if any, benefits to Puerto Rico if it were to become a state. On the contrary, he saw the following disadvantages for the island: the unsound economic system with its heavy emphasis on sugar would be continued, Puerto Rico would lose customs receipts and other forms of tax revenue that then returned to the insular treasury, and the state government would likely collapse under the burden of having to contribute eight or nine million dollars to the federal treasury, assuming that there were no replacement funds in the form of grants and relief. If Puerto Rico became a state, he argued, the federal government would become "one more absentee extractor of the wealth produced by the Puerto Ricans."[30]

The leader of the ASI proceeded to point out why he favored independence. He said that a colonial empire was built around two motives: economic exploitation and the "white man's burden." The second was often used to cover up the first. However, Muñoz Marín believed that the "white man's burden" could reflect a sincere desire to help the people of the colony, and he had no doubt that the period of the Roosevelt administration was one of those rare times in United States history when sincerity was evident, even though it had been somewhat marred by the "state of mind of one individual"—referring, of course, to Gruening. But he was concerned that future administrations would revert to "protecting exploitation of the people of Puerto Rico by a few privileged interests." For this reason alone, he felt that Puerto Rico should be given independence.[31]

The future leader of the PPD then went on to spell out the specific benefits of independence to Puerto Rico. As a sovereign power, Puerto Rico would have tariff-making and treaty-making powers to implement a desirable economic policy: by creating a class of small landholders, and thereby ending the heavy emphasis on sugar; by beginning a program to produce tropical foods; and by rehabilitating the coffee industry for the European market. Without the threat of a Congressional veto, the government of the island would have the power of broad policy-making over such matters as birth control and emigration. Among other things, the island's independence would put an end to the "spiritual havoc" created by the colonial status. It would eliminate a situation in which "patronage and pie" tended to develop "an attitude of bootlicking, toadying, proclamation of a 100% americanism."[32]

Muñoz Marín reassured the secretary on two important aspects: the United States would be permitted to retain military bases on the island; and the Puerto Ricans, after their thirty-eight years of experience under American democracy could be trusted not to elect bad governments. He did not seek to sever ties with the United States, but sought to take full advantage of its markets for Puerto Rican commodities by means of reciprocal arrangements.[33]

Fully aware of the way in which independence was offered in the Tydings bill, Muñoz Marín described at length the procedure by which sovereignty could be extended to the island. The most notable features of this procedure were his insistence on a referendum among Puerto Ricans on the question of independence, and the adequate representation of Puerto Rican views on the terms to be incorporated in mutual agreements.[34]

The memorandum did not discuss many other important aspects of the status question: how long the process should take, what should happen if Puerto Ricans rejected independence, Congressional willingness or lack of it to grant the island independence or statehood. Furthermore, Muñoz Marín was overly optimistic as to what Puerto Rico could achieve economically as a sovereign entity. One fact, however, emerges clearly from the document: the future leader recognized that the status issue, far from being a political question, was actually an economic one. And his broad thinking on economics was going to be incorporated in the program of the PPD.

In the months after the 1936 elections, both Barceló and Muñoz Marín were under pressure from elements among their supporters to call for an open break. Neither desired to be held responsible for the disintegration of the Liberal party. Barceló, however, was the first to fire the shot when he expelled Muñoz Marín on May 31, 1937, in an informal meeting at a farm called Naranjal. When Muñoz Marín challenged this move, the Barceló group struck back by dissociating Muñoz Marín, the ASI, and the former senator's newspaper *La Democracia* from the Liberal party, retroactive to December, 1936. Thereafter, the Liberal party's central board under Barceló's directive declared Muñoz Marín and his followers enemies of the party.[35]

Charging that the party's executive committee had become a "closed corporation," Muñoz Marín and his followers met on June 4, 1937, and announced the formation of the Pure Authentic and Complete Liberal party (*Partido Liberal Neto Auténtico y Completo*).[36] Twenty-three days later Muñoz Marín called a giant rally at which the new political group elected members to its central committee and Muñoz Marín as its president. Its platform called for independence. Muñoz Marín said in his speech, ". . . there shall be social justice and independence for all . . . . Deny it or not, we are the seed of Puerto Rico's independence."[37] The platform also included opposition to forced instruction of English in the school system, and an appeal to the authorities for the release of Nationalist prisoners in custody.[38]

Even though Muñoz Marín's new group was for all intents and purposes a new political party, he still left the door slightly ajar for reconciliation with the Liberal party, as the unconventional name of the group suggests. Barceló, however, was not persuaded that there could be reconciliation. Instead he made subtle overtures to the Coalition, which was also experiencing dissension within its ranks. In the months after June, 1937, Muñoz Marín proceeded to convert the Pure Authentic and Complete Liberal party into a full-fledged organization, completely separate and independent from the Liberal party. The new party was named the *Partido Popular Democrático* (PPD), and adopted as its emblem the profile of a *jíbaro* (countryman) wearing the traditional Puerto Rican straw hat, the *pava*. For the next three years Muñoz Marín and his faithful band of supporters traveled the countryside and campaigned for endorsement of the PPD. They stressed the party's commitment to improve economic, social, and health conditions, because they believed that living conditions were of greater concern to the *jíbaros* than the issue of political status.[39]

By the time the constituent assembly of the PPD met at San Juan on July 21, 1940, the party leadership was convinced not to emphasize the status question in the forthcoming elections but instead to concentrate its energies on economic and social issues. The new party's decision to minimize the status issue had two reasons: one, Muñoz Marín desired not to turn the elections into some sort of a referendum on the political status question—he was only too aware of what had happened in the 1936 elections—and, two, to attract the widest possible support. The party platform included independence as an objective at a special plebiscite, but it was considerably weakened by stating that the party considered statehood as of equal dignity.[40] Indeed, Muñoz Marín thwarted some members from sending a message to the Pan American Conference seeking recognition of Puerto Rico's right to sovereignty. Besides, the language on the status question was such as to leave open the possibility of either statehood or independence.[41]

Even if the platform was vague on the question of status, it was generally believed that the party leadership favored independence. And the *Popular* campaign booklet with a question-answer format, *The People's Catechism,* left little doubt that its author, Muñoz Marín, advocated independence.[42] Much of the fervor among the leadership, however, had abated since 1936, probably as the leaders became more aware of the economic implications surrounding status solutions. The shift is noticeable in the rest of the party's platform. It called for enforcement of the 500-acre land limit law; minimum wage laws; social security for the unemployed and the physically disabled; liberalization of credit to farmers, workers, businessmen, and manufacturers; a program for the development and utilization of water resources; laws to protect union rights; and, finally, legislation to make

Spanish the official language of instruction in public schools, without undermining the teaching of English.[43]

Muñoz Marín campaigned strenuously, carefully playing up his image as the "people's man." The party platform was heavily oriented towards the interests of the laboring class and the middle class. Those persons that Muñoz Marín could not personally visit he hoped to reach through party newspapers like *La Democracia* and the newly established *El Batey*. The *Popular* leader, however, preferred to see and talk to the people, and he covered 500 of the 786 electoral districts. Among those he visited were the *jíbaros* in the hills and valleys of the island, urging them not to sell their votes for two dollars, as had been the general practice in past elections, but to give the PPD the votes in return for "justice" long overdue to them. He talked to them in his shirtsleeves, went without meals, slept at odd times, and generally ran the campaign on much good will and little money, or so at least two of his sympathetic biographers say.[44]

To further impress upon the electorate's mind the party's sincerity and conviction in its program, the PPD called a massive rally on September 15, 1940, in San Juan, at which all the bills the party had campaigned for were approved and each *Popular* candidate took an oath to vote for the bills if the party came into power.[45]

In the meanwhile, Ramírez Santibáñez had taken over the leadership of the Liberal party after Barceló's death in October, 1938. He moved to capitalize on the difficulties within the Coalition. The new Liberal leader joined forces with a dissident Republican faction under Miguel Angel García Méndez and an insurgent Socialist faction under Prudencio Rivera Martínez to form a new political group, the Tripartite party. The new party's platform included statehood, which it considered "the supreme ideal of Puerto Rico."[46]

The PPD was not completely happy with the 1940 election results, but it nevertheless proclaimed victory. The Coalition polled 222,423 votes compared to 214,857 for the *Populares* and 130,299 for the Tripartite party. The PPD failed to elect its own resident commissioner—that post went to Socialist leader Bolívar Pagán—but captured ten of the nineteen Senate seats, and shared equally thirty-six of the thirty-nine House seats with the Coalition, the three being won by the Tripartite party.[47] Its success is remarkable when one considers that it was organized slightly over two years before the elections and that it had pitted itself against a group well entrenched politically and well backed financially.

There are several possible reasons for the PPD's success. The dissension among the Coalition and the disintegration of the Liberal party doubtless helped it. Muñoz Marín predicted before the elections, "When the wolves begin to fight among themselves, there's a chance the lambs will get through safely."[48] The vigorous campaigning by the PPD candidates had an enormous impact on the minds of the voters. But perhaps the most important factor was the personality of Muñoz Marín himself. His charm and persuasiveness were a great political asset. The Puerto Rican leader could as easily move among *jíbaros* as he could mix with high-ranking government officials. George A. Malcolm, the attorney general of Puerto Rico at the time of the PPD's victory, later wrote of Muñoz Marín, "One either surrenders unconditionally to his charm or as thoroughly dislikes him." "Don Luis captivated me, as he has many other persons."[49] No less impressed was William Brophy, legal counsel for the Interior department, who commented about Muñoz Marín in his diary: "His eloquent hands hypnotize. A clever, shrewd, calculating politician, not in the sense of a job seeker or job giver, but in the sense of a philosophy [philosopher?] politician . . . ."[50] He had a rare quality of engendering trust and understanding in most people who came into contact with him.

Such a man was bound to command attention and respect among a people who traditionally looked up to strong men to lead them,[51] especially since two veteran politicians, Antonio Barceló and Santiago Iglesias, had died within the space of a year.

After the Tydings bill, a number of bills were introduced in Congress purporting to give the island either independence or statehood, none of which had the backing of the administration or the enthusiasm of many Congressmen. On February 18, 1937, Congressman Wilburn Cartwright, Democrat from Oklahoma, introduced a bill enumerating steps to make the island a sovereign state.[52] Gruening opposed it, saying that there could be no solution of Puerto Rico's status until the island was "rehabilitated economically."[53] On several other occasions, Resident Commissioner Iglesias sponsored bills to turn Puerto Rico into an "incorporated territory" and to provide for its admission into the the Union as a state, without any success.[54] Iglesias' failure did not discourage Bolívar Pagán, who replaced the Socialist leader after his death in December, 1939. Pagán introduced in Congress two bills at the same time, one providing for statehood, and the other for greater autonomy, neither of which was acted upon by the Committee on Insular Affairs.[55]

The Roosevelt administration did not wish to support legislation concerning Puerto Rico's status without investigating its political, legal, and economic implications. There are a number of special reports in the files of the Office of Territories and the Department of the Interior records, at least one of which was undertaken at the specific request of the administration. The first of these reports was submitted by H. Murray-Jacoby to Secretary of War Harry H. Woodring. The 65-page report, prepared on March 11, 1937, ruled out independence and statehood but recommended steps by which the island could arrive at dominion status. Drawing upon his study of British colonial policy, the author described a series of four two-year stages by which Puerto Rican autonomy could be increased. The most notable aspect of the report was its emphasis on gradualism, the next two-year stage being contingent upon satisfactory performance during the stage immediately preceding.[56]

In another report, Benjamin Horton, a lawyer on the staff of PRRA, offered his opinion as to the island's legal status. He maintained that Puerto Rico was a "territory" of the United States enjoying the same legal status that the states then in the Union did when they were "territories." It had never been the intention of the United States, he continued, to withdraw its sovereignty, especially since it had extended United States citizenship to the islanders in 1917.[57] Later in 1937, Walter F. McCaleb, special advisor to the Department of the Interior, prepared a 173-page report. It lacked any merit and appeared to be superficial in its investigation and sometimes wild in its conclusions, as in the assertion that Muñoz Marín and Gruening had conspired to jockey themselves into power and position.[58]

The most important of the reports to appear by 1940 was the Zimmerman report. The study was requested by the Interdepartmental Commission, consisting of six high interdepartmental officials, among them Interior's Assistant Secretary Chapman, who served as the chairman. Dr. Erich W. Zimmerman was placed in charge of the investigation. The 308-page report was published in September, 1940. Its findings were not encouraging. The report stated that the island lacked industrial resources, and was heavily dependent upon agriculture. It also stated that, because of natural conditions and the desire for access to an expanding market, sugar was the best crop, though not necessarily ideal. Furthermore, there was little room for expansion of agricultural resources, which was discouraging because of the rapid rate of the island's population growth. The report recommended that the island's trade restrictions with its Caribbean neighbors be relaxed.[59]

Even though the Zimmerman report did not give adequate attention to truck-farm products and pineapples, which would thrive given the same conditions under which sugar cane thrived on the island,[60] the implications of its findings were ominous: the island's economy was stagnant because of its dependence on sugar, and yet, under the circumstances, it was the best crop. It was apparently with this in mind that the administration appointed Tugwell, then chairman of the Planning Commission of New York City, and formerly assistant secretary of Agriculture, to undertake an investigation of the possibilities of enforcing the 500-acre land limit law in Puerto Rico,[61] especially since this was the avowed objective of the newly elected PPD. Tugwell's recommendations and the PPD program will form the subject of the next chapter. It is sufficient to say here that the call for an investigation of the island's economic problems would indicate the administration's concern for Puerto Rico's economic stability rather than political status. This was a far cry from the 1936 Tydings bill. Since then, the European war had entirely changed the complexity of the situation.

CHAPTER THREE

Delayed New Deal under
Muñoz Marín and Governor Tugwell

The year 1941 marked the beginning of a new direction in Puerto Rican affairs. The newly formed PPD assumed control of insular political affairs, and a new governor in the person of Tugwell helped the *Populares* in their efforts to implement programs and policies for which they had campaigned in the 1940 elections. In Tugwell, Puerto Ricans found a champion of greater autonomy and administrative reforms. The governor partly succeeded in instituting administrative reforms, but his attempts to grant the islanders wider self-government ran afoul of Congressional opposition generated by wariness that comes with the excessive powers of the administration during wartime, and by some Congressmen's suspicions of New Dealers.[1] Indirectly, Tugwell's contribution to the islanders' political freedom was enormous: in helping the PPD to carry out its forward-looking policies, he aided in politically consolidating the party under which the greatest political autonomy was to come in the postwar period.

Although the *Populares* were able to persuade the three Tripartite members in the insular House to support their cause, thereby maintaining a tenuous majority,[2] they needed a cooperative governor if they hoped to succeed in their policies. Both

39

Governor Tugwell and the *Popular* leader Muñoz Marín were New Deal enthusiasts who broadly agreed on the manner in which the island's economic and social problems should be corrected. The governor appointed like-minded *Populares* to important government posts, which had the effect of reducing Puerto Rico's traditional friction between the elected legislature and the appointed executive, and generating considerable agreement and coordination between the two.[3]

A controversial figure in American politics, Tugwell did not escape scrutiny and criticism at the time he was nominated for the governor's post. A number of Coalition representatives insisted at the Senate hearings on Tugwell's nomination that the former Agricultural undersecretary's appointment as governor would inject disharmony into Puerto Rican politics, not only because he was a close friend of Muñoz Marín's but also because his economic views were certain to run counter to the interests of the sugar corporations, and thus of Puerto Rico's.[4] The strongest opposition came from Senator Robert H. Taft of Ohio, who accused Tugwell of being an opponent of the "traditional American system of individual initiative and enterprise" and therefore incapable of representing American ideals. Taft sharply questioned Tugwell's competence as an administrator, asserting that nothing in the New Dealer's record since 1933 could be regarded as "successful accomplishment."[5]

It was presumably the administration's strong backing and Muñoz Marín's endorsement that led the Senate narrowly to approve Tugwell's nomination.[6] He took the oath of office on September 19, 1941, two days after he had resigned his post as the chancellor of the University of Puerto Rico.[7]

Tugwell brought to the office of governor a varied background of knowledge and administrative experience. A professor of economics at Columbia University in 1931, he had become known for his economic views through a series of books and articles. He felt that laissez-faire capitalism was doomed, and should make way for "undoctrinaire planned economy."[8] Tugwell drew national attention when he was appointed in 1932 as one of the original members of the "brain trust" in the Roosevelt administration. A year later, Tugwell was assigned to the post of assistant secretary of Agriculture, and later became undersecretary of Agriculture. In 1935 he organized the controversial Resettlement Administration, which was designed to handle rural poverty. This venture brought him much notoriety, and he left the administration in 1936. Two years later Mayor Fiorello H. La Guardia of New York City appointed him the first chairman of the Planning Commission of the city, a post he held until 1941 when Muñoz Marín offered him the chancellorship of the University of Puerto Rico.[9]

Soon after Tugwell was inaugurated he was confronted with the problem that all his predecessors had faced in Puerto Rico, namely, the question of patronage. The *Populares* had elected their men to key legislative positions, the most important of which, the Senate presidency, was held by Muñoz Marín himself. With the help of the Tripartite members, the PPD leader secured the election of fellow–party-founder Samuel Quiñones as Speaker of the House. Governor Tugwell, like his immediate predecessor, Guy J. Swope, realized that no appointments opposed by Muñoz Marín could hope to be confirmed by the Senate.[10]

Thus, when a Coalition delegation, consisting of Bolívar Pagán, Celestino Iriarte, and José Balseiro, visited the governor for assurances that he would appoint Republicans and Socialists to government posts, at least in proportion to their legislative strength, he flatly turned it down. He could not but favor the *Populares,* he argued later in his book, because they controlled the legislature. He explained, "If I had to make a choice, I should have to choose the *Populares* because that party had control of the Senate, which, after all, did the confirming. If, however, I was pressed to choose, I could often appoint *Republicanos* and bargain for their confirmation."[11] The Coalition naturally became piqued about it, and soon declared the governor *persona non grata.* What made it particularly difficult for the Coalition to accept Tugwell as governor was his endorsement of *Popular* policies, which clashed with the interests of other groups that it traditionally represented.[12]

Tugwell hoped to institute administrative reforms that would give the executive a measure of freedom from the politics of patronage. The Puerto Rican Senate wielded enormous influence over even minor appointments by virtue of its power of confirmation; and cabinet members sedulously complied with the wishes of the party in legislative control, even though they were in theory directly responsible to the governor. In investigative functions, too, the legislature had encroached on the powers of the executive. And as to the executive powers over appropriations, the legislature had clearly circumvented them by creating a host of permanent appropriations and many more special funds.[13]

Tugwell made some progress in his reform attempt. The former practice of formally submitting to the governor lists of possible appointees was discontinued in favor of informal consultations between the majority party leaders and the governors.[14] The governor added specialists and technical experts to his staff to help him in his administrative duties. Within a year of his taking the office, his staff had doubled. In May, 1942, the Office of Statistics was established, followed a month later by the Office of Information. The Bureau of the Budget was created in August, 1942, to help him in fiscal matters, followed soon thereafter by the appointment of a coordinator of Insular Affairs and a coordinator of Federal Affairs. These offices were designed to expedite the administrative efforts of the territorial and federal capitals. The annual appropriations for the office of the governor more than doubled, from $100,000 to $250,000, by the end of 1946.[15]

Muñoz Marín was fearful that the increased powers of the governor would undermine his position as leader of both his party and the insular legislature. Furthermore, he was concerned about the long-term effects of such reform measures, and many times he invoked the name of "Ole Gandule," the mythical bad governor of the future.[16] Tugwell reflected later in his book, ". . . he [Muñoz Marín] felt he could not give up his control. He fought me insistently to keep intact the political machine. Moreover, he now continually called in cabinet members and gave them orders without consulting me."[17] The *Popular* leader did, however, begin to support Tugwell's civil service reforms by 1944, when he felt sufficiently strong politically;[18] but real progress in this area came only after Muñoz Marín was elected the governor and leadership in the executive and legislative branches was centralized in the majority party.[19]

The governor's appointment of young, educated, talented, and dedicated men to the various administrative posts was to serve Puerto Rico's long-term interests. In hiring young Puerto Ricans to do work that would normally be done by non-Puerto Ricans in a typically colonial situation, Tugwell pointed to the political maturity and responsibility of the islanders in general. He hoped that their appointments would augur well for Puerto Rico's cause for greater self-rule by making available competent personnel ready to serve administratively when the time came.[20] Most of these men continued working in their positions after he left the governorship in 1946, many of them reaching prominent positions under the last appointed governor, Jesús T. Piñero, and the first elected governor, Muñoz Marín.[21]

The leader of the *Populares* proceeded to implement a far-reaching program of economic and social development with the help of Governor Tugwell. In compliance with their campaign promise, the *Populares* had succeeded in establishing the Land Authority in April, 1941 (before Tugwell became governor), to implement an equitable land policy along the line suggested by the previously discussed Chardón Plan of 1936. The United States Supreme Court had ruled in March, 1940, that the 500-acre land law was constitutional. It was now the task of the Land Authority to decide what should be done with the total of 580,788 acres of land, 249,000 of which were held by fifty-one corporations, owned in violation of that law. Muñoz Marín realized that no matter how the land was to be acquired and redistributed he would need the wholehearted support of the governor.[22]

Tugwell had investigated, at Secretary Ickes' direction, the whole question of the 500-acre law months before his appointment as governor. His report, officially submitted to the secretary in December, 1941, maintained that the land should be acquired by purchase and redistributed by the Land Authority. He did not elaborate as to how this might be done, but he did maintain that in eliminating illegal large-scale sugar operations, efficiency should not be sacrificed. The governor also suggested that the Land Authority be given assistance from the Farm Security Administration.[23] As it happened, the Puerto Rican agency received the help of such federal agencies as the Agricultural Adjustment Agency, the Farm Credit Administration, and the Insular Experiment Station.[24]

The Land Authority, authorized by the insular legislature and approved by Secretary Ickes, decided to redistribute the purchased land in three ways. First, under the Individual Farm plan it hoped to create small farm units between five to twenty-five acres in size, to be purchased by individual households at a price to be determined by the Authority, plus 5 percent interest, and payable in installments over a period as long as forty years. Second, the "Proportional-profit" farm, ranging from 100 to 500 acres, was designed to combine justice with the administrative efficiency necessary in large-scale operations. The farm was to be run by an experienced manager and workers, all of whom were to receive wages plus proportionate shares of the profits for the whole operation. Third, the homesteading program for the *agregados* (landless peasants) was to provide small tracts of land made available nominally, one of the conditions being that the owner of the land was to build or move his house on the land within 120 days.[25]

Tugwell cooperated fully in implementing the *Popular* land policy. On several occasions between 1942 and 1946, the Puerto Rican legislature amended the Land Law of 1941 upon the governor's advice to clarify certain provisions and to broaden the scope of others to include a wider section of the people. By June 30, 1946, the Land Authority had acquired 2.9 percent of the total land area of the island, almost all of which it redistributed in the following way: 2,000 *cuerdas* (1940 acres) to 148 individual farmers, 44,897.99 *cuerdas* (43,551.05 acres) as "Proportional-profit" farms, and 15,648.83 *cuerdas* (15,179.37 acres) as homestead plots to the landless.[26]

The Water Resources Authority (WRA) was created before Tugwell took office, but its final organization was completed during his governorship. Its function was to facilitate irrigation and to develop energy resources to produce cheaper electricity. Tugwell recommended to the president the purchase of three private utility companies. When the companies refused to sell their properties, the federal government expropriated them. The companies filed litigation against the government, and the matter was not resolved until January, 1944, when, subsequent to the court decision, the three companies were permanently transferred to WRA.[27] The Tugwell administration created several public utilities. The Transportation and Communications Authorities were intended for improved roads and streets and for better public conveyances at cheaper rates. Another public utility, the Aqueduct-and-Sewerage Authority, was established in 1945. Its function was to install and operate a modern system of sewage disposal and to supply pure water to residents in towns and cities.[28]

At the governor's request, the Puerto Rican legislature consolidated in 1942 several insular authorities into a central body known as the Puerto Rico Housing Authority (PRHA). Despite the interruption of federal loans because of the war, the PRHA was able to undertake the development of new housing projects;

and under the direction of the Planning, Urbanizing, and Zoning Board, it was able to institute slum clearance programs. By June, 1946, the PRHA had built projects at a cost of over $4.5 billion and had housed over 2,000 families.[29]

An ambitious industrialization program was undertaken when the Puerto Rican Development Company (after 1946 the body was known as the Puerto Rican Industrial Development Company, PRIDCO) was established in 1942. The company was modeled closely after the Chilean *Corporacion de Fomento,* except that the former concentrated its efforts in fostering industrial and commercial enterprises. The organization was authorized to direct research into the island's resources, to make available loans and technical information to persons willing to establish new industrial enterprises or expand old ones, and to train personnel that would be required for working the new facilities.[30]

The funds necessary to expand PRDCO's activities were made available by an insular agency, the Development Bank. Under Teodoro Moscoso as its general manager, PRDCO organized five subsidiary corporations in the next four years. These were the Pureto Rico Glass Corporation, the Puerto Rico Cement Corporation (first organized in February, 1938, under the Puerto Rican Reconstruction Administration), the Puerto Rico Clay Products Corporation, and the Puerto Rico Shoe and Leather Corporation.[31] By June, 1946, PRIDCO, as it was then called, owned properties estimated at $11,743,456, giving employment to 1,379 persons.[32]

The industrialization program was an attempt to tap fully the benefits of the mineral-based industries and to utilize "idle capital."[33] It was a bold scheme made possible by the fantastic rum "bonanza" during the war years (rum taxes netted the insular treasury $160 million more than in normal times). However, except for the Cement Corporation, the other government ventures were failures. They were plagued by lack of technical personnel, the difficulties of operating subsidiaries owned by the government, such as debilitating labor disputes, and the competition from United States markets. Furthermore, PRIDCO failed in its promise of creating thousands of jobs for the island's workers.[34]

The Chardón Plan had maintained that the Puerto Rican economy could improve only if an industrialization program accompanied plans for diversifying insular agriculture. The Land

Authority hoped to break the monopoly over land that could otherwise be used for growing other agricultural products; the Puerto Rican Agricultural Development Company, organized in 1945, sought to use government efforts along the lines of PRDCO to introduce to the island food crops other than those existing already, and to improve upon those already being grown.[35] The *Populares* and the Tugwell administration succeeded partially in striking a reasonably happy balance between industry and agriculture. This indeed must be the conclusion from the figures given by Harvey Perloff in writing about Puerto Rican economy for the periods 1939–1940 and 1945–1946, considering the fact that this was the first concerted effort in Puerto Rican history and that trends do not clearly emerge over a short period of six years.[36]

But the increased economic activity in Puerto Rico came during wartime, when it was able to capitalize on the rum industry and the absence of aggressive mainland capital. Furthermore, the government-sponsored enterprises had been plagued by a variety of problems. A need was felt, therefore, to reorient its industrialization drive to accommodate the postwar economic exigencies. After 1946 the insular government shifted its policy to rely less upon government-sponsored programming and more upon privately organized efforts. The new policy, known as "Operation Bootstrap," involved selling three of the PRIDCO-managed corporations to a private Puerto Rican industrialist and inviting mainland capital to the island.[37] The decision to bolster Puerto Rican industrialization with United States private capital was a clear recognition of an already existing fact, namely, that the island's economic future depended upon its continued relationship with the giant of the North. It was to have significant implications for Puerto Rico's political future.

The *Populares* and the Tugwell administration relied upon bold and innovative methods that sometimes showed good results but always raised a storm of controversy among insular and continental politicians. The pitch of political acrimony seldom reached the point it did in the first two years of Tugwell's governorship when *Coalicionistas* were crying "Socialism, Communism, Dictatorship!" in an attempt to dislodge the governor from his office.

When the Coalition succeeded neither in its attempts to win

Tugwell's political favor nor in its drive to deprive the *Populares* of the support of the Tripartite party,[38] it called upon the tireless assistance of the resident commissioner in Washington, Pagán, who belonged to the Coalition group. Together they hoped to bring to the administration's and Congress' attention their opinion that Tugwell was undesirable as governor and should be removed.

On February 17, 1942, Pagán had printed in the *Congressional Record* a resolution adopted at a mass Coalition convention. The resolution accused Tugwell of being partisan, charged that his policies were anti–sugar industry and pro-labor, and called for his dismissal.[39] A day later the resident commissioner inserted into the records a letter that Coalition leaders Iriarte and Lino Padrón Rivera had written to Secretary Ickes. Puerto Rico was, the letter said, "sick and tired of undesirable Federal appointees whose incumbency would not be tolerated by any American community."[40]

The resident commissioner accused Tugwell of being "an American Quisling" because he was sowing disunity among the islanders loyal to the United States and causing them to feel "digust and distrust" towards American institutions.[41] Even though the charges by Pagán were distorted, many newspapers in the United States appeared to be at least sympathetic to Coalition complaints. And the Puerto Rican representative did not hesitate to have printed in the *Congressional Record* newspaper editorials that were favorable to his cause.[42] The *Washington Evening Star* spoke disapprovingly of the PPD's "secessionist or independence plank" and of its program of "communistic distribution of land" among the poor farmers and peasants of the land. The *New Republic* echoed Pagán's disapproval of Tugwell because he had fostered "disunion and hatred" among the Puerto Ricans and pointed out that an "overwhelming majority" of them desired his removal.[43]

In addition Pagán wrote to congressmen and senators whenever the opportunity presented itself. On February 24, 1942, he addressed a letter to Senator Harry S. Truman—in response to what he called a "sneak letter" by Muñoz Marín to the senator—in which he accused the PPD leader of collaborating with Tugwell in seeking to establish a "communistic 'new order.' " The resident commissioner revealed what was probably the real reason for his opposition to Tugwell: the governor was "disregarding and kicking the rights of the Coalition" and was "playing all the political game exclusively with Luis Muñoz Marín."[44]

The anti-Tugwell campaign reached its peak by the middle of 1942. The governor's resolve to hold the office weakened somewhat, and his resignation was rumored.[45] Tugwell was persuaded to continue as governor by the strong endorsement he received from the *Populares* and Secretary Ickes. The PPD leader explained to the president in a cable on January 19, 1942, that the move to oust the governor was the work simply of a few "reactionary Republican and Socialist politicians."[46] About a month later he wrote to Senator Truman, telling him that Pagán's attacks were "false in [their] irresponsible allegations."[47]

Muñoz Marín at the same time worked to get the insular House to adopt and forward to President Roosevelt a resolution denouncing Pagán's activities in Washington as unrepresentative of the majority will.[48] Soon thereafter the Puerto Rican Senate, under Muñoz Marín's leadership, adopted a resolution endorsing the governorship of Tugwell.[49] In addition, a petition bearing over 300,000 signatures was presented to Tugwell in support of his administration of the island.[50]

Secretary Ickes consistently supported Tugwell. On January 27, 1942, the secretary informed the governor that he was not going to trouble to respond to Tugwell's critics because to do so would simply give "currency and dignity to an effort to put you in a false light."[51] When Tugwell suggested that Pagán had an "unlimited drawing account with the sugar producers association" and that "serious" attempts were being made to "bore" into the "Army, Navy, Interior, and Agriculture" departments,[52] the secretary directed Federal Bureau of Investigations director J. Edgar Hoover to investigate the matter.[53] Relations between the secretary and the resident commissioner were at best strained. When Pagán requested in somewhat intemperate language that the secretary veto an insular law already approved by Tugwell, Ickes rebuked him in a similar vein for even suggesting such a move.[54] Four months later the head of the Department of the Interior publicly chided two of Tugwell's critics who were also members of Tugwell's cabinet. They were two continentals, Patrick J. Fitzsimmons as auditor and George A. Malcolm as attorney general,[55] both of whom later testified before Congressional investigating committees.

The attacks on Tugwell coincided with the difficulties created by the war and added to the fodder of Coalition cannons. The Puerto Ricans suffered directly and indirectly as a result of the shortage of shipping space. The War Shipping Administration (WSA) fixed the monthly tonnage to the island at a much reduced quota of 30,000 tons, the major portion of which was reserved for essential items such as food. The Agricultural Marketing Administration (AMA), later the Food Distribution Administration (FDA), was a federal agency that undertook to distribute the food supplies on the island to ensure fair distribution and to prevent profiteering. Puerto Rican business interests and insular representatives of mainland food processors complained about unnecessary interference. They maintained that the AMA policy was undermining the business activities of the private interests, which would lead to inefficiency and the supplying of low quality food. Furthermore, they argued that the allotment of 30,000 tons per month needed to be increased. (The tonnage in normal times was 110,000 per month.)[56]

It was in response to the food crisis in Puerto Rico that Senator Dennis Chavez of New Mexico introduced on October 20, 1942, Senate Resolution 309 to investigate the social and economic conditions resulting from the war.[57] When the resolution reached the Senate floor, Senator Arthur Vandenberg of Michigan insisted that the investigation be broadened to include the policies of Tugwell, whom he referred to as the "chief commissar of Puerto Rico" and the "Don Quixote of the New Deal," to find out whether Tugwell's "half-baked" projects were the real causes of Puerto Rico's problems.[58] A similar sentiment appeared to prevail in the House Committee on Agriculture, which had a week before approved a measure to provide an additional $15 million to encourage the production of foodstuff in Puerto Rico and the Virgin Islands, with the provision that the Puerto Rican part of the money could not be used so long as Tugwell remained the governor.[59]

However, because many senators were opposed to taking political advantage over the island's food problem, and Secretary Ickes objected to any kind of investigation,[60] the Chavez Subcommittee of the Committee on Territories and Insular Affairs decided to limit its study to the food problem only. Even though *Coalicionistas* like Pagán did not miss the opportunity to take swipes at Governor Tugwell in their testimony at the hearings, the Chavez Subcommittee's report exonerated Tugwell and Ickes from responsibility for the shipping shortage and the food crisis. The report maintained that the investigation was far too general for the subcommittee to say whether the other charges against Tugwell were valid.[61]

The anti-Tugwell forces, having been thwarted by the administration's backing of the governor, decided to remove him by legislative fiat. Senator Vandenberg and Resident Commissioner Pagán capitalized on the anti-Tugwell momentum that had built up in Congress by introducing S.40 and its companion bill H.R. 784. The bill did not specifically refer to Tugwell, but provided that upon its enactment the term of office of the incumbent governor would expire and that the new governor would hold office for a period of two years. The senator's remarks, however, left little doubt that the bill was aimed specifically at Tugwell. He said, "Governor Tugwell's removal has been prayerfully sought by petitions from numerous Puerto Rican groups and other students of Puerto Rican affairs who believe that his swiftly expanding bureaucracy and his superlatively expensive administration—with all its implicit national socialization—is a fateful threat to our Island wards and is related to the Island's serious predicament."[62] Eleven days later the Senate Committee on Territories and Insular Affairs approved S.40 with two amendments: the governor's office was to expire sixty days after enactment of the bill, and future governors were to hold office for four years. The committee chairman, Senator Tydings of Maryland, did not think the bill was an ouster of Tugwell.[63]

But the administration thought otherwise. In a letter to Senator Tydings, Secretary Ickes strongly stated his objection to S.40: it was aimed specifically at Tugwell; and since the responsibility of removing an executive-appointed official was that of the president and not of the legislature, it was unconstitutional. The legislature did have the right, he continued, to impeach, but S.40 circumvented this provision and sought to punish a public official without a judicial trial. Besides, the secretary pointed out, the committee had acted hastily: it had succumbed to the insistence of a vocal minority in Puerto Rico, it had not held hearings or sought the opinion of the departments of State and Interior, it had not considered the implications that the bill would have on the Caribbean and Latin America.[64]

At a press conference on February 4, 1943, Ickes lived up to his nickname "Old Curmudgeon" in attacking Pagán for his attempt to remove Tugwell. He said, "We think that that ought to be a two-year term rather than a four-year term, and in that connection we have in mind the [fact that the] legislature of Puerto Rico sent a memorial to Commissioner Pagán asking him to introduce a bill providing for his recall. But he's too busy trying to tear down other people to introduce a bill that the people of his own Territory asked him to introduce."[65]

On February 9, 1943, the secretary of Interior stated in a long letter to Congressman Jasper Bell of Missouri, chairman of the House Committee on Insular Affairs, his reasons for opposing H.R.784. In addition to some of the reasons he gave in his letter to Senator Tydings, the secretary expounded on others: Tugwell had the backing of the insular legislature; 568,747 persons had signed a memorial supporting him; and he was therefore a popular governor; the controversial laws in Puerto Rico had been presented before the New Dealer took office; and governors in the past had become the centers of great political controversy, irrespective of their political views. Furthermore, H.R.784 would have the effect of superficially changing the Organic Act when a thorough investigation of the law was necessary. The secretary intimated that the Department of the Interior was studying how the Organic Act might be revised.[66]

In the hearings on H.R.784 that followed a week later, no new arguments were produced either for or against the bill's passage. They were highlighted by the showdown between Secretary Ickes and the resident commissioner, which presumably discredited Pagán and killed all hopes of the bill's success. Having the advantage of testifying over a week after the resident commissioner, the secretary came well prepared with a rebuttal.[67] Ickes questioned Pagán's integrity by accusing him of misrepresenting facts to serve his own interests and those of a minority. ". . . [T]his attack upon Governor Tugwell," the secretary charged, "by Mr. Pagán and his associates has bigger game as its objective . . . . They are attacking the wisdom of the people of Puerto Rico in electing to the legislature a majority which is opposed to Mr. Pagán's Socialist party and its Coalition allies. And they are attacking the Legislature of Puerto Rico because it has passed laws with which they do not agree and which are being faithfully executed by Governor Tugwell as he is charged to do." The bill, Ickes continued, was meant to build Pagán's own "political fences," and as soon as the administration told Pagán that it was considering a bill for an elective governor, he "came in with a badly digested, badly constructed bill. I think it is just politics."[68] The administration was able to beat back the attempt to oust Tugwell. There were two other similar attempts, the first in April, 1944, and the second in December, 1944.[69] Neither had much chance of success.

Since the administration staunchly opposed Tugwell's removal, the United States Congress sought to assert its authority in other ways. On January 11, 1943, four days after Senator Vandenberg introduced S.40, Representative Fred Crawford of Michigan introduced a bill to annul a whole range of sweeping laws passed by the insular legislature. These laws were: the Land Law, Water Resources Act, Puerto Rico Transportation Authority Act, Puerto Rico Industrial Development Company Act, Puerto Rico Communication Authority Act, and the Development Bank Act. Crawford explained his bill in this way, "Inasmuch as the administration for some strange reason seems reluctant to remove him [Tugwell] in spite of the flood of violent criticism and the disruption of economic life in Puerto Rico, the least we can do at this time is to undo some of the evil he has perpetrated in our territory."[70] Crawford sought to undo with one legislative stroke the entire PPD program.

Crawford's bill raised deep and serious questions of Puerto Rican autonomy. The United States Congress was seeking to exercise its authority over insular affairs to the extent of annulling laws duly passed by a popularly elected body, unless Crawford merely intended to pressure the administration into firing Governor Tugwell. There was widespread opposition to the bill among all Puerto Rican political groups. Muñoz Marín is reported as having said, ". . . [it would be] resisted with the same tenacity and the same determination with which the free nations of the world are resisting the attempts of the dictator Adolph Hitler to destroy democracy."[71] The bill was opposed by the administration, at least as it is reflected in the diary of the Interior department's legal counsel William Brophy.[72] Crawford's bill probably strengthened the position of the *Populares* rather than weakened it.[73]

In yet another way Congress felt obliged to exercise its powers. Both the Senate and the House called for investigations of the political, economic, and social situation in Puerto Rico. That the two bodies should initiate within a month of each other two separate investigations seemed a strange waste of Congressional energy and public money. The Senate approved, in January, 1943, Senate Resolution 26, which called for a study of "Economic and Social Conditions in Puerto Rico"; while the House authorized the Committee on Insular Affairs, by House Resolution 159 in April, 1943, to undertake the "Investigation of Political, Economic and Social Conditions in Puerto Rico."[74]

The Senate Subcommittee, known as the Chavez Subcommittee, after its chairman Dennis Chavez, approached its task in a fairly impartial manner. Senator Chavez and four other senators, among them Taft of Ohio, were interested in getting a cross-section of Puerto Rican views and opinions. They visited the island and attempted to meet and hear all interest groups. In all they heard forty-five witnesses testify before their subcommittee.[75] By far the most interesting development was Senator Taft's appreciation of the sincerity of the attempts by the PPD and Tugwell to eliminate the island's problems. He was impressed with the magnitude of Puerto Rico's problems and was willing to permit bold approaches to solve them. "I'm not exactly a radical," he is reported by Tugwell as having said, "but after all I object to being classed with those who think public ownership unconstitutional. I may not be in favor of it, usually, but Puerto Rico is a very special case."[76]

Indeed, the Chavez Subcommittee's evenhanded approach is reflected in its report. Far from being overly critical of the *Populares* and Tugwell, it underscored the need for federal aid to help alleviate conditions resulting from unemployment. The report also stressed that programs for increasing food production should be undertaken. Soon after the subcommittee's return to Washington, it secured the adoption of Senate Resolution 981 to appropriate funds ($25 million each for fiscal years 1943–1944 and 1944–1945) to ensure the continuation of the Works Progress Administration.[77]

The House subcommittee, under Congressman Bell, conducted its investigation in a different fashion, on the other hand. In contrast to the Chavez Subcommittee, which sought to hear all shades of political opinion, the Bell Subcommittee relied heavily upon witnesses who were opposed to Tugwell and the *Populares*. The hearings were stretched over a period of more than a year, the subcommittee's purpose apparently being to keep the Tugwell administration in Puerto Rico under constant watch.[78]

Its report certainly does not do justice to the massive and sometimes complex testimony that the subcommittee heard, presumably because the subcommittee did not consider it necessary to obtain the professional help of an economist, a statistician, or a historian.[79]

The report concluded that the insular government was increasingly encroaching upon private enterprises, which, in the subcommittee's opinion, corresponded with the situation of Fascist Italy under Mussolini. The leaders of the island, the report continued, had embarked upon policies and programs bound to destroy "individual liberties of the people and enslave them eventually by setting up a form of government wholly alien to our own."[80] It recommended that the teaching of the English language in public schools should be expanded, that the island's industrialization policies should be re-examined, and that the House Committee on Insular Affairs should be given full authority to consider all legislative matters affecting Puerto Rico.[81]

There is truth in Tugwell's assertion that the Bell Subcommittee proceeded about its business with prejudged notions[82] and that it was not sympathetic to the administration's explanation of why government-sponsored projects were necessary, given the conditions on the island.[83] Far from desiring to increase the island's autonomy, the Bell Subcommittee sought to impose stifling Congressional controls over the manner in which Puerto Rico was going to handle its problems, especially where federal funds were involved. When the Chavez Subcommittee sponsored Senate Resolution 981 to provide work relief for the unemployed in Puerto Rico and the Virgin Islands, Congressman Bell argued for an amendment that would have appropriated a portion of the internal revenue taxes on rum that were returned to the insular treasury to go to the Federal Works Agency, where the funds would have been controlled by Congress. Secretary Ickes and the Puerto Rican leaders of all parties registered strong protests, and the bill was shelved until February, 1944.[84]

The Vandenberg-Pagán bill, the Crawford measure, the two Congressional investigations, and the intended amendment to Senate Resolution 981 indicate Congress' desire to have a greater say in the administration of the island. So long as Puerto Rico was under the United States flag, and so long as it received federal funds, Congress should exercise its supervisory powers over insular affairs, according to many Congressional members. At a time when the executive had assumed wide powers, such Congressional reaction seems understandable. But those legislators who sought to remove Tugwell from the governorship one way or another were confusing the constitutional issue of Congressional prerogative and the political issues surrounding his incumbency. They overlooked the fact that Tugwell had the support of the insular legislature, that the policies they were attributing to the governor originated in nearly all cases with the *Populares,* and that the island's problems were such that bold and innovative methods were necessary to handle them. But above all, in singling out the New Dealer and the *Populares,* who after all represented the majority will of the Puerto Rican electorate, they neglected questions about the island's desire for self-government and greater autonomy.

Ironically, the man who insisted that the islanders be granted at least the right to elect their own governor was the appointed representative of the United States, Governor Tugwell. His experience with the United States Congress underscored the need for such a reform measure.

CHAPTER FOUR

An Attempt to End "Humiliating Suspense": The Elective Governor Bill of 1943

Coalition attacks upon Tugwell strengthened the governor's resolve to work for an amendment to the Organic Act to provide for an elective governor. A popularly elected governor would end some of the bickering over political patronage and pave the way for a smoother and less confused administration by the party in power, as it would normally control leadership in both the executive and legislative branches. An appointed governor was answerable to the president and the United States legislature, a fact which confused and confounded his duties in the minds of the Puerto Rican people, and made difficult his relationship with the popularly elected insular legislature. Besides, the United States was morally obliged to advance political freedom in its Caribbean possession in terms of the professed Allied aim during World War II to extend greater self-government in the colonial world.

Throughout 1942 and 1943 Tugwell worked towards this end, even though he was given no active encouragement from a skeptical Muñoz Marín, who was at this time preoccupied with consolidating his political power.[1] In a letter to President Roosevelt on March 11, 1942, Tugwell suggested that the president announce support for a change in Puerto Rican status after the war. Allowing the Puerto Ricans to elect their own officials, Tugwell continued, would "abjure colonialism not in words but by a deed," while the United States could retain military and naval privileges, as in the case of Cuba and Guantánamo.[2] Apparently sensitive to Caribbean criticism of colonialism, he prevailed upon the Caribbean Advisory Committee, organized jointly by the United States and Britain, to address a similar message to the president in June, 1942.[3]

The administration was prodded into some action only after Resident Commissioner Pagán introduced on July 6, 1942, H.R. 7352 to provide for an elective governor in Puerto Rico.[4] Secretary Ickes told Pagán, however, that the matter of revising the Organic Act needed to be carefully studied before decisions could be taken,[5] while Undersecretary Abe Fortas advised the chairman of the Committee on Interior Affairs that the bill required substantial revision.[6] On the same day that the secretary responded to Pagán, he requested Tugwell to consider preparing legislation for the election of a governor beginning in 1944 and every four years thereafter, and for any other changes to the Organic Act that were necessary.[7] It is not known what steps Tugwell took after receiving this communication. In November, 1942, the president reassured Pagán that the Department of the Interior was studying the question,[8] which suggests, if nothing else, that the administration had not forgotten about the subject of insular autonomy.

There was increased reference to Puerto Rican autonomy only after the Vandenberg-Pagán bill was introduced in January, 1943, seeking to remove Tugwell. The governor spoke briefly about self-government for Puerto Rico in the fifteenth insular legislature in February, 1943.[9] He was more specific about what steps should be taken when he testified at length before the Chavez Subcommittee about the necessity of ending "older approaches to colonialism." The United States should permit the election of a governor, who in turn should have the power to appoint the auditor, the commissioner of education, the attorney general, and the judges of the Supreme Court, all of these appointments then being submitted to the president for confirmation. The governor warned that this step should be taken soon or else there would be "grave administrative difficulties," but he ruled out independence for the island as a "cruel and delusive ideal."[10] The secretary of the Interior endorsed Tugwell's stand in a press conference on February 4, 1943.[11]

The Puerto Rican leaders, too, backed the sentiment. A joint cable was dispatched a day later by Muñoz Marín, Celestino Iriarte, and Ramírez Santibáñez, leaders of the PPD, the Union Republican party, and the Liberal party, respectively. They called for an end to Puerto Rico's colonial status in accordance with the anti-colonial affirmation as embodied in the Atlantic Charter.[12] This was followed up by a concurrent resolution adopted by the island's legislature urging Congress to terminate "the colonial system of government . . . totally and definitely."[13]

On March 9, 1943, the president, upon Ickes' recommendation, sent a message to Congress.[14] "It has long been the policy of the United States," President Roosevelt said, "progressively to reinforce the machinery of self-government in its territories." In accordance with this policy he asked Congress to consider amending the Organic Act so as, among other things, to permit the Puerto Ricans to elect their governor. The president informed Congress that he had appointed a committee—subsequently to be known as the President's Committee—consisting of an equal number of Puerto Ricans and mainland residents to advise the administration as to how the Organic Act might be changed.[15]

Undersecretary Fortas was made the chairman of the President's Committee. Other continental members were: Benjamin W. Thoron, director of DTIP, Governor Tugwell, and the Reverend R. A. McGowan, assistant director of the National Catholic Welfare Council. The Puerto Rican members were Muñoz Marín, Iriarte, Ramírez Santibáñez, and Puerto Rico's Supreme Court Justice Martin Travieso.[16] Neither the Socialist nor the Nationalist parties was represented by members on the committee. While the first had joined in a coalition with the Union Republican and therefore was presumably considered as having been represented, the second was excluded apparently because its goal was absolute and total independence and its members wished to have nothing to do with the committee.

Administration officials, in particular Fortas, wanted a "balanced" committee in which all the dominant parties were represented. Tugwell did not think that choosing party presidents because of their loyalty and responsibility to goals and organizations was a good idea. He preferred selecting prominent leaders. In addition, he wished to have a mixed executive-legislative committee in which the United States Congress would also be represented. This was, in retrospect, a good idea, because the administration measure on the elective governor emerging from the committee's recommendation ran into endless trouble with the Congress. At the time, however, the Interior department was opposed to the suggestion because of the anti-Tugwell sentiment in Congress.[17]

The governor succeeded at least in prevailing upon the administration to exclude Pagán because, Tugwell argued, the Socialist leader had "almost no following left and so counted for nothing at home."[18] Pagán naturally protested his exclusion to the president. After all, as resident commissioner he was the official representative of the islanders.[19] The Puerto Rican legislature agreed with Pagán, for it adopted a resolution asking the secretary to broaden the membership of the committee.[20] Some insular leaders accused Ickes of harboring a grudge against the resident commissioner.[21] But the secretary withstood all pressures to include Pagán in the committee. Relations between him and the resident commissioner had never been good, and Ickes probably believed that Pagán's violently anti-Tugwell stance in Congress would jeopardize the work of the President's Committee.

The appointment of the President's Committee was received by some Puerto Ricans and Congressional leaders with doubt and skepticism. Iriarte feared that making provisions for an elective governor was a ruse to keep Tugwell in office and that such a change would postpone the Coalition's ultimate goal of statehood.[22] Senator Tydings, who held the chairmanship of the Committee on Territories and Insular Affairs, and who had since 1936 advocated independence for Puerto Rico, stated that nothing short of complete political freedom could solve the island's political status issue.[23] In response to these criticisms, Undersecretary Fortas advised Secretary Ickes to make clear at one of his scheduled press conferences that the final political status of Puerto Rico would be considered only after there had been "some experience under an elective governor."[24]

Despite the administration's insistence that it was willing to consider only an elective governor then, Senator Tydings introduced on April 2, 1943, a bill designed to give Puerto Rico independence. The bill (S.952) provided for a three-year period in which the transference of power was to take place constitutionally. It was considerably different in its economic arrangement from the independence bill of 1936. The measure provided for a twenty-year transition period to regulate the export-import relationship between the United States and Puerto Rico at a duty-rate graduated at 5 percent per year. The bill did not change matters concerning United States military and naval installations, and the presence of its armed forces on the island, nor did it seek to alter United States control over Puerto Rico's foreign affairs.[25]

Secretary Ickes opposed S.952 in a letter to the senator on April 23, 1943. The reasons he gave for his opposition were, among others, that the bill restricted Puerto Ricans' choice to only independence, and that it came at an inopportune time when the islanders were fighting on the side of the Allies.[26] The Puerto Rican leaders appeared to agree with the secretary about having several options from which the people of Puerto Rico should be allowed to choose. A day later, the island's legislature adopted a concurrent resolution establishing a Puerto Rican commission to study the possible status options open to Puerto Ricans. Governor Tugwell approved the measure.[27]

In spite of these developments the chairman of the Senate Committee on Territories and Insular Affairs proceeded to hold hearings on S.952. It soon became apparent that there was little support for the bill from some other departments in the administration or from some of the senator's colleagues. Assistant Secretary of War John T. McCloy categorically stated the Army's opposition to independence for Puerto Rico during the war because the island was a "bulwark in the defense" of the Caribbean, but he was unwilling to say what position the Army might take after the war. "We ought to have a 'look-see,'" he said, "in regard to what the Caribbean area is at the end of the war . . . ."[28] Senator Homer T. Bone of Washington, a member of the committee, was not satisfied that there would be a clear distinction of responsibilities between Puerto Rico and the United States if the island became independent. Another member of the committee, Senator Taft of Ohio, would rather leave the question until after the war because he felt it was related to the entire range of semi-autonomous states in the Caribbean and elsewhere.[29]

Puerto Rican and non-Puerto Rican advocates of insular independence were given ample opportunity to state their views. Puerto Rico was, they maintained, culturally and historically Latin American and should be made sovereign so that it could more rightly affiliate itself spiritually with the rest of Latin America. Their testimonies glibly passed over the question of what might happen to the island economically if it became a separate republic. In contrast, statehood adherents pointed out that the bill did not take sufficient cognizance of the economic realities in Puerto Rico. The island would be subjected to economic disaster if it were to sever its ties with the United States, they predicted.[30]

Ickes wrote to Tydings a second time and pointed out, among other things, that serious economic consequences might affect the entire Caribbean if Puerto Rico was granted independence, and that the president was in favor of extending only autonomy in local matters for the time being.[31] Muñoz Marín, who had not yet indicated his position on S.952, stated to reporters that the bill did not fully accommodate Puerto Rico's economic needs, and that reforming the Organic Act appeared to him to have a greater potential then.[32] Shortly thereafter, he sent a cable to Tydings jointly with the president of the insular House, Rafael Arrillaga Torrens, advising the senator to incorporate other forms of status options besides independence from among which Puerto Ricans could make a choice.[33] In July, 1943, the Tariff Commission forwarded to Tydings its findings, which were that serious repercussions would follow the reduction of trade and federal benefits.[34] In the same month the secretary of the Treasury, Henry J. Morgenthau, Jr., pointed out to the Senate committee chairman the bill's unsound fiscal provisions, and the difficulties it would cause in the application of United States navigation and coastwise laws.[35]

Senator Tydings was possibly aware of all this. Puerto Rico's position was considerably different than that of the Philippines, which he had helped in 1935 to set on a ten-year road to independence. The Philippines could sustain independence economically, and its inhabitants had indicated their support for it. On the other hand, Puerto Rico's economy was so closely integrated with that of the United States that the islanders stood to suffer from any plan that provided for abrupt or gradual severance of ties without proper economic safeguards. Nor had there been any test of Puerto Rican public opinion on the status question. Moreover, there was hardly any support for the independence bill in Congress. Why, then, did the Maryland senator introduce the bill in the midst of a concerted effort by the administration? One must assume that Tydings was piqued about having been bypassed by the administration. After all, he *was* the chairman of the Senate Committee on Territories and Insular Affairs, and his committee *was* constitutionally responsible for sharing in the administering of Puerto Rico.

The administration proceeded, however, with the President's Committee. Preparatory work by Governor Tugwell and the staff of the Department of the Interior and DTIP gave Undersecretary Fortas a general idea as to the anticipated positions of his Puerto Rican colleagues. Tugwell warned, according to one memorandum, that all leaders would attempt to disagree with the committee's recommendations so as to emphasize to their followers that they had not abandoned the search for a final solution to the status question. The memorandum also pointed out that the Puerto Rican leaders were opposed to the federal representative on the island being termed "High Commissioner."[36] In his memorandum to the Interior secretary, Fortas intimated his desire to see Puerto Rico achieve goals of self-government beyond those to be provided by the anticipated elective governor bill. Anxious to see that this trend of greater self-government continued after the Puerto Ricans had an elected governor, Fortas believed that it was necessary for the United States to reserve certain "essential executive powers" with respect to the insular legislature that might have serious consequences on the island's basic internal organization and its external relations. Fortas perhaps implied that it was the United States' responsibility to prevent things from going wrong by means of "essential executive powers," thus averting a setback to the policy of greater autonomy.[37]

The Puerto Rican members of the President's Committee were able to agree in a couple of meetings that the elective governor should be given powers greater than those enjoyed by the appointed governor. Some other aspects upon which they agreed were: electing a governor in 1944, increasing loan margins of municipal and insular governments, creating a Department of Public Welfare and Social Security, empowering the governor to appoint all heads of the executive departments, permitting the legislature to fix uniform salaries for all department heads, electing two resident commissioners instead of one, increasing the Supreme Court justices from five to seven, allowing appeals direct from the insular Supreme Court to the United States Supreme Court, and giving no authority to the coordinator of federal activities over insular officials. The Puerto Rican group reached no agreement concerning the island's political status in the future.[38]

By the time that the President's Committee met for the first session on July 19, 1943, the continental and insular members were substantially in agreement as to what changes should be made to the Organic Act. The members knew fairly well which issues would generate disagreement. The committee's function did not include resolving questions about Puerto Rico's final status, although its discussion could hardly be avoided. Still, the secretary felt obliged to remind the members at the opening session that it did not constitute a "Constitutional Convention but an advisory body."[39]

The President's Committee met for twelve days between July 19 and August 1, 1943. Its proceedings run over 300 pages in fine print. On many occasions the Puerto Rican members insisted that the committee could not discuss amending the Organic Act without considering the larger question of the island's future political status. Abe Fortas reminded his Puerto Rican colleagues that the committee's function was restricted to the discussion of the elective governor and to matters related to his powers and office. He pointed out further that providing for an elective governor then would not prevent solving Puerto Rico's final political status later.[40]

Another point of disagreement between the continental and insular members was whether Congress' prior approval was necessary before the Puerto Rican people were asked to choose from among several options. Fortas contended that no status solution could hope to succeed if Congress did not at first approve of it. If Congressional endorsement was necessary, the Puerto Ricans countered, it raised serious questions about insular autonomy and the value of a popular referendum. In the end the committee decided to recommend the creation of an advisory council of Puerto Ricans and United States residents, whose function it would be to report within a period of time further desirable changes in the Organic Act.[41]

As had been anticipated, there was disagreement as to what the federal coordinator might be called. Undersecretary Fortas looked upon the official as being responsible for the smooth functioning of federal agencies and representing the president. He chose the term "Commissioner-General," which the Puerto Ricans accepted on the understanding that the office had little in common with that of a "High Commissioner" in British colonies, and would not carry powers of intervention in matters that were strictly insular.[42]

In addition, the President's Committee agreed upon the

following aspects: a governor was to be elected in 1944 and every four years thereafter; he was to have increased powers—this at Tugwell's insistence—such as naming the cabinet, including the auditor, and the justices of the Supreme Court, with the advice and consent of the insular Senate. The executive council as a corporate body was to be abolished. The committee accepted Tugwell's argument that a weak executive in Puerto Rico would hamper efficient administration, and that the elective governor should therefore have wider powers than those he wielded as an appointed governor.[43]

The committee's recommendations were incorporated in a bill by the Department of the Interior and forwarded to the president on August 31, 1943, for him to approve and send to Congress. The bill proposed amending various sections of the Organic Act and adding new ones. It provided for the creation of a joint advisory council of twelve members to "assure constant review" on the status question. Section I of the bill stated, "It is further declared to be the intention of Congress that no further changes in the Organic Act shall be made except with the concurrence of the people of Puerto Rico or their duly elected representatives." The president retained the power of absolute veto over insular laws that he considered in conflict with the "security and international relations of the United States and Puerto Rico." Furthermore, the United States reserved the right to intervene "to prevent or suppress invasion, insurrection, rebellion, or (upon the request of the Governor) lawless violence."[44]

President Roosevelt submitted to Senator Tydings on September 28, 1943, the proposed bill without any changes, accompanied by a brief message concerning the desire and need for self-government in Puerto Rico. He reassured the senator that Congress would not be giving up its ultimate power of legislating on the territory by its passage, nor would it threaten United States strategic dominance in the area.[45] Three days later Senator Tydings introduced the bill as S.1407 to the Committee on Territories and Insular Affairs.[46]

The Puerto Rican press and public hailed the measure as progressive, especially as it came in the midst of a war.[47] Congress, however, was not so favorably disposed to submit to the administration's wishes. The Chavez Subcommittee had just completed its investigation of insular matters, and had not shown too great a concern about granting greater political autonomy. The Bell

Subcommittee was in the process of conducting its own investigations, with unmistakable hostility towards the Tugwell administration. It was also clear that the anti-Tugwell sentiment among certain other elements in Congress had not subsided. That the administration measure was going to run into difficulties became apparent soon.

A subcommittee of the Senate Committee on Territories and Insular Affairs under the chairmanship of Senator Chavez of New Mexico conducted hearings on S.1407. Despite the testimonies of Secretary Ickes and DTIP director Thoron, members of the subcommittee remained doubtful and skeptical about some of the bill's provisions. Senator Ralph O. Brewster of Maine doubted the constitutionality of the provision that stipulated that changes in the Organic Act could not be made except in consultation with the Puerto Ricans. The present Congress, he argued, could not bind future Congresses to the decisions it made. Senator Taft of Ohio stated that the bill confused two separate issues, namely, autonomy and Congressional sovereignty. Since the bill was considering only autonomy, he continued, there was no question about Congress' power to oversee insular affairs. The Puerto Rican witnesses, on the other hand, argued that the bill circumvented the real issue, that is, whether Congress was willing to grant independence or statehood to the island.[48]

Administration officials hoped to get Tydings to extend the hearings so that some of the Puerto Rican members of the President's Committee might be able to be present to testify on behalf of the bill, but met with no success.[49]

The extent of S.1407's troubles became known two months later in February, 1944, when the Senate subcommittee reported it out with extensive changes. The subcommittee struck out the provision concerning Congress' obligation to consult Puerto Ricans before changing the Organic Act. One Congress could not bind those succeeding it, it declared. The provision creating a joint advisory council was omitted because, in the words of the subcommittee, it was the responsibility of Congress "to study and resolve on the relationships between the United States and Puerto Rico and to determine for itself at the proper time and through its regular procedure the ultimate destiny of the island." To emphasize this point, the subcommittee added an amendment to section two of the bill. The amendment stipulated that any excise or sales taxes levied on "articles, goods, wares, and merchandise" imported into Puerto Rico for the purpose of re-exportation would be refunded.[50]

The subcommittee drastically cut the powers of the elective governor, in most cases to the advantage of the insular legislature. The terms of office for cabinet and lesser officials were to be decided by the Puerto Rican legislature, which was also to be given the power to decide on the fate of the executive council. Further to weaken the powers of the governor, the subcommittee increased those of the auditor, and made the office of the attorney general elective. The subcommittee was opposed to any increases in insular departments and agencies, and limited to two the increase in the number of Supreme Court justices. The bill was amended accordingly. Nor was it in favor of the governor appointing the new justices; it provided for the president to continue doing so with the advice and consent of the United States Senate. The Senate group eliminated the office of "Commissioner-General" and replaced it with that of the "Federal Coordinator," its fear being that the first might become a "supergovernor." Lastly, it reinserted section 34 of the Organic Act, which read, "All laws enacted by the legislature of Porto Rico shall be reported to the Congress of the United States as provided in section 23 of this Act, which hereby reserves the power and authority to annul the same."[51]

There was strong reaction to the Senate subcommittee's amendments. Muñoz Marín was reported as saying, "It would be better not to have any reform at all. In this way the problem would remain open for prompt consideration and could be solved in consultation with the Puerto Rican people in an honorable, democratic and definite manner." Iriarte and Pagán criticized the omission of the policy statement regarding the consultation of Puerto Ricans, and Ramírez Santibáñez believed that the amendments eliminated the fundamental recommendations made by the President's Committee.[52] Tugwell's unfavorable reaction to S.1407 as amended was relayed to Undersecretary Fortas upon the latter's request, first briefly, and later in a twelve-page memorandum.[53]

Whether or not Senator Chavez received official administration reaction to the much-amended S.1407, he introduced the bill in the Senate on February 15, 1944, for the deliberation of his not-too-enthusiastic colleagues. Senator Vandenberg, anxious to see that Tugwell did not become the first elected governor, inquired why the president could not appoint a native Puerto Rican as governor for a few years before the islanders were permitted to elect one. Senator Taft commented that the Puerto Ricans were dissatisfied because the bill did not go far enough to determine the island's "ultimate status," but he believed that the United States could not do so, at least while the war continued. On the other hand, Senator Tydings was convinced that only "complete, absolute, and unconditional independence" was the solution because the "lines of cleavage in culture, speech, and thought is [sic] wide as between Latin on the one hand [and] the predominant Anglo-Saxon, characterized by the United States, on the other." The Puerto Ricans, he believed, were being kept in "slavery because of a few investments there by persons in this country who are reaping handsome dividends as a result." Despite such sentiments, the Senate passed the bill. Three days later it was referred to the House Committee on Insular Affairs.[54]

But the House Committee on Insular Affairs was not in a friendly mood at all. It brought up for discussion in February and March a bill (S.981) that, as amended by the committee in November, 1943, provided for returning 50 percent of the revenues on rum, tobacco, cigarettes, and cigars to a special fund to be controlled by the federal government.[55] The bill sought to introduce a drastic change in the fiscal arrangement between Puerto Rico and the United States that had operated for forty years. It was an ominous sign of how the committee might further amend S.1407.

It would appear, furthermore, that the House committee sought by direct and indirect ways to make known to the administration that the price of approving the elective governor bill—and that, too, in its amended form[56]—was the ejection of Tugwell from the governorship. On a number of occasions members of the committee made public such a desire. Republican Representatives Sterling Cole of New York and Fred Crawford of Michigan appealed to Secretary Ickes on March 15, 1944, to fire Tugwell. A day later, the committee's Democratic chairman, Jasper C. Bell of Missouri, joined his colleagues in a similar gesture stated somewhat more strongly.[57] About two weeks thereafter, Democratic Representative Dan R. McGehee of Mississippi, also a committee member, introduced House Resolution 496 requesting the president to dismiss the governor.[58]

The Union Republican party joined the chorus by adopting

on April 30, 1944, a resolution condemning Tugwell, Thoron, Fortas, and Ickes.[59] And Pagán, fearing that honest elections could not take place while Tugwell governed, approached Undersecretary Fortas with the proposal of postponing the 1944 elections to 1945, which was rejected in no uncertain terms.[60] It is not known whether other House committee members supported Pagán's move.

As late as June 9, 1944, the administration did not know whether the House Committee on Insular Affairs was going to hold hearings.[61] Committee chairman Bell claimed that other important business had delayed consideration of S.1407.[62] The Department of the Interior moved to pressure Bell into taking action, even though Tugwell was of the opinion that the administration should not urge passage of the bill in its emasculated form.[63] The secretary wrote to Bell on June 23, 1944, urging him to support S.1407 as originally introduced. The Senate amendments, he argued, would restrict insular efficiency in government.[64]

More than two months later the House committee held a hearing. Undersecretary Fortas appeared as a witness for the administration. The Interior department appeared to be willing to accept S.1407 in its amended form,[65] because, as Fortas explained it, it would still be a significant step forward in self-government for Puerto Rico. The islanders had reached "political maturity," he continued, and an elective governor would add to their sense of responsibility and confidence. Beyond that, the bill's passage would reflect well in the eyes of Latin America and the rest of the world.[66] Even though Fortas had tried through Tugwell to persuade the Puerto Rican members of the President's Committee to come to Washington to testify, none had come.[67] It was in part because, as Tugwell explained to Fortas, the insular leaders did not wish to come to Washington if it involved the political risk of bringing nothing home.[68] Two persons representing the *Populares,* however, did appear to urge the bill's passage. They were Representatives Elmer Ellsworth and Jesús T. Piñero.[69]

On the same day that he testified before the House Insular Affairs Committee, Undersecretary Fortas addressed a letter to presidential advisor Samuel Rosenman stating that a communication to Bell about the desirability of passing the elective governor bill would prove effective. Fortas' letter was accompanied by a draft message for the president to send to Bell.[70] A couple of days later, the undersecretary urged Congressman Richard J. Welch of California to use his good offices with Bell to obtain quick action on S.1407.[71]

The president wrote to Bell on August 29, 1944 (made public September 4, 1944), pointing out to the Congressman that the bill had widespread Puerto Rican support, and that its passage would "multiply the good will we have already gained throughout the Western Hemisphere."[72] Bell replied on September 5, 1944, intimating to the president that Congressional preoccupation with two other measures, which were in conference stages, had brought the two Houses to a "standstill." Many of the twenty-six Congressmen serving on the House committee, he continued, were absent, thus making quorums difficult to obtain. If under these circumstances the committee were to clear the bill, the "objections which would be raised on account of the quorum would in all probability result in the defeat of the bill on the floor of the House."[73] By December 9, Bell believed it impossible to report out S.1407 in time for it to pass before the Congress adjourned.[74]

By December, 1944, however, the political scene in Puerto Rico had changed. The *Populares* had won thumping majorities in both Houses in the November, 1944, elections, and had elected one in their ranks, Jesús T. Piñero, as resident commissioner-elect. An elated Muñoz Marín reported to Ickes that the electoral majorities had vindicated the *Popular* policies, Tugwell's governorship, and the administration's backing of both. There was, therefore, no need for hurried action. The bill, he told Secretary Ickes, was "generally and deeply unsatisfactory." He had supported it "only on the certainty . . . [that] it would receive a veto." The *Popular* leader continued, ". . . I am convinced that we should wait until the people have spoken and then work out a detailed solution on the basis of the wishes they may express."[75]

Ickes agreed about letting S.1407 die because any hope of its passage, he said, was "academic." He was a little puzzled, however, as to what the Puerto Rican leader intended doing. Did he want the elective governor bill reintroduced in the next Congressional session, or did he desire that the Organic Act remain unaltered until a plebiscite was held in Puerto Rico? Whatever it was that Muñoz Marín wanted to do, the secretary added, he would have to review it first.[76]

Tugwell's enemies in Congress, repeatedly thwarted in their

moves to displace him, did not quite give up by the end of 1944, although much of the wind out of the anti-Tugwell sail had dissipated. In December, 1944, Representative Cole of New York introduced H.R.5570 to terminate Tugwell's governorship sixty days after its enactment.[77] The House Committee on Insular Affairs cleared the bill hastily, even though a quorum was allegedly not present. This prompted Secretary Ickes to write two letters to majority floor leader John W. McCormack of Massachusetts. The first denounced the bill as unconstitutional. He was particularly angry at the hasty action on H.R.5570, when the same committee had allowed the administration-sponsored S.1407 to lie "dormant" since February, 1944. He asked the majority leader to have the bill "watched so that it will not be taken up with unanimous consent and also to endeavor to prevent the granting of a rule that would authorize its consideration." In the second letter, Ickes pointed out to Representative McCormack that the committee had capitulated to a vocal minority that had been thoroughly beaten in the 1944 elections.[78] In any case, the bill had little chance of passage because the House Democratic leadership was determined to block any attempt to obtain unanimous consideration of the bill.[79]

There are a number of reasons why Congress dealt a cruel blow to Puerto Rican aspirations of greater self-government. Congress desired to exert its authority especially at a time when it felt that the administration had assumed wide powers, some of which encroached upon its traditional prerogatives. The House Committee on Insular Affairs was particularly sensitive about this, as it sought by means of its powers over appropriations to share in the administration of Puerto Rico. In part the administration was responsible for failing to cultivate harmonious relationships with Congressional leadership. The administration might have invited both the Senate and House committees to participate in the President's Committee. The differences in points of view among the administration, Congress, and the Puerto Rican leadership might conceivably have been ironed out before the measure, emerging out of such deliberations, reached Congress for its consideration. As it happened, Congress virtually ignored the recommendations of the President's Committee and proceeded to chop and change S.1407 in a great show of its constitutional prerogative.[80] But beyond this, there are other reasons that lie in public opinion, ignorance, and politics.

The twenty-three members of the House committee and the sixteen of its Senate counterpart were not directly responsible to the Puerto Rican people, and any pressure of public opinion as to their responsibility could only come from mainland citizens. The continental citizenry remained indifferent and ignorant about matters concerning Puerto Rico. And few questioned the spirit of paternalism that prevailed among the more powerful members of the two committees.[81]

Under these circumstances it was easy for Congress to become entangled with the administration and insular politics rather than policies. No doubt some of the members of the two committees sought to use every instance to embarrass and oppose the administration.[82] In this they found a cause in Tugwell's occupancy of the island's governorship. A controversial figure, the New Dealer's policies and support of the *Popular* program easily made him the target of politicians who had never been too fond of New Dealers. In this connection, Tugwell was more a hindrance than a help because Congress refused to pass the elective governor bill, fearing his eligibility as the first elected governor. Thus, the 1943–1944 attempt by the United States to extend to Puerto Rico greater self-government became sidetracked by the administration's endorsement of Tugwell's governorship and some Congressmen's desire to displace him.

CHAPTER FIVE

Muñoz Marín's Shift
from Independence to Autonomy,
1944-1946

Those among the *Populares* who believed in independence for Puerto Rico were encouraged by the international situation. The Atlantic Charter had reaffirmed the colonial peoples' rights to choose whatever form of government they desired; the Yalta Conference in February, 1945, had agreed upon reviewing the existing mandated territories; and at the San Francisco meeting where the United Nations Organization was being formulated, considerable attention was given to the whole colonial question. Eventually the document that emerged from the San Francisco meeting, the United Nations Charter, was to reserve three chapters for colonies and their aspirations. Chapter XI was entitled "Declaration Regarding Non–self-governing Territories," while chapters XII and XIII dealt with the "International Trusteeship System" and the "Trusteeship Council," respectively.[1] On a number of occasions, *independentista* leaders in Puerto Rico capitalized on the situation to appeal to the international body and to major Western leaders.

Their main efforts, however, were concentrated on domestic politics in the hope of pressuring *Popular* leader Muñoz Marín into seizing the opportunity to win independence for the island. Soon after Senator Tydings introduced in Congress the independence bill discussed in the previous chapter, a pro-independence assembly of 200 persons was held in April, 1943, in San Juan. The majority of those present were *Populares,* although Liberals, Nationalists, and Communists were also present.[2] The insular advocates of independence turned out in force at the hearings in May, 1943, to demonstrate to Congress the widespread support for the Tydings bill. But the PPD leader did not openly endorse the bill, thus leaving doubt in the minds of many United States Congressmen as to how much support the *independentistas* had. More importantly, there was little support for independence in the administration or the Congress of the United States.[3]

Indeed, Muñoz Marín stated on a number of occasions his qualified opposition to either statehood or independence. One such occasion was at a roundtable conference at the University of Chicago radio in July, 1943, when he expressed his desire to see the "colonial" status ended, but ruled out independence and statehood on economic grounds. It was more realistic, he argued, to work for an elective governor at the time.[4]

Undaunted, the *independentistas* prepared for the organization in August of 1943 a Pro-Independence Congress (CPI). Muñoz Marín was fearful that the CPI leadership, among whom were prominent *Populares,* might develop into a new party. He called, therefore, an informal meeting of the party leadership, including the *independentistas,* and announced that he would not attend the scheduled meeting because the PPD was officially neutral on the status issue. The *Popular* leader cautioned the *independentistas* that "the only interest which the *Popular* party as such could have would be in the resolutions or actions of the Congress that might be prejudicial to the party's work or lead to confusion among the voters."[5]

The *independentistas* proceeded to organize the Pro-Independence Congress. Muñoz Marín wished the Congress "much success in the expression before the people and the Government of the United States of the ideals that without doubt are those of large numbers of Puerto Ricans."[6] The 1800 delegates at San Juan hammered out statements of purpose and goal. The delegates expressed their desire in these statements to work for independence by peaceful methods, in part by means of marshaling public sentiment behind, and lobbying for, their goals. Dr. Juan Augusto Perea, once a political associate of Nationalist leader Albizu Campos, was elected president.[7] He and Dr. Sergio Peña were later named to represent the CPI in Washington, and Gilberto Concepción de Gracia, residing in the United States, was appointed the group's legal advisor.[8]

Differences between the CPI leadership and Muñoz Marín were soon to emerge. The CPI condemned the elective governor bill (S.1407), then being considered by Congress, as a "smoke screen" for colonialism.[9] The more radical among the *independentistas* moved in March, 1944, for the creation of an independence party, but were thwarted by those who felt that the establishment of a new party would only divide and weaken their forces and benefit the Coalition. Dr. Augusto Perea and his followers charged that the CPI had become a branch of the PPD and resigned. Late in 1944, the CPI presidency was given to Concepción de Gracia.[10] For the moment, a measure of harmony was restored between the CPI and the *Populares*.

Muñoz Marín could not afford a rupture just before the 1944 elections. He proceeded as gingerly as he could to keep the status question out of the elections. As early as October, 1943, he had maintained that independence would not be an issue in the elections a year hence. He said he was not willing to discuss the status issue until Congress conceded that Puerto Rico had the right of plebiscite to determine its final status.[11]

In this endeavor, the Puerto Rican senator could point to the opposition to independence and statehood among United States Congressmen. Rafael Soltero Peralta, representing the Masons of Puerto Rico, interviewed influential legislators on the island's future status. Representative Crawford of Michigan, who was a member of the House Committee on Insular Affairs, was interviewed several times. Crawford stated that Puerto Rico should not think of statehood or independence for the next twenty-five years. He said bluntly, in a later interview, "I'm going to explain the real reason. Puerto Rico cannot be independent because the United States has to maintain an army, and a navy in the island to defend the territory against the Russian menace, which after this war will try to dismember this continent to take possession of South America." To give Puerto Rico a free hand in making treaties, he continued, would be to run the same risk as in the case of Argentina.[12] He was apparently referring to Argentina's resistance to supporting the Allied war effort.

Senator Allen J. Ellender of Louisiana echoed some of Crawford's sentiments. He doubted whether the Puerto Ricans were capable of self-government, and would rather grant autonomy in small doses.[13] Representative Cole of New York believed that the United States could not give up control, especially as Puerto Rico depended upon federal funds.[14] Nebraska's Senator Hugh Butler believed that to grant the island independence would be to abandon United States responsibility towards it.[15] Several other senators and representatives were opposed to giving either independence or statehood to the island. A few supported whatever the islanders desired. But the only influential legislator willing to give Puerto Rico independence was the chairman of the Senate Committee on Insular and Territorial Affairs, Senator Tydings.[16]

Partly in response to the challenge of the *independentistas,* the November, 1944, PPD platform contained a promise to hold a plebiscite on the definite status of the island "no later than the moment of the structuring of world peace." But the PPD insisted during the campaign that status was not an issue in the elections.[17] In a pamphlet called *People's Catechism,* Muñoz Marín directed his remarks about the island's status to "impatient" *Populares*:

> Then, if a Popular elected by the people on November 7, 1944, tries to use the position to which he was elected to vote for independence, statehood, or any other form of definite political status, would he be violating the people's mandate?
>
> Yes, clearly he would be violating the people's mandate. No Popular will act that way. He who would act that way would no longer be considered a Popular by the people.[18]

The PPD won a landslide victory in 1944. The Republicans and Socialists were effectively excluded from their positions of power. Furthermore, a *Popular,* Jesús T. Piñero, was elected to the post of resident commissioner. Muñoz Marín's power could not now be threatened by the Coalition. The challenge to his power came, however, from members of his own party who had *independentista* leanings. For instance, newly elected *Popular* representative Benjamin Ortiz, soon to become the House majority leader, declared his belief in independence for Puerto Rico and offered financial support to the CPI. Another prominent *Popular,* Antonio Pacheco Padró, argued in a newspaper article that since the issue of independence could disrupt the PPD Muñoz

Marín, the only man capable of achieving independence, should take the initiative.[19]

On December 10, 1944, the Pro-Independence group held another meeting. It was attended by leading *Populares*.[20] A resolution was adopted by the CPI calling upon the insular legislature to raise the issue of independence before the Congress of the United States.[21] Two weeks later the CPI president, Concepción de Gracia, wrote letters to President Roosevelt, Prime Minister Winston Churchill, and Marshal Stalin informing them about Puerto Rico's desire for independence.[22] Muñoz Marín was concerned that the CPI political structure was gradually assuming permanence in the form of delegations throughout the island. To him it appeared too much like activities preliminary to the organization of a new party, despite the CPI leadership's assurances to the contrary.[23]

The CPI's intention was, as Tugwell explained, to maneuver the *Popular* leader into announcing something concrete about his 1944 plebiscite promise. The governor advised Muñoz Marín to play down the plebiscite issue until he had discussed the matter with the Department of the Interior. Tugwell told Undersecretary Fortas, "He [Muñoz Marín] wants something beyond it [the elective governor bill then bogged down in Congress]—though just what that something is, is not quite clear, and could best become clear, I believe, through conversations between Muñoz, the Secretary, and yourself."[24] Fortas replied to the governor after consulting with Secretary Ickes,[25] expressing the belief that Muñoz Marín should come to Washington to reach some understanding with the department on the elective governor bill, specifically, and the status question, generally. Fortas preferred for the Puerto Rican leader not to make a public statement, for fear of arousing "unwarranted hopes."[26]

Apparently impressed by the *independentista* agitation in Puerto Rico, Senator Tydings introduced on January 10, 1945, a bill (S.227) to provide for the island's independence.[27] Like his independence bill of 1943, the present measure provided for the election of a Puerto Rican constitutional convention and the writing of a republican constitution. A year after the president of the United States endorsed the constitution, a twenty-year transition period was to follow. As in the earlier bill, the United States was to reserve the right to expropriate insular land for defense purposes and to maintain military and naval bases in Puerto Rico.

Section 3 (n) of the bill provided for United States intervention in insular affairs under emergency situations.[28]

Encouraged by the Tydings independence bill, the CPI moved quickly to capitalize on the international situation. CPI leader Concepción de Gracia and Representative Vito Marcantonio of New York announced their intention of presenting Puerto Rico's case before the forthcoming United Nations conference in San Francisco.[29] On March 26, 1945, the *independentista* leadership prevailed upon Representative Marcantonio to introduce an independence bill that incorporated some of the changes to the Tydings bill requested by the CPI.[30] In May the CPI requested a seat in the future United Nations Organization as a prelude to recognizing the island as an independent state.[31]

Muñoz Marín could not ignore the activities of the CPI, among whose numbers were many *Populares*.[32] On January 21, 1945, Resident Commissioner Piñero declared that Congress should clarify its position on the status question by permitting the islanders to decide on a plebiscite.[33] Governor Tugwell echoed Piñero's sentiments in his message to the Puerto Rican legislature on February 13, 1945. He said, "Fairness to everyone requires that the Congress offer the choices it is willing to accept rather than to require that Puerto Ricans should petition for status with the risk of rejection."[34]

The *Popular* leader persuaded other insular legislators of the wisdom of Tugwell's argument, as he explained to Secretary Ickes,[35] for on February 20, 1945, the Puerto Rican legislature passed a resolution requesting Congress to offer options of political status from among which the islanders could choose. But the resolution insisted that it be done in such a manner "that our people may have clear knowledge of the mutual economic relationships and the recognition of mutual moral obligations that would exist under each of the alternative forms that Congress may present to them."[36] Copies of the resolution were sent to the president, the secretary of the Interior, the chairmen of the Senate and House committees responsible for insular affairs, and others.[37]

But if Muñoz Marín had hoped to dissuade Senator Tydings from proceeding with his independence bill, he was disappointed, for the senator opened hearings on S.227. Tydings did, however, postpone the hearings once he had heard *independentistas* until after the insular legislative session came to an end. He sought to give all an opportunity to testify.[38] Secretary Ickes had made clear the administration's position even before the hearings had started. "I have repeatedly said," the secretary wrote on March 3, 1945, "that I consider it not only right but desirable that the people of Puerto Rico should be given an opportunity to express freely and democratically their desires in regard to their ultimate relationship to the United States. This expression might well be given in a plebiscite to be held under conditions prescribed by the Congress of the United States, but it should be only after a full consideration of alternatives which the Congress may be willing to grant to the people of Puerto Rico and full exploration and exposition of the economic consequences to each of them, both to Puerto Rico and to the United States."[39]

To explore all possible avenues for a definitive solution to the status issue, the Puerto Rican legislature named members to the Joint Legislative Committee that it had created in 1943. Muñoz Marín was appointed as chairman of the committee. The remaining eight members represented all political groups and parties except the Nationalists.[40]

The administration in Washington took steps to be informed about the possible status alternatives and their economic implications. In April, 1945, special assistant to the secretary of the Interior, Jack B. Fahy, prepared an eleven-page memorandum. He illustrated both United States and Puerto Rican interests with facts and figures and considered how they would be affected in the following alternatives: "quick statehood," "quick independence," "provisional statehood," and "provisional independence." In listing United States interests, Fahy pointed out that 94 percent of the island's goods came from the mainland, making Puerto Rico its seventh-best customer. In 1940, for instance, United States farmers received $20 million for food consumed on the island, while mainland manufacturers and processors sold $100 million worth of merchandise. There were likewise interests in United States railroads, truckers, and steamship lines. Continental sugar industry, too, had money invested in Puerto Rico (no figures were given), but Fahy pointed out that United States cane- and beet-sugar growers probably desired to see the island become independent, and thus end insular competition.[41]

The memorandum went on to point out the extent of Puerto Rico's interests tied with the island's continued relationship with the United States. Without tariff-free access to United States markets for the island's sugar, tobacco, rum, fruits, and so on, Puerto Rico would lose $50 million, which it was not likely to make up as an independent country because it had very little to offer other countries. Puerto Rico also desired to retain United States excise revenues on its rum, which came to $25 million yearly, and it also sought to be exempted from United States tariffs on imports like rice, beans, and textiles because it would save the island about $7 million. The list of benefits Puerto Rico wished to retain was long: exemption from United States Coastwise Navigation Laws so as to utilize cheaper foreign rates and thus save $8 million; exemption from the Sugar Act of 1937, which in 1938 cost the island 25,000 in unemployed, 100,000 in idle acres, and $20 million in income; change in agricultural policy because the existing policy was exacerbating problems of unemployment; and, finally, protection from State department tariff concessions to other countries. In 1939, for example, the United States treaty with Cuba seriously affected the Puerto Rican pineapple industry.[42]

Given these facts, Fahy continued, both "quick statehood" and "quick independence" would be disastrous for the island. Under immediate statehood the total drop in federal and state expenditure in Puerto Rico would be from $51 per capita to $39. With immediate independence the per capita insular government expenditure would fall from $39 to $20. The island's population density, its need to increase agricultural production, and other special problems made it necessary that either "provisional statehood" or "provisional independence" be tried out for ten years, at the end of which the whole situation should be reviewed. If there was no satisfactory progress, then greater autonomy should be implemented. Fahy ruled out dominion status because Puerto Rico's present state of productivity could not sustain it.[43]

The memorandum completely ignored the island's potential in industrialization, as was pointed out in a critique offered by Interior's legal counsel William Brophy.[44] Nor did it explore in any detail the dominion status. But Fahy's memorandum clearly showed the extent to which Puerto Rico depended upon the United States. Under such conditions the Department of the Interior could not possibly accept independence programs along the lines suggested by the Tydings bill.

In the same month that Fahy prepared his memorandum, Governor Tugwell addressed another to Secretary Ickes. His conclusions about Puerto Rico–United States relationships were the same as those of Fahy. Tugwell discussed what he considered to be the ten essential points in the matter of status. The long association between the two, the governor said, made it impossible to deal with the island's problems except with the help of the United States. Puerto Rico needed special treatment in social security benefits, aid in education and health, and relief for the unemployed. Therefore, Tugwell continued, the island should not expect a political arrangement in which control of the expenditure of federal funds would be in extent greater than in the case of a state. So long as Puerto Rico received federal money, the islanders should expect a measure of supervisory control by the United States. Tugwell insisted, however, that changes in the Organic Act should be subject not only to Congressional action but to ratification by a convention of insular representatives.[45]

Muñoz Marín's thinking was much like that of Fahy and Tugwell to the extent that it was primarily concerned with economic matters. Early in May, 1945, the *Popular* leader and the rest of the Joint Legislative Committee members arrived in Washington. Before Muñoz Marín testified at the Tydings hearings on S.227, he met with administration officials to clarify his position on status. The Puerto Rican leader told Fahy, Interior's legal advisor Fowler Harper, and DTIP director Benjamin W. Thoron that he desired permanent economic ties with the United States accompanied by maximum political freedom—"sovereign home rule," he phrased it.[46]

"Here lives a free man," not "here lies a man," was the way he summed it up. The Puerto Rican senator did not question the United States' right to maintain military installations on the island, nor its control in insular foreign affairs. But he insisted that Congress should offer several alternatives, each one with economic guarantees clearly spelled out. The PPD leader pointed out that an elective-governor bill at that stage would not please the islanders because they disliked "absentee sovereignty." The memorandum from Thoron summed up Muñoz Marín's position in this way, ". . . he desires an economic arrangement that will be at least as favorable as the present one, with as many of the attributes of complete independent sovereignty as possible. He wants to be free to reject any proposal that does not appear sufficiently generous, but wants to avoid making the choice between divorce without alimony and a wardship with generous maintenance allowance."[47]

Much the same caution was expressed by Undersecretary Abe Fortas in an article in the *Washington Post*. Puerto Ricans, he said, were in a "hopeless struggle with the Malthusian law: there are just too many people on too little and too poor land." Political solutions must adjust to economic realities, he argued. "Perhaps the Puerto Ricans," he concluded, "do not want to sue for divorce and perhaps we should not propose that the ties between us be dissolved. But there is one thing we can all agree upon: Puerto Rico should have complete home rule."[48]

The Puerto Rican Joint Legislative Committee addressed a letter to Senator Tydings as chairman of the Committee on Territories and Insular Affairs. The independence bill (S.227), the letter said, should be amended so as to include other political alternatives: statehood, and a "form of dominion government based on full and final political rights." In all cases the bill should provide for "certain minimum economic conditions," which were stipulated: one, free trade between the island and the United States, regulated by bilateral agreements periodically; two, exemption from United States internal-revenue taxes for insular exports to the mainland, provided that Puerto Rico collected export taxes on such products at the same rates imposed by the United States; three, maintaining for a period of time favorable conditions for the island's cane farmers; and four, temporary continuance of other grants and aids to the island, to be stopped only when the island's productivity and commerce reached a certain level.[49]

In his testimony before the Senate committee on May 7, 1945, Muñoz Marín argued that while he personally favored the dominion status he did not approve any status alternative that did not have the backing of the Puerto Rican people. But he insisted on economic guarantees. "It could be this or that, and submit that to a vote of the people of Puerto Rico, with their knowledge that under any circumstances they would have minimum economic conditions."[50] Senator Tydings believed that the Puerto Rican Joint Legislative Committee's request was fair-minded, and he asked its members to formulate a plan in accordance with its recommendations. This the insular committee did. Its program included a referendum on three options, each one to be accompanied by adequate economic guarantees. They were: independence, statehood, and dominion.[51]

The insular committee's recommendations were incorporated

in a bill, S.1002, and introduced by Senator Tydings on May 15, 1945. A day later the resident commissioner co-sponsored a companion bill, H.R.3237.[52] The Tydings-Piñero bill, as it came to be known, amplified greatly the Maryland senator's independence bill, S.227. It provided for the Puerto Rican electorate to choose from among independence, statehood, and dominion, each with the necessary economic guarantees suggested by the insular Joint Legislative Committee.[53] The procedures for organizing a constitutional convention and drafting a constitution were the same for independence and dominion. The independence status, however, differed in one important economic provision from the dominion status: under the first, federal aid was to be gradually reduced on the recommendations of a five-man economic commission and effected by presidential proclamations; while under the second, federal aids and benefits were to continue on the basis then prevailing.[54]

Although Secretary Ickes supported the Tydings-Piñero bill in principle,[55] the Department of the Interior was not certain about some of its legal aspects. It was still not sure a month after the bill's introduction whether the dominion status would require a constitutional amendment.[56] Muñoz Marín, apparently concerned about the hesitancy in the administration and Congress, wrote to Harry S. Truman, who had succeeded to the presidency after Roosevelt's death in April, 1945. He requested President Truman to urge Congressional action on S.1002. "I do not request," he went on to elaborate, "that you urge the approval of the bill, as you may not wish to commit yourself on all details, but that you send a message supporting the principle of self-determination under economic conditions that shall be workable in Puerto Rico."[57]

The *Popular* leader faced a barrage of criticism by the CPI. He had, the *independentista* organization argued, deliberately sabotaged the Tydings independence bill (S.227) by sponsoring the Tydings-Piñero measure. The CPI believed that Muñoz Marín had sufficient influence among circles in Washington to win independence for Puerto Rico.[58] By August, 1945, the CPI leadership was accusing Muñoz Marín of supporting "colonialism" dressed up in a "new package."[59]

Governor Tugwell, in Washington at the time, believed that the Tydings-Piñero bill was lengthy and complicated and that a simplified procedure would help to speed up Congressional consideration of a plebiscite in Puerto Rico. On August 29, 1945, his aide dispatched for the president's consideration a seven-page joint resolution to be adopted by Congress. The joint resolution spelled out more clearly what each of the three status options included in the Tydings-Piñero bill meant. The "Associated State" (dominion) alternative envisaged, for instance, the continuation of existing relationship between the island and the United States in all major respects, except that the supreme executive power was to be vested in an elective governor who would have the authority to appoint executive heads and judges of all insular courts. Under this status Congress could not nullify laws enacted by the Puerto Rican legislature. Tugwell's plan called for permitting the Puerto Ricans to decide in a plebiscite which one of the three they preferred, after which Congress would enact legislation effectuating the islanders' choice at the earliest possible time.[60]

Upon Truman's request, presidential advisor Samuel Rosenman took the matter up with Senator Tydings and chairman Bell of the House Insular Committee.[61] Rosenman found Tydings "violently opposed" to Tugwell's suggestion. Congress, Tydings insisted, would not accept the proposal because for one thing it was not disposed to grant statehood. Instead, the senator suggested that the president make a general statement that Congress grant, "within such limits as may be set" by it, the kind of government that Puerto Rico desired. The president should include in his message, Tydings insisted, the stipulation that Congress should not submit any proposition it was not willing to carry into execution.[62]

Even though Muñoz Marín was at this point considering the establishment of a commission to study the status question[63]—much to the annoyance of Tugwell, who thought the suggestion was tangential[64]—Rosenman prepared a draft message for Congress after consulting Secretary Ickes, Senator Tydings, and Governor Tugwell.[65] On October 16, 1945, President Truman delivered his brief message to Congress. The time had come, he said, for the Puerto Ricans to decide on their political status. Congress should permit the Puerto Ricans to choose from among four possible alternatives: the right to elect their own governor, with a wider measure of local self-government; statehood; "complete independence"; and a dominion form of government. The president cautioned Congress not to submit any proposal that it was not prepared to enact finally into law.[66] The president's message included elective governor as one of the alternatives, perhaps out of the realization that Congress might not be willing at that time to consider the other three alternatives.

And indeed, Senator Tydings had become by this time extremely doubtful about the referendum bill. As early as September, 1945, he had reservations about the bill, which he himself had sponsored, and hinted that his independence bill, S.227, should be considered instead.[67] A day after President Truman's message, he made known his intention to submit only two alternatives, namely, independence and elective governor with greater autonomy, because there was no support for statehood, and dominion status had not been properly defined.[68] It was a very skeptical chairman of the Senate Committee on Territories and Insular Affairs who a week later sent four-column questionnaires to his colleagues in the committee with the intention of discovering their positions on President Truman's four alternatives. There was no point, Senator Tydings told his colleagues, in holding hearings if there was no support for statehood and dominion.[69] Apparently there was little sentiment among the rest of the committee for statehood or dominion, for on November 27, 1945, Senator Tydings canceled hearings on S.1002 that he had scheduled for January, 1946. He was going to offer the island independence once more if the majority of the insular legislators should request it.[70]

Popular leader Muñoz Marín cabled Tydings on December 1, 1945, relaying to him the unanimous decision of the Permanent Commission of Puerto Rican Legislature on Political Status that hearings on S.1002 should be held as scheduled. The insular leader also requested a "round table conference" to discuss economic conditions to accompany the various status alternatives. Tydings replied two days later: he was not prepared to consider anything but independence, and Muñoz Marín should submit more liberal economic provisions than those set forth in S.227. His party's pledge was, the *Popular* leader wrote back, to have "the broadest possible alternatives for the plebiscite under sound, workable economic conditions."[71] Muñoz Marín's appeal to Representative Bell elicited a more categorical response: the Congressman did not think that the House Committee on Insular Affairs would act favorably on the referendum bill.[72]

The Puerto Ricans continued, however, to exert pressure on

Congress. A petition bearing 300,000 signatures was forwarded to the United States legislature;[73] Resident Commissioner Piñero announced his intention to confer with Congressional leaders;[74] and the Puerto Rican legislature authorized Muñoz Marín to lead a delegation to Washington to discuss with Senator Tydings and Congressman Bell all aspects of the status question.[75]

But the most dramatic demonstration of Puerto Rican displeasure was shown when in February, 1946, the insular legislature passed two bills, S.195 and S.196. S.195 provided for a plebiscite in July, 1947, of Puerto Ricans on the island's political status; and S.196 provided for taking a poll among the qualified voters of Puerto Rico as to who should be recommended to President Truman as the next appointed governor, should that office become vacant.[76] (Governor Tugwell had indicated in December, 1945, his desire to resign, and was expected to do so soon.)[77] Tugwell vetoed S.195 on the grounds that it interfered with Congress' power to legislate on the matter of status, and indeed would jeopardize the chance of Congressional authorization of a plebiscite. The governor vetoed S.196 as well, arguing that the bill constituted an interference with the powers of presidential appointment and senate confirmation.[78] Promptly the Puerto Rican legislature passed the bills over Tugwell's vetoes.[79] On only two other previous occasions since 1898 had this happened, and both times the president had upheld the veto.[80]

Meanwhile, Muñoz Marín visited Washington in April, 1946, as head of the ten-man delegation created by the insular legislature in December, 1945.[81] Newspaper reports spoke of his meetings with Senator Tydings and of their discussions of economic arrangements to accompany each status alternative. Tydings agreed to incorporate the delegation's request in the new bill.[82] But disagreements emerged soon between Senator Tydings and Muñoz Marín, specifically over what is not clear.[83] Muñoz Marín no doubt met with administration officials, too, and their discussions must have included the matter of Tugwell's vetoes, although there is no record of this in the files of the Office of Territories or the Department of the Interior.

Administration officials were uneasy about the vetoes. While the Department of Justice approved the vetoes, DTIP's legal advisor Irwin W. Silverman believed that there would be serious implications if the president upheld the vetoes on the two bills, especially on S.195, because it would be construed as disapproving the principle of self-government.[84] Secretary of the Interior Julius A. Krug, who had been appointed to the office after Ickes' resignation in February, 1946, wrote to F. J. Bailey, assistant director of the Bureau of the Budget, on May 3, 1946. He said he agreed with Tugwell's action on S.196. "Unless and until," he explained, "the Congress decided to permit the people of Puerto Rico to elect their governor, or itself enacts a measure authorizing an advisory poll such as the bill contemplates, the appointment of a governor should be strictly complied with." He disagreed with Tugwell's veto on S.195, however. The secretary conceded that a "unilateral plebiscite" had an element of "unreality and a wishful thinking quality," because Congress was sure to balk. There was, however, the larger question of the right of self-determination involved in the matter. Krug continued, ". . . a sustaining of the veto would be regarded by Puerto Rico, South America and the European nations both large and small as a denial in practice of an oft-expressed principle."[85]

The new secretary of the Interior minimized the dangers pointed out by Tugwell in his veto. He argued that a plebiscite could be preceded by "an educational campaign" so that the voters could "clearly and intelligently realize the precise character of the alternatives to be placed before them." Greater care should be given, Krug argued, as to the political, economic, and social consequences of the alternatives offered, since Congress would regard the result of the plebiscite as a "conclusive expression of the will of the Puerto Ricans." He concluded, "If the voters come to the polls with such an understanding of the implications of their choice, the plebiscite may well be a valuable guide to the Congress and need not jeopardize the proposal made by the President to that body in October [16, 1945], that it offer the Puerto Ricans alternative forms of status."[86] Two draft letters with a similar message were prepared by the Department of the Interior for the president to send to Tugwell in the event that he accepted Krug's recommendations.[87]

But the president chose to follow the advice of Governor Tugwell. On May 16, 1946, President Truman sustained Tugwell's vetoes on both bills. The approval of S.195 might have been interpreted erroneously to mean that the United States was willing to accept any plan selected by the Puerto Ricans. And the acceptance of S.196 "would [have] constitute[d] an interference with the powers of the President and the Senate of the United States."[88]

Truman's action put a final damper on the hopes of a plebiscite, which had been raised nearly a year ago when S.1002 was introduced.

Whatever lessons Muñoz Marín learned from his experience with the Tydings-Piñero bill, one thing emerged clearly. He realized that he could not have either independence or statehood with the kind of economic guarantees necessary to sustain a tolerable standard of living. Given the choice, he would naturally select both political sovereignty and economic safeguards. But he did not have the choice. Even if Congress were willing to grant independence, it was unlikely that it would generously extend for an indefinite period of time federal benefits that the *Popular* leader considered adequate. Statehood was ruled out because there was hardly any sentiment for it in Congress. Furthermore, by most accounts the economic arrangements that would accompany statehood would spell disaster. There was much talk of dominion status among prominent Puerto Ricans and non-Puerto Ricans. But this alternative was yet politically vague and constitutionally uncertain, thus causing Congressmen to shy away from it.

These were the realities that faced Muñoz Marín by 1946. In contrast to his guarded enthusiasm and optimism for independence apparent in the previously discussed memorandum to Secretary Ickes in January, 1937,[89] he had serious doubts in 1946 about independence as a practical goal even for the foreseeable future. This is not to say that he had no reservations about complete political separation in 1937. Indeed, they must have been partly the reason why he called for a moratorium on the status issue in 1940. And his first years with the political responsibility of carrying out the *Popular* programs must have added a few more. But try as he might to avoid the issue of political independence, it was thrust before him in 1943 when Senator Tydings introduced his independence bill. Muñoz Marín remained cool to it, even though the bill had incorporated many of the provisions requested by the Puerto Rican in 1936 when the senator first offered the island independence. The PPD leader was even less enthusiastic when Senator Tydings offered independence again in 1945 and persuaded the senator to sponsor instead the referendum bill (S.1002). There was no point, he told officials of the Department of the Interior, in being concerned merely about political labels.[90] No doubt his lack of enthusiasm was partly because Congress did not show any either. Besides, he was unable to obtain from Senator Tydings the kind of economic assurances that in his opinion were necessary for the island to survive.

Muñoz Marín's growing disenchantment with independence as an appropriate solution, at least for the time being, correlates significantly with the widening political rift between him and the CPI. If before November, 1944, he did not feel politically safe to challenge the *independentistas,* he felt sufficiently powerful by the end of 1945 to demand strict loyalty from his followers on the status question and to confront the CPI directly with some of the reservations he had always harbored about independence. You are a *Popular* or an *independentista,* not both, he told his followers by the end of 1945.

The hardening of positions occurred after Muñoz Marín supported the Tydings-Piñero referendum bill instead of the independence measure introduced earlier by Senator Tydings. In a newspaper polemic in September, 1945, between CPI leader Concepción de Gracia and the PPD head, Muñoz Marín was accused of being an obstacle to the *Popular* party's goal of independence. Why include statehood in the bill, the *independentista* leader asked, when there was no backing for it in Congress. Dominion status, Concepción de Gracia continued, was a device to perpetuate the "colonial" status. He charged that Muñoz Marín had become the sole arbiter of the PPD. In reply, Muñoz Marín insisted that the party was not opposed to independence and accused the CPI, by veiled references, of disrupting his efforts to get Congress to approve the referendum bill.[91] In October, 1945, the CPI formally repudiated the plebiscite measure and called for the reconsideration of Tydings' S.227.[92] Soon thereafter, Muñoz Marín declared that is was incompatible for a *Popular* to be a member of CPI. Some of the *independentistas* determined to organize the CPI into a new political party, but were thwarted by moderate members in the organization.[93]

By February, 1946, the *Popular* leader was willing to force a showdown. He classified the CPI as a partisan political movement whose goal of independence was in conflict with the aims of the PPD. The *Popular* party's central committee endorsed Muñoz Marín's declaration. The CPI denounced the move and directed its members not to abandon the PPD. Only the general assembly of the PPD, the *independentista* leaders argued, could make a decision that amounted to the expulsion of a group of followers.[94]

At the same time that he virtually expelled the *independentistas*, Muñoz Marín laid the philosophical grounds for the switch from independence to autonomy by writing a series of articles in the San Juan daily newspaper, *El Mundo*. United States aid to the island, he pointed out, had increased from $3 million in 1933 to $35 million in 1943. The benefits included increased United States expenditure in the military and naval activities in the island, and production heightened by war needs. He called these benefits "artificial aids" because they were generated by the war. Puerto Rico had to develop without "artificial aids" if it was going to be able to accommodate the needs of a projected 3,000,000 people in 1960.[95]

In succeeding articles he criticized those who would ruin everything in order to resolve hastily Puerto Rico's future status. The island's future lay in industrialization, for which it needed United States markets and dollars absolutely. This meant that the existing relationship could continue for some time and that there was no pressing need to resolve the island's status right then.[96]

The insular leader's conclusions were borne out by the findings of the Tariff Commission, which had investigated the economic aspects of the various political status alternatives. The Tariff Commission reported that mere political change would not solve the island's fundamental problems. It cautioned against seeking quick solutions to problems that required long-term planning and consideration. Independence, the Tariff Commission report concluded, would cause a depression, making it necessary for the United States to reestablish its authority over the island. Nor would the lengthening of the transitional period be of any help because Puerto Rico's fundamental problems would remain unaffected.[97]

In June of 1946, Muñoz Marín left no doubt as to the shift in his position that was in evidence in February, 1946. He wrote another series of articles, under the title "New Paths Toward Old Objectives." This time he openly abandoned plans for independence or statehood in the immediate future and argued for the continued relationship of United States and Puerto Rico. The Puerto Rican leader admitted that the existing relationship was not perfect but pointed out that it had been largely beneficial to the island. He elaborated on arguments he had presented earlier concerning Puerto Rico's drive for industrialization, its need for

United States markets, and so on. These benefits could not be continued by highly favorable bilateral treaty agreements under independence because such arrangements tended to be inflexible.[98]

A political solution, the insular chief continued, could be worked out without destroying the existing economic benefits that accrue to Puerto Rico, outside the framework of the known classical forms of independence and statehood. This would be "Pueblo Asociado de Puerto Rico," a status under which Puerto Ricans would have complete internal authority, and one which would serve as transitory for some status in the future. The future status, independence or statehood, would be considered when certain economic indexes would be reached and when it would be clear that the island could sustain its implementation.[99]

For many *Populares*, Muñoz Marín's new policy was hard to swallow when for so long they had believed that the PPD's goal was independence. But the central committee officially endorsed the change signaled by the articles.[100] For the CPI, whose members had been effectively excluded from influential positions within the *Popular* structure, the parting of the ways had come. So, too, for many die-hard *independentistas*. After mass rallies and executive meetings by the CPI in the months after July, the *Partido Independentista Puertorriqueño* (PIP) was organized on October 20, 1946.[101]

The defeat of the referendum bill raises questions of motives. Why did the Department of the Interior agree upon including independence and statehood when it realized that economically neither was practical and that Congress was not favorably disposed to granting either one? It was ironic, furthermore, for Interior's secretary to object to Tydings' independence bills but not to independence when it was offered with other status options. The same might be said about statehood. In part, the ambivalence stemmed from the United States' moral obligation to honor the principle of allowing colonial peoples to choose their own government, and from the specter of possible economic and political chaos on an island that had assumed strategic importance in postwar global politics. Besides, there was no clear and firm indication as to what Muñoz Marín, the island's most powerful politico, desired. Beyond demanding absolute economic guarantees, he was saying that the people should decide.

Then what did he hope to achieve by supporting the referendum bill? He, too, did not accept independence and statehood as workable solutions. Muñoz Marín presumably hoped to diffuse the challenge to his leadership by the *independentistas*. More than that he hoped to get Congress to accept the principle of consulting with the Puerto Ricans to decide on the status question. When he did not quite succeed in either, he decided to reorient his whole approach to the issue. He consolidated his position by expelling the *Independentistas* from the PPD and shifting his party's platform to some kind of dominion status, the details of which were to be formulated in the next few years. Meanwhile, he concentrated his efforts on getting a compatible Puerto Rican appointed to the governor's post soon to be vacated by Tugwell and urging Congress to permit elective governorship.

CHAPTER SIX

Self-Government "Little by Little":
The Appointment of Governor Piñero,
and the Elective Governor Act of 1947

When Harry S. Truman came to the presidency in April, 1945, he was confronted with a long history of tardiness and non-progress on Puerto Rico's political status. The United States had passed only two important pieces of legislation since the Caribbean island was acquired in 1898. These were the Foraker Act of 1900 and the somewhat more liberal Jones Act of 1917. Other major initiatives ended in failure: the 1936 attempt to grant Puerto Rico independence never got off the ground; the efforts by the Roosevelt administration in 1943 to provide for an elective governor became ensnarled in politics and personalities; and the 1945 Tydings-Piñero bill's provisions for substantial changes in Puerto Rico's status found no support in Congress.

In view of Congressional conservatism and cautiousness on self-government in Puerto Rico, the Truman administration decided to proceed on a gradualist basis and to shelve the issue of the island's ultimate political status *per se* until such time as conditions and circumstances might indicate how its solution was to be approached.

The opportunity to formulate a new approach came when Tugwell announced in December, 1945, his intention of resigning as Puerto Rico's governor some six months later.[1] DTIP's new

93

director, Edwin G. Arnold, who had succeeded Thoron in June, 1945, believed that Tugwell's intended departure might serve a dual purpose. He suggested that a bill be introduced in Congress combining the features of the 1943 elective governor measure and the 1945 referendum bill. Such a bill would permit the Puerto Ricans to elect their next governor and at the same time allow them to indicate which of the following they would prefer by 1950: independence, statehood, or dominion.[2]

Not knowing, however, whether his suggestion of a dual-purpose bill would lead anywhere, Arnold addressed another memorandum to the secretary on January 31, 1946. In it he listed the names of people who might be considered for the governor's office if legislation making the next governor elective could not be passed before Tugwell left his post. He insisted that the next appointee be, first, a Puerto Rican, and, second, in sympathy with the program of the PPD, the party that was in control of the insular legislature. Arnold proceeded to consider, one by one, the six persons on his list of likely nominees.[3]

The first name was that of Piñero, whom he considered to be "far and away the best" person for the post. His experience in government, Arnold believed, would help in securing "amicable" executive-legislative relations. Piñero had been an official in municipal government between 1928 and 1932, and an insular PPD Representative between 1940 and 1944, and he had been popularly elected in 1944 as the resident commissioner, with a convincing majority of 174,764 votes. Furthermore, his experience in sugar cane and dairy farming would make him realistic in his handling of the island's economic problems. Arnold listed a few other factors in Piñero's favor: his friendship with PPD leader Muñoz Marín; his "ingratiating" personality, which had won him many friends in Congress and the administration; and the fact that he had few enemies.[4]

Arnold ruled out five other candidates for one reason or another. He considered Pedro del Valle, a Marine general who had given a good account of himself as a soldier at Guadalcanal and Okinawa. Arnold believed that del Valle's war record made him ineligible, by which he presumably meant that he was not suitable for government work. A third candidate, Justice Cecil Snyder of the Puerto Rican Supreme Court, had the support of Muñoz Marín, but Arnold surmised that the *Popular* chief's endorsement was likely connected with the fact that "several suits challenging the constitutionality of the Authorities set up" under the PPD program were about to be reviewed by the insular Supreme Court. The director of DTIP did not believe that Snyder's colleague, Justice Martin Travieso, was suitable because he was a "reactionary" whose legal opinions were colored by his political beliefs. And Muñoz Marín? Arnold thought it unlikely that the *Popular* head would relinquish his party leadership to become an appointed governor. The last candidate was commissioner of education José Gallardo. His disappointing record in office, Arnold asserted, placed him out of the running.[5]

While these names were being considered, the matter about the dual-purpose bill was being aired among United States and Puerto Rican officials in government. Mason Barr, chief of the newly created Caribbean Branch under DTIP, found both Resident Commissioner Piñero and Muñoz Marín favorable to the idea.[6] However, because Congressional leaders had so recently balked on the notion of a referendum, DTIP's legal counsel Silverman advised caution. He suggested to the new secretary of Interior, Krug, who had succeeded Ickes in February, 1946, that he should consider instead appointing a committee of continentals and Puerto Ricans to review all facets of the relationships between Puerto Rico and the United States. The committee would advise how the Organic Act might be revised.[7]

Secretary Krug agreed. He communicated to the president his intention of appointing such a committee, and even named possible candidates to serve on it.[8] President Truman, Director Arnold, and Interior's Undersecretary—until May, 1946, an assistant secretary—Oscar L. Chapman were all pleased to learn of Krug's decision.[9] But nothing further was heard about the matter. Presumably, as the emphasis shifted to autonomy, considerations on the island's final status became less urgent, and the committee plan was abandoned.

As it became apparent that the Truman administration was considering the appointment of a native Puerto Rican as governor, insular leaders moved to make known their preferences. Muñoz Marín, the most important among them, naturally desired to have a man who was sympathetic to the *Popular* program. If he could persuade the White House to appoint a PPD member, so much the better. In the months after February, 1946, he increasingly applied pressure on administration officials to make the appointment from among candidates he found acceptable.

In the middle of February, the **PPD** leader wrote to President Truman, pointing out candidates he considered eligible. The names he suggested were: Piñero; Justice Cecil Snyder; Esteban Bird, a liberal Puerto Rican banker; and Calvin B. Baldwin, at one time an administrator of the Farm Security Administration and then an executive of the Congress of Industrial Organization's Committee on Political Action. The primary consideration in the selection of the next governor, he added, should be "the sincere possession of views as to policy similar to those overwhelmingly supported by our people," that is, the policy of the PPD. "Birthplace," the *Popular* leader asserted, "is an entirely secondary matter."[10]

Although Muñoz Marín did not include the name of Pedro del Valle as one of the acceptable candidates, the Marine general had influential backers in the United States and Puerto Rico. Senator Chavez of New Mexico had early supported del Valle's candidacy, and the United States Navy found him at least appealing because of his Marine background. In Puerto Rico the Republican-Socialist coalition strongly supported del Valle.[11] His chances were obviously boosted when President Truman interviewed him on February 19, 1946.[12]

The possibility that the president might appoint a candidate not agreeable to the *Populares* precipitated the PPD-dominated insular legislature to adopt on February 21, 1946, a joint resolution, and to pass two bills, S.195 and S.196.[13] The first measure (S.195) was intended to pressure Congress into committing itself to a referendum on the political status of Puerto Rico. It provided for the authorization of a plebiscite to be held in July, 1947, to decide on the question. The joint resolution and the second measure (S.196) concerned themselves directly with the possibility that the next governor might still be appointed. The joint resolution provided that a candidate with popular approval, or an elected representative, or a cabinet member should be appointed if the governorship became vacant. If this was not possible, S.196 provided for a special election on July 4, 1946, through which the people of Puerto Rico would express their preference for the person they wished to recommend to the president as the next appointed governor. Muñoz Marín forwarded the joint resolution and the two bills to Interior's Chapman.[14]

In a letter accompanying the documents, Muñoz Marín explained to Chapman, "Since governors as a matter of reality must be recommended by some one, it is obvious that the best recommender . . . would be the people of Puerto Rico themselves, either through the action already taken at the past elections or through consultations provided for in our bills." The *Popular* leader reiterated that birthplace of the next appointee was not important. "We are interested in the democratic significance of a policy," he asserted. "We would rather have, if it came to that, a liberal Chinaman than a reactionary Puerto Rican." He categorically rejected the candidacy of del Valle, arguing that "his public utterances lead to the fear that the relationship between his military and civil abilities is somewhat the same as in the case of General Ulysses S. Grant." Muñoz Marín openly endorsed Piñero's candidacy. If the president did not appoint the resident commissioner, he asserted, Governor Tugwell should be persuaded to approve S.196.[15]

But Tugwell vetoed both bills on March 2, 1946, on the grounds that they interfered with the constitutional prerogative of the president.[16] Hence, the governor and Chapman felt an added obligation to get President Truman to appoint Piñero as the next governor. Chapman pointed out to Tugwell that, since Senator Chavez was doing his best to get del Valle appointed, it was important to get "our viewpoint to the President before things had gone too far and any commitments were made."[17]

Even by the time President Truman sustained, on May 16, 1946, Tugwell's vetoes on S.195 and S.196, he had not reached a decision as to whom he was going to appoint. It is not clear why the president was hesitant. Certainly Secretary Krug was not happy about Piñero. Muñoz Marín feared that the secretary was considering del Valle and Justice Travieso and reminded Krug that both fell in the "category of persons inimical" to the *Popular* program. In response to Krug's question about the propriety of appointing an elected man for a post designated as appointive under the Organic Act, Muñoz Marín pointed out that if Piñero resigned his post as resident commissioner he would become a private citizen and thereafter would be eligible for any position offered by the president.[18]

Secretary Krug's reluctance stemmed, in what measure it is uncertain, from the criticism by the National Democratic Committee chairman Robert Hannegan and "his crowd," who charged that Piñero would turn out to be a "stooge" of Muñoz Marín. He even thought of submitting the names of Esteban Bird and Cecil

Snyder.[19] Further conversation between Krug and Chapman two days later revealed that the president was not firmly committed to appointing a native Puerto Rican at all.[20] One can only surmise that the president and the secretary worried over Piñero's close association with the PPD head and how the Senate might interpret this at the time of his confirmation.

What probably decided the matter was the action of the Puerto Rican legislature. In a special session on July 9, the insular legislature recommended, by a vote of 54 (all *Populares*) to 3, the appointment of Piñero as the next governor.[21] Secretary Krug realized that a non-*Popular* governor would run into endless trouble with the PPD-dominated insular legislature. A week later he recommended to the president the appointment of Piñero,[22] and made public his endorsement a few days later.[23] The president accepted the secretary's recommendation. On July 25, 1946, he announced the appointment of Piñero as the next governor of Puerto Rico. The Senate confirmed the appointment on July 31, 1946.[24] For the first time since 1898, when the island came into United States hands, Puerto Rico was going to have a native resident as governor.

The *New York Times* called it a "courageous forward step."[25] The *Washington Post* commented, "To the rest of the world, and to the Western Hemisphere in particular, Mr. Truman's decision cannot fail to seem a practical application of the liberal colonial policies which this country has preached, and lately practiced."[26] Said the *Washington Evening Star*, ". . . Puerto Ricans in general will read into his appointment an encouraging confirmation of our resolve to help them achieve a greater and greater measure of self-rule; nor can that fact fail to reflect creditably on us throughout Latin America."[27] *La Prensa* in New York, on the other hand, believed that Piñero would have a "double preoccupation": one, to solve the island's profound economic and social problems, and two, to demonstrate his worth as the first Puerto Rican to fill the post.[28]

As significant as the step was in the advancement of Puerto Rico's political rights, the appointment in itself fell short of the aspirations of the island's people, as Governor Piñero himself pointed out in his inauguration speech on September 3, 1946.[29] From the point of view of the Truman administration, however, it was a necessary stage because of the stalemate that had been reached on Puerto Rico's final political status. The next stage would be the election of the governor. Such a gradualist approach meant that the eventual settlement of Puerto Rico's status would be postponed until some future date. Both Muñoz Marín and the Truman administration were broadly in agreement with this new approach.

The *Popular* leader's virtual control over insular politics was vitally important to the administration. Piñero, even though he was an appointed governor, belonged to the same party as Muñoz Marín and was his close associate. Furthermore, Muñoz Marín had expelled diehard *independentistas* from the party; and he faced no challenge to his authority from the Coalition forces, traditional advocates of statehood, because they were weak and divided. The Truman administration could therefore go to Congress with its new approach in the sure knowledge that it had the support of the most powerful man on the island.

For its part, the Truman administration had to make sure that procedurally it did not offend the Eightieth Congress, dominated as it was by Republicans,[30] in presenting the case for greater political autonomy for Puerto Rico. It might capitalize, incidentally, on the friendlier atmosphere that possibly followed the departure of such controversial figures as Ickes and Tugwell, whose relations with earlier Congresses were difficult. The administration succeeded, in point of fact, in striking very good relations with the Congress. It benefited from the services of the active and alert Antonio Fernós-Isern, who had been appointed as the new resident commissioner.[31] He, together with such top officials as Undersecretary Chapman,[32] Arnold, and Barr, maintained close relations with Republican leadership in Congress, consulting it frequently before undertaking major actions concerning Puerto Rico.

Congress offered close bipartisan support in the passage of the elective governor bill of 1947. There was little or no opposition that had accompanied earlier attempts at granting political freedom to Puerto Rico. Indeed, the climate in the Congress for insular autonomy was remarkably favorable. This was probably because the postwar position and role of the United States in international politics placed a certain obligation upon the legislators in Washington to show its commitment to the cause of self-government everywhere. The Truman administration and insular leadership fully exploited this friendly disposition in the Congress. They combined careful consultation with clever parliamentary maneuver and compromise to overcome Congressional caution and secured passage of the elective governor measure.

Neither the Truman administration nor the Puerto Rican leaders were deflected from this new approach by the language issue, which once more surfaced following the insular legislature's passage of a language bill (S.51) in April, 1946. (The bill provided that, beginning with the school year 1946–1947, instruction in all public schools on the island, including the University of Puerto Rico, would be in Spanish, except in certain special cases.) Tugwell vetoed the measure just before his resignation on the grounds that, as Krug reported to Truman, "no dispassionate study of the desirability and consequences of the bill from a pedagogical standpoint preceded its enactment." Furthermore, Truman and Krug believed that the language issue might better be postponed until the status question had been clarified. Congress might misconstrue its passage as indicative of Puerto Rico's desire for independence. Both Piñero and Muñoz Marín agreed. Indeed, Muñoz Marín did not see Truman's upholding of the veto on October 26, 1946, as indicating the president's lack of concern for Puerto Rican aspirations, although the insular protest groups probably interpreted it as such.[33] Whatever his intentions in supporting the bill in April, Muñoz Marín did not allow them to get in the way of the new approach when President Truman sustained the veto on the measure six months later.

Governor Piñero and Muñoz Marín separately visited Washington in January, 1947. In the conferences that the two had with Congressional leaders, they agreed that an elective governor measure should precede a referendum to test insular opinion on the final status.[34] But the effort to enact an elective governor measure began, according to Fernós-Isern, with a meeting called by Chapman in the last days of January. The undersecretary told Muñoz Marín and Fernós-Isern that the administration had abandoned any referendum plan temporarily and that it was considering an elective governor measure, for which it desired the cooperation of the Puerto Rican leaders. They agreed.[35]

While Governor Piñero announced upon his return Congress' friendly disposition towards an elective governor,[36] Chapman prepared to initiate the administration measure. He told reporters that he was going to study the abortive elective governor bill of 1943, and informed them of his intention to confer with Senator Taft of Ohio, a powerful Republican leader in the Congress.

Meanwhile, Resident Commissioner Fernós-Isern laid the ground-work for Congressional support by writing to all congressmen and senators about the proposed measure.[37]

Despite the favorable attitude of leading members of Congress, the Senate Public Lands Committee decided to visit Puerto Rico to see insular conditions for themselves.[38] Chairman Hugh Butler from Nebraska, of the Senate Public Lands Committee, announced on February 11, 1947, that he and five other senators (all but one were Republicans) would journey to Puerto Rico.[39] The Congressional visiting team was broadened a week later to include ten representatives of the House Public Lands Committee. The joint investigating committee of fifteen United States legislators—one of the senators had dropped out—visited the island to discuss economic, social, and political questions with insular officials. The visitors returned some six days later, considerably impressed by Puerto Rico's needs and achievements.[40]

More importantly, the legislators came back firmly persuaded that Congress should permit the people of Puerto Rico to elect their governor.[41] Senator Butler told a *La Prensa* reporter that he believed Congress would pass such a bill. He insisted, however, that the United States continue to review fiscal matters on the island by retaining the presidentially appointed auditor for Puerto Rico. Clearly, Congress still wished to act cautiously, despite its commitment to self-government in Puerto Rico.[42]

The administration proceeded to prepare the necessary legislation to forward to Congress. In March, 1947, Barr presented a draft of an elective governor bill to Senator Guy Cordon of Oregon, a Public Lands Committee member. Copies of the draft bill were also sent to Senators Taft and Butler. The draft measure provided for an elected governor every four years, with the power to appoint the entire cabinet, including the commissioner of education, the attorney general, and the auditor, as well as the justices of the insular Supreme Court. All of these positions were then being appointed by the president. Obviously, the administration desired to incorporate in the bill as much as it dared, even though it was aware that Congress was not favorably disposed to some aspects of the measure.[43]

The departments of the Interior and of State added to the gathering momentum by expressing their support for self-government in Puerto Rico.[44] The administration was not prepared, however, to give serious consideration to a statehood bill introduced in January, 1947, by Republican Senator William Langer from North Dakota,[45] or to the independence bill sponsored on April 24, 1947, by Maryland's Democratic Senator Tydings. Tydings believed that Puerto Rico could easily achieve independence. He said, "If the people of Puerto Rico want independence, there is a very simple way in which they can get it. If the legislature of Puerto Rico will ask the Congress of the United States to give them independence there is no doubt in my mind that Congress will accede to the wishes of the people of Puerto Rico."[46] Undersecretary Chapman did not agree, and stated the administration's opposition to the bill some three months later.[47] In any case, the administration had become too firmly committed to a policy of autonomy to revert to one of final political solutions.

On April 29, 1947, Senator Butler introduced the elective governor bill (S.1184). It was presumably the same bill that had been drafted by Barr. Three days later Representative Crawford of Michigan co-sponsored a companion bill (H.R.3309).[48] The measure was subsequently referred to as the Butler-Crawford bill.[49]

A subcommittee of the House Committee on Public Lands, under the chairmanship of Congressman Crawford, conducted a hearing on May 19, 1947. Among those who testified on behalf of the bill were Secretary Krug and Governor Piñero. The secretary urged the passage of the bill in line with the administration's policy of honoring Article 76 of the United Nations Charter, concerning the aspirations of the inhabitants of territories. He cautioned, however, that self-government should be given "little by little." As to the island's final political status, the secretary believed that the Puerto Ricans should decide for themselves sometime in the future by means of a plebiscite. Governor Piñero regarded the bill as a "necessary step" in the solution to the problem of the island's political status, pointing out that it left the door open for Puerto Ricans to choose from among independence, statehood, and dominion when conditions warranted a referendum.[50]

Advocates of independence and statehood opposed the Butler-Crawford bill on the grounds that it was not necessary in the solution to the island's final status, and saw it as a diversionary and delaying tactic. PIP's president, Concepción de Gracia, called it a "colonial reform" and a "fraud." Former Puerto Rican Governor James R. Beverly, an *estadista,* was doubtful whether the measure still left open the possibility of statehood. And a diehard continental member of the American League for Puerto Rico's Independence, Ruth M. Reynolds, interpreted the bill thus, "It merely transfers from the President of the United States to the people of Puerto Rico the questionable privilege of selecting one more servant of the empire."[51]

There was no opposition to the bill among members of the subcommittee, except to certain aspects of it. Congressman Crawford endorsed the bill when he opened the hearing, although he objected to the governor appointing the auditor.[52] Representative William Lemke of North Dakota did not like, Fernós-Isern wrote later, the justices being appointed by the governor. He wanted them to be elected by the Puerto Rican people, but apparently there was no backing for his position among other members of the Public Lands Committee.[53] On May 26, 1947, the bill was referred to the Committee of the Whole House on the State of the Union with one major amendment: namely, that the post of the auditor was to continue being appointed by the president.[54] The amendment indicated caution, not objection to the idea of self-government.

However, New York's Congressman Cole intended to object to the consideration of the bill, a move that would have meant defeat of the bill. When Fernós-Isern learned of this, he enlisted the help of Crawford and of Cole's fellow-Republican Congressman Dean P. Taylor of New York. The two gentlemen persuaded Cole to offer instead an amendment later when the bill would move from the Consent Calendar to the House floor for debate. Crawford, it was agreed, would introduce the amendment on Cole's behalf to eliminate the internal revenue taxes on Puerto Rican rum sales on the mainland, which by special fiscal arrangement had been reverting to the insular treasury. Cole must surely have known that the Puerto Ricans would not agree to an amendment that threatened to cripple the insular economy; his apparent intention was to defeat the bill. Meanwhile, Fernós-Isern, Taylor, and Crawford planned, upon consulting the parliamentarian, a strategy that would defeat the amendment: Crawford would introduce the amendment, and Congressman Antonio M. Fernandez of New Mexico would ask the speaker of the House to rule it invalid because it was not relevant to the bill.[55]

The bill came up for debate on the House floor on June 16, 1947. Crawford duly offered the amendment as agreed, and Congressman Fernandez—supported unexpectedly by Representative Marcantonio of New York—asked the speaker to rule it inadmissible because it was not germane. The speaker agreed, and the bill was passed with one major amendment about the auditor as recommended by the Public Lands Committee. Except perhaps for Cole, no other representative opposed the measure seriously enough to block its passage. Marcantonio called the bill "an embellishing facade of an ugly and rotten colonial structure." But even the American Laborite, an advocate of Puerto Rican independence, supported it because, as he explained, ". . . I do not want to deprive the people of Puerto Rico of even this gesture after we have deprived them of so much and so often."[56]

Perhaps Undersecretary Chapman explained most succinctly and accurately the reason for the bill's success in the House: ". . . the entire course of the bill was noteworthy for the cooperation and understanding of the issues and of the broad significance of the bill shown by representatives of the executive and legislative branches."[57]

The passage of the elective governor measure in the Senate is marked by a similar kind of cooperation and understanding, although the additional amendments offered by the senators would suggest that the degree of caution was much greater in the upper chamber.

A day after the House passed the bill, it was referred to the Senate Committee on Public Lands.[58] Senator Butler had not planned to hold any hearing but had been persuaded to do so, Chapman told Muñoz Marín, by several communications from Puerto Rican *independentistas*. No hearing, however, was held on the scheduled day of June 21, 1947.[59] Instead, Senator Butler solicited Secretary Krug's views on the bill by correspondence. The secretary endorsed the measure strongly, saying that its passage would place the Puerto Ricans "further along the road to self-government."[60]

The Senate Committee on Public Lands, however, requested clarification on certain aspects concerning continental United States citizens and the insular court system. DTIP's chief legal counsel, Silverman, responded by stating that mainland citizens would not be discriminated against by insular laws. In subsequent memoranda, Silverman explained how the court system of Puerto Rico operated in relation to the District Court of the United States, the United States Circuit Court of Appeals, and the United

States Supreme Court. Silverman stated that cases involving mainland citizens and begun in the courts of Puerto Rico might be removed to the Federal District Court and proceed higher up. Even in cases where the United States was not a party to the action as originally brought in the Puerto Rican courts, it could become a party "by intervention and thus eligible to remove the cause to the Federal Court."[61]

Assurances notwithstanding, the Senate Committee on Public Lands reported the Butler-Crawford bill out on July 2, 1947, with two new sections designed to clarify federal authority on the island. Section 7 provided for a "Coordinator of Federal Agencies" responsible for correlating the activities of federal bodies on the island, and for requesting from the governor reports concerning insular affairs. Section 8 added the following: "The rights, privileges, and immunities of citizens of the United States shall be respected in Puerto Rico to the same extent as though Puerto Rico were a State of the Union and subject to the provisions of paragraph 1 of section 2 of Article IV of the Constitution of the United States."[62] Puerto Ricans had no objection to section 8.

But they were unhappy about the creation of a federal coordinator. Governor Piñero and Resident Commissioner Fernós-Isern both hoped that the amendment would be dropped in a House-Senate conference. Fernós-Isern preferred that the Department of the Interior continue to assume the role of a federal coordinating agency.[63] Indeed, Executive Order No. 9383 had empowered the Interior department to do just that, and a special position as provided by the amendment, Chapman believed, would be duplication. Opposition to it, Fernós-Isern recalls, would have placed the bill in jeopardy, especially as the idea of a federal coordinator came from Senator Taft, who had considerable influence in the Senate.[64] Muñoz Marín did not believe the amendment important enough to risk failure of the bill, especially since only three days remained in the session. Chapman agreed but believed that opposition to it should be registered. And Silverman duly expressed the Interior department's disapproval.[65]

The bill was placed on the Senate Calendar for July 26, 1947, the last day of the legislative session. It would appear that its success or failure at this stage depended almost entirely on Senator Taft. Fernós-Isern claims that he had known of Taft's opposition to the governor's appointing the insular Supreme Court Justices, but that he did not know until a few hours before the legislative session whether the senator's intention was to kill the bill "outright" or to offer an amendment about the justices at the last minute and thus force the House to accept the amended bill without a conference of the two chambers.[66] H. Rex Lee, who was a DTIP official responsible for Alaskan matters, discovered on July 25, while canvassing for the bill, that Senator Taft wished to amend it at the eleventh hour. If Lee did know about Taft's intention, he apparently did not disclose it to the resident commissioner. Lee, by his own account, consulted both Crawford and Butler and elicited their prior approval,[67] a statement that is contested by Fernós-Isern, who insists that Taft did not make his position clear until the final hours of July 26 and that Crawford first learned about the amendment from him.[68]

In any event, Crawford, Butler, and Fernós-Isern could not do otherwise but accept the Taft amendment. When the bill was called up the second time for debate at 11:45 P.M., July 26, fifteen minutes before the end of the legislative session, it was passed in the Senate without debate. Crawford got the Senate president to sign the bill, and at 11:55 he and Fernós-Isern rushed the bill back to the House. Fortunately, three minutes before midnight the House had decided to prolong the session so that all the Senate amendments could be considered. The amendments were accepted, and the bill was passed—the last measure to be cleared by the House.[69]

The administration and the insular leaders accepted the three major amendments: the auditor and the justices of the Puerto Rican Supreme Court were to continue being appointed by the president, and the post of federal coordinator was created.[70] Puerto Ricans could enjoy in the elections of 1948 the long-sought right to choose their governor. President Truman lamented the fact that the islanders had not won complete autonomy but still considered the measure "a great step toward complete self-government" when he signed, on August 15, 1947, the Butler-Crawford bill into Public Law 362.[71]

The striking fact about the elective governor measure is the relative ease with which it sailed through Congress. It contrasts sharply with a similar measure a few short years before, in 1943, which suffered from conservatism and caution, political bickering and misunderstanding. Or again in 1945, the Tydings-Piñero referendum bill hardly generated more than a casual interest among congressmen and senators in Puerto Rico's right to self-government. Congress reacted unfavorably in large measure because of the absence of a properly articulated policy and program for Puerto Rico's autonomy. To be sure, the Truman administration did not appear to have one either until about the time Piñero was appointed governor. But by January, 1947, a major feature of its policy was the separation for practical purposes of the issues of autonomy and the final political status of Puerto Rico, to the extent to which these inextricably intertwined questions could be separated. Herein lies the reason for the elective governor measure's success.

Congress was in a conservative mood and acted with extreme caution. The act did not introduce drastic changes in Puerto Rico's political, constitutional, and fiscal status. The United States retained the power of the purse in the appointive auditor; and it reserved final responsibility in the insular legal machinery.

An undated, anonymous report entitled, "Work of the Senate Committee on Interior and Insular Affairs," suggests further that the revocability of the Elective Governor Act was an important factor in some of the lawmakers' supporting it. The generally paternalistic report argued that a decision was not being made on the final status of the island, which meant that Congress was still in a position to take action if the need arose. "The elective governor bill for Puerto Rico . . .," it stated, "can be repealed if Communists should gain control of the Island government, or for any other reason." It would be quite another thing, the report continued, if Puerto Rico were being granted statehood. That would have meant "that the new state could send Senators and Representatives to Congress and would share in a selection of a President. Such an ideal goes far beyond the ideal of self-government."[72]

Nor did the act impair Puerto Rico's strategic value to the United States. In a period of heightened security-consciousness, many legislators in the Capitol must have felt reassured that the Navy and Army holdings and operations would remain unaffected on an island that guarded the entrance to the Caribbean. The departments of the Navy and the Army held large amounts of land as naval and military bases, and had the power to acquire more. The Navy reclaimed, for instance, an entire half of Vieques island in 1947, which had formerly been turned over to the insular government by the Department of the Interior. It was able to do this under the provisions of the National Security Act of 1947.[73]

Secretary of the Navy James Forrestal explained the need for acquiring such lands in the following way:

> In developing its post-war plans, the Navy Department has found it necessary to give careful consideration to the requirements of the Atlantic Fleet for adequate training areas in the Caribbean area, particularly for amphibious operations and firing practice. Its studies demonstrate conclusively that this area will assume great strategic importance in the post-war era, that the Atlantic Fleet must be maintained in a high state of readiness, and that amphibious training and shore target exercises must be continued on an extensive and realistic basis.[74]

All this is not to deny that Congress recognized its duty in terms of the United States' obligation towards the advancement of self-government. Many members of Congress felt that the Puerto Ricans had earned the right to self-government by their loyalty to the United States through times of war and peace. Furthermore, the new breed of administrators as exemplified by Piñero and Muñoz Marín would prove worthy because it had shown what Gordon K. Lewis calls a new "sense of public duty" and "massive incorruptibility."[75]

Indeed, Congress could not easily reverse the trend towards greater self-rule in Puerto Rico, which it had established in enacting the law. Its action was morally binding. In this sense the act paved the way for the successful implementation of the Commonwealth of Puerto Rico between 1950 and 1952.

CHAPTER SEVEN

"Polititiation Mutation":
Public Law 600, July, 1950

Although definite outlines of the Commonwealth status first appeared in 1946, the concept of such a dominion-like plan was not new. Groups of Puerto Ricans had advocated some form of dominion status ever since the island fell under United States rule. There were proposals in the 1920s and the early 1940s that were somewhat like the Commonwealth concept. In 1922, the Union party, which had earlier supported independence, adopted a political formula it called "Associated Free State."[1] It merged in 1924 with the Republican party whose earlier platform of statehood did not prevent the new alliance from working under the common slogan, "sovereignty within the American sovereignty."[2] The status position of the alliance did not appear to make a significant impression upon either the United States or the insular electorate by the time that it ruptured in 1930.[3]

In 1943 two groups of Puerto Ricans separately submitted bills to the Roosevelt administration providing for the establishment of a dominion status. Their proposals were in part prompted by the scheduled meeting of the President's Committee then authorized to consider ways of reforming the Organic Act, and by Senator Tydings' independence measure then before Congress.[4]

The first group consisted of Enrique Campos del Toro, formerly a professor at the University of Puerto Rico, and four others who also had a professional and legal background. It suggested in a twenty-page memorandum that Puerto Rico might develop "a higher degree of statehood" in its relationship with the United States, much as that of Canada, Australia, and New Zealand with Britain within the Commonwealth. The bill accompanying the memorandum proposed extending complete self-government in insular matters, and permitting the Puerto Rican government to enter into trade agreements with foreign governments. The measure also proposed repealing coastwise laws that were adversely affecting Puerto Rican trade.[5]

The second group to offer an alternative bill to the Tydings measure consisted of Teodoro Moscoso and seven other Puerto Ricans representing the professional and business classes. The bill reflected greater concern with economic aspects of the envisaged relationship between Puerto Rico and the United States. The "Free State" proposed by the group was roughly equivalent, by its own description, to the Irish Free State within the British Commonwealth. Under such a status, the United States would continue "Free State" relations with Puerto Rico for at least fifteen years. In addition, the United States was to provide for protective measures to help insular industries, establish a minimum sugar quota, and continue refunding customs duties on Puerto Rican goods for twenty years. It was not made clear what was to happen thereafter.[6]

Neither group's proposal was seriously entertained by the administration, largely because it was limiting itself at the time to the consideration of permitting the Puerto Ricans to elect their own governor. Furthermore, Congress was not favorably disposed towards considering at that time any question that involved major changes in the island's political status as long as World War II continued. Nor did the Puerto Ricans show much enthusiasm, primarily because most of them continued to think in terms of independence or statehood.[7]

Two years later Muñoz Marín succeeded in persuading Senator Tydings to incorporate dominion in his 1945 independence bill as one of the alternatives from among which Puerto Ricans could choose. The measure that emerged was the Tydings-Piñero referendum bill. The bill did not adequately define in practical terms what the concept of dominion involved, which was one of the reasons why it failed to excite enthusiasm among members of the United States Congress. In any case, Senator Tydings himself abandoned it in favor of his conviction that only independence was the right solution to the status question.[8]

By 1946, Muñoz Marín was convinced that both independence and statehood were impractical goals for the immediate and even the near future, the first because of economic reasons and the second because Congress was not favorably disposed to it. The *Popular* leader was fully aware that he had to wean his supporters gradually from the "either independence or statehood" syndrome. He had to persuade Puerto Ricans, many of whom looked to the *Popular* party for the cherished goal of independence, that a dominion status was an honorable alternative that would not compromise their sense of what Tugwell called "dignidad."[9] Furthermore, the United States, too, had to be persuaded that such a status was a practical solution that in no way would detract from the island's strategic value.

The campaign to reorient the thinking of Puerto Ricans began in earnest in June, 1946, when Muñoz Marín wrote two articles in the San Juan newspaper *El Mundo* at about the time he expelled *independentistas* from the PPD, and to which reference has been made earlier in this study. In these articles, he pointed out Puerto Rico's absolute need of the United States for its economic survival. He argued that production had not kept pace with the population growth, and that the island needed to step up its pace through increased industrialization. Such a program, Muñoz Marín continued, required Puerto Rico's continued free access to United States markets. Since Puerto Rico could not afford to give up its economic relations with the United States, a political solution had to be found outside of the "known classical forms" of independence and statehood. One such solution that the *Popular* leader suggested was what he called *Pueblo Asociado de Puerto Rico*. He did not give any details about it except to say that under it the Puerto Ricans would enjoy complete internal authority, and that sometime in the future, when the island reached certain economic indices, its inhabitants could decide between independence and statehood.[10]

As co-founder and member of the governing body of the PPD, Fernós-Isern also played an influential role in the formulation and implementation of the Commonwealth. He wrote an article in the July 4, 1946, issue of *El Mundo* proposing what was to become later the Commonwealth status.[11] On February 27,

1947, by which time Fernós-Isern had been appointed the new resident commissioner in Washington, he spoke about a "third point of view" at Rollins College, Florida. Careful not to offer the formula as officially that of the insular government, he raised the question, "Why they [the advocates of the "third point of view"] ask, cannot Puerto Rico become a self-governing community with its own democratic constitution, and still retain its present economic relationship with the United States within an adequate political association pattern?"[12]

A year later President Truman visited Puerto Rico (and the Virgin Islands), but it is not known whether insular leaders discussed with him the new plan for dominion status.[13] In May, 1948, however, Fernós-Isern translated the "third point of view" into what he called the "Federated Free Commonwealth" in an address before a group of graduate students from Princeton. In contrast to his Rollins College speech, the resident commissioner openly declared that the Puerto Rican government favored this new status, although not as a permanent but an intermediate solution. He described the process by which the "Federated Free Commonwealth" could be achieved. First, Puerto Ricans must be permitted to appoint their own auditor and justices of the Supreme Court, positions then being named by the president. Second, the limits to which the federal government could intervene in insular matters should be established. Third, the islanders should be permitted to write their own constitution. Fourth, the political and economic relations between the island and the mainland should be perfected, subject to change only by mutual consent.[14] The speech contained the essential features of what was to be the constitution bill two years later.

Muñoz Marín followed up the resident commissioner's suggestion with a major address on July 4, 1948.[15] It also served as a basis for the PPD's campaign in the forthcoming insular elections. The question of political status, the *Popular* leader said, was part of the "whole problem of life" for the Puerto Ricans. Whoever promised to achieve immediate independence or statehood, he continued, "would not be a liberator; he would be an enslaver, a destroyer of freedom in the life of men and women who make up our people; he would be an annihilator of all hope of being able to add political liberty permanently to the other essentials of freedom of the people of Puerto Rico." Muñoz Marín suggested dominion form of government, and urged Congress to "complete by law" self-government in Puerto Rico without making it a state, but "within the constitutional structure of the United States." By this he meant that Congress should authorize the Puerto Rican people to draw up their own constitution.[16]

The economic relations between Puerto Rico and the United States, Muñoz Marín continued, must remain basically the same except for lifting the restriction upon the refining of insular sugar. When all this was done, self-government in Puerto Rico would reach the "maximum point," "which sometimes under the name of autonomy, sometimes under the name of dominion, and sometimes under other names, has been one of the solutions which have, in the past, been put forward in Puerto Rico." The *Popular* leader clearly stated that this status was to be transitional, for he wanted Congress to pass a law authorizing the insular legislature to submit to a plebiscitary vote the question as to whether Puerto Rico desired independence or statehood "at any time when the Legislature may judge that the economic development will allow it."[17]

Muñoz Marín's Fourth of July address was incorporated in the *Popular* party's platform on August 15, 1948, and therefore also served to initiate the campaign in the first elective governor's contest in 1948. The PPD platform called first, for the preservation of the economic and fiscal relationship between the island and the mainland. Second, it made public its intention of seeking a constitution drafted by the Puerto Ricans themselves. Third, the party promised that the island's legislature would convoke, "when it deem[ed] that favorable conditions exist[ed]," a plebiscite to poll Puerto Ricans on three alternatives: independence, statehood, and continuation of dominion status because economic conditions were not yet ripe. The party was having the electorate believe that it did not rule out independence under certain circumstances, partly to undermine the strength of the *independentistas*. Fourth, it would call upon the Congress of the United States to act in accordance with the wishes of the people of Puerto Rico as reflected in the plebiscite on the third point.[18] The PPD nominated Muñoz Marín to run for the governor's post and Fernós-Isern to continue as the resident commissioner.[19] The mainland Democratic party platform of 1948, incidentally, promised "immediate determination by the people of Puerto Rico as to their final form of government and their ultimate status with respect to the United States."[20]

The *Partido Estadista Puertorriqueño* (PEP) joined forces with the Socialist party of Bolívar Pagán, and the newly-formed Reform party of Santiago Iglesias Silva, the last party consisting of followers of the defunct Liberal party.[21] The Coalition's candidates for the posts of governor and resident commissioner were Martin Travieso and Luis Ferré, respectively.[22] Its platform advocated statehood as an eventual goal, which was in conformity with the plank offered by the Republican party on the mainland advocating eventual statehood for Hawaii, Alaska, and Puerto Rico.[23]

In contrast, the PIP promised in their platform the appointment of a legislative committee to decide how indpendence for Puerto Rico was to be instituted. Its two candidates for governor and resident commissioner were both formerly prominent members of the PPD. They were Dr. Francisco Susoni and Rafael Arjona-Siaca.[24] Corresponding to the PIP's aspirations was the plank of the mainland Progressive party, which stated that the people of Puerto Rico had a right to independence, and that the United States had "an obligation toward . . . [them] to see that they [were] started on the road toward economic success."[25]

The 1948 elections were significant because it was the first time in Puerto Rico's 450 years of history since Columbus' time that its citizens were being permitted to elect their own governor. Furthermore, the island's 872,114 registered voters were being called upon to choose from three major sets of candidates, each one fairly clear on where it stood on the status question.[26] The *Popular* party injected, perhaps deliberately, some confusion by advocating a plebiscite on three alternatives sometime in the future. For the moment, however, Muñoz Marín referred to *independentistas*[27] as dreamers because they failed to realize that Puerto Rico needed the United States for its economic well-being.[28]

Fernós-Isern emerged in the campaign as a leading spokesman for the party's goal of dominion status. Twelve days before the elections, he addressed Puerto Ricans over the air. The resident commissioner spent considerable time explaining how Puerto Rican's fixation with statehood and independence had made their advocates "worshippers in separate sects" when in fact neither was immediately realizable because of the island's economic conditions and because neither could be obtained from Congress. He suggested, therefore, a political and economic union in the form of a dominion "founded on complete equality" with the United States. Fernós-Isern did not believe that such a status was not "a respectable political status," or that Puerto Rico would deserve to be referred to as a "colony" thereafter. He pointed to the Commonwealth of British Nations and to the statuses of Canada, Australia, and New Zealand within it. "You cannot say," he insisted, "they are inferior or politically subordinate to Britain. They live united by common allegiance to the British Crown. But they live under a democratic regime where the Crown merely represents common citizenship." Fernós-Isern told his listeners how the new status might be implemented: obtaining the right to draw up their own constitution and the authority to elect their auditor and appoint their justices of the Supreme Court. Furthermore, a statute would replace that part of the Organic Act that then served to regulate Puerto Rico–United States relations. He also suggested adjustments to clarify the application of federal laws in Puerto Rico.[29]

The Coalition pointed to the advantages that would follow statehood. With Puerto Ricans in the Senate and the House of the United States, the island would be able to secure the best possible terms for all its marketable commodities, including the lifting of restrictions then on sugar acreage and refining. The PIP accused Muñoz Marín of having abandoned independence as a goal and said that the status could be achieved with the close cooperation of Untied States legislators.[30]

The PPD scored victories even more convincing than its achievements in 1944. In the gubernatorial contest it received 392,386 votes (over 61 percent), as opposed to the combined votes of 248,328 for the opposition parties. The votes for the opposition were distributed thus: PEP 89,441, Socialist party 64,396, Reform party 29,140, and PIP 65,351. The *Populares* won 17 of the total 19 seats in the Senate and 37 of the 39 seats in the House.[31]

Governor-elect Muñoz Marín interpreted the support his party received as endorsement of the dominion status, and the day after the elections he made public his intention of asking Congress to allow the islanders to write their own constitution.[32] In his inaugural address on January 2, 1949, the governor argued that colonialism was "obsolete" but that ending it with "narrow nationalism" was bad. He pointed out that it was Puerto Rico that needed the United States, and not the other way around, and promised that traces of colonialism in United States–Puerto

Rican relationships would soon be ended.[33] Undersecretary Chapman, who was present at the inauguration, read to the assembly the president's message of felicitation and expressed his faith in the leadership of Muñoz Marín and in the islanders' ability to run their own affairs.[34]

Congress appeared generally willing to extend greater responsibility to Puerto Rico. On January 17, 1949, for instance, Senator Butler of Nebraska introduced a bill to establish in a single man the post of resident commissioner for Puerto Rico and the Virgin Islands, and to extend to him, together with delegates from Alaska and Hawaii, the right to vote in the House of Representatives.[35] Governor Muñoz Marín was not too happy about having one man representing both Puerto Rico and the Virgin Islands.[36] Besides, the Puerto Rican government based the island's unique tax structure, in part, on the general principle that the islanders could not be taxed without representation. Giving a vote to the resident commissioner might open the door in the future for the Puerto Ricans to become eligible for federal taxation and for the tax-exemption laws to be ruled invalid.

In any event, Undersecretary Chapman opposed the bill. In a letter to Senator Joseph C. O'Mahoney, chairman of the Committee on Interior and Insular Affairs, he pointed out that there were nearly 2,000,000 Puerto Ricans in contrast to 30,000 Virgin Islanders. Under such circumstances, the needs of the two groups of people could not be adequately represented by one resident commissioner.[37]

In pursuit of the insular government's announced intention of clarifying the rule regarding the application of federal laws in Puerto Rico, Fernós-Isern introduced H.R.3848 in Congress in March, 1949.[38] The bill proposed amending section 58 of the Organic Act so as to provide that all laws originating in Congress should be made specifically applicable to Puerto Rico. The measure aimed at preventing "indirect, automatic, undetected, and accidental amendments" to the Organic Act, the resident commissioner explained to DTIP's new director, James P. Davis. In Fernós-Isern's opinion, the Organic Act was not a general but a special law operating both as a constitution for Puerto Rico as well as a statute of relations between the island and the mainland.[39] The bill did not make any headway, and its provisions would be written into the constitution bill a year later.

In July, 1949, Governor Muñoz Marín visited Washington

to take up the constitution project.[40] On July 5, he discussed it with President Truman. He referred to Puerto Rico, according to Secretary Krug, as a "new state," not in a legal or formal sense but in the sense that it was in charge of its "own destiny." There were also references in the memorandum to Puerto Rico's desire to participate in the Point Four program then being developed by the United States.[41] The governor's desire to offer technical aid to under-developed countries reflected Puerto Rico's pride in its progress and confidence in its future. The offer was made partly in response to Puerto Rico's detractors who claimed that the island was still a colony of the United States. The reactions of the president and the secretary to Muñoz Marín's "new state" at this stage are not known, but Krug reported later to the president that the State department was favorable to Puerto Rico's joining the Point Four program.[42]

The governor's optimism in the coming days suggests that his July 5 meeting with President Truman and Secretary Krug was a favorable one. At a press conference on July 9, 1949, he told reporters, "Our new state is not defined by law but it is already a reality. There are no documents which say that Puerto Rico is a forty-ninth state, but we have facts not documents to demonstrate it." Since Puerto Rico was already a "new state," the next step was for the islanders to write their own constitution as in the case of established states, the governor added.[43]

Three days later Muñoz Marín appeared before the House Public Lands Committee to report to it Puerto Rico's progress. The major part of the more than one hour he spent before a well-attended meeting of the committee was devoted to describing the island's economic program. Muñoz Marín referred only briefly to the matter of the constitution, assuring the congressmen that the Puerto Ricans' writing their own constitution did not signify a step toward statehood but the extension of self-government. He concluded, ". . . I would like to leave it [the constitution idea] with you gentlemen for your consideration for action during a future session."[44] The governor also spoke to full attendance of the House Ways and Means Committee, and was met by individual congressmen interested in Puerto Rico.[45]

Muñoz Marín made an overwhelming impression upon the legislators. The Public Lands Committee, for instance, broke tradition by giving the governor a standing ovation.[46] Secretary Krug noted in his memorandum to the president that the *Popular* leader had been received by congressmen with "extraordinary cordiality." The secretary continued, "On the whole there is no question that our relations with Puerto Rico are very much better than at any previous period."[47] The reason for the governor's popularity, *La Prensa* reflected, was his ability to be both idealistic and practical, and his emphasis upon the importance of Puerto Rico as a link between Latin America and the United States. Besides, Muñoz Marín was living proof, in the minds of many congressmen, that the United States was opposed to a policy of territorial expansion.[48] The governor himself was pleased with the favorable response that the constitution project had received from congressmen.[49]

But other Puerto Rican leaders were not wholly satisfied about the constitution plan. PEP's leader Celestino Iriarte said that if the new constitution was merely a change in the Organic Act it was not consequential. Socialist leader Pagán argued that true sovereignty could be attained only under statehood or independence. And PIP head Concepción de Gracia insisted that the constitution would not be Puerto Rico's own, but merely an addition to the Organic Act. Two leading insular newspapers were also critical. *El Imparcial* believed that the so-called "new state" was neither "new" nor a "state," while *El Mundo* charged that Muñoz Marín was falsely claiming that Puerto Ricans were in agreement with his plan when he had not consulted them in deciding on the new status.[50]

The governor replied to these charges to the United Press in Washington. He said he was sure that the islanders supported his plan because he was doing no more than fulfilling the program he had campaigned for in 1948. In any case, whatever the final political solution, Puerto Ricans would have the opportunity to decide for themselves in a referendum. Resident Commissioner Fernós-Isern also claimed that the Puerto Rican people knew and understood the distinct type of political state envisaged by the insular government as reflected by their support of the PPD in the 1948 elections.[51] Despite his confidence in the wide support for the constitution plan, Fernós-Isern announced that the bill providing for the constitution would not be presented in 1949 because he wanted Congress to have the maximum time and attention in considering it.[52]

No further reference to the projected constitution appears in the records until December, 1949, when presidential aide Philleo

Nash dispatched a memorandum to one of his colleagues, Stephen J. Spingarn. Nash informed Spingarn that the Interior department had received a request from Muñoz Marín to make an announcement about the constitution plan. The aide believed that the governor had injected a "new note" into the unending debate on political status largely as a reaction to pressures he was feeling from *independentistas* and *estadistas*. He also felt that the project would take about two to three years to complete. It does not appear as if Nash was fully acquainted with the details of the Puerto Rican plan.[53]

On December 28, 1949, the chief of the Caribbean Division of DTIP, Mason Barr, addressed a memorandum to Nash. Barr did not feel that the projected constitution would differ much from that part of the Organic Act providing for autonomy. He felt that its great merit lay in the "psychological advantage" it held out for Puerto Ricans and the rest of the world as another example of the "progressive attitude of the United States toward its territories and so-called 'non–self-governing' areas." He seemed to have some reservations about the dominion concept. Barr said, ". . . dominion, federated state, autonomous state or some other semantical juggling, would be a difficult concept for either Congress, the American people, or the Puerto Rican people to understand."[54] The drafting of the constitution, on the other hand, would not meet opposition, and Barr recommended that the president support this general principle in his State of the Union address.[55] The president, however, did not refer specifically to Puerto Rico or the projected constitution plan in his annual message to Congress in January, 1950, but simply endorsed the policy of a greater measure of self-government for all of the island possessions of the United States.[56]

In January, 1950, Governor Muñoz Marín announced that he would be visiting Washington to work out, among other things, the details of the constitution plan.[57] A few days thereafter, the governor described the process by which Puerto Rico had naturally evolved into a "new kind of statehood" as "polititiation [of polity?] mutation" and stated that the time had come for formalizing it by deliberate action. Three factors, according to Muñoz Marín, had helped in bringing about the "new kind of statehood": first, the island's racial affiliation to Latin America and its political connection with the United States, which made it culturally a "harbor [of] understanding for both main cultures of the hemisphere"; second, Puerto Rico's practically complete self-government; third, its unique fiscal and political arrangement with the United States.[58]

He listed in the same memorandum two ways by which the evolved state could be formalized into a constitutional reality. One, the people of Puerto Rico should be authorized to draft their own constitution and to establish a procedure for amending it, subject only to the limitations continued in Congress' enabling act, such as a bill of rights. Two, Congress should elicit the consent of the insular legislature or of the Puerto Rican people before passing laws that concerned the island's affairs.[59]

Fernós-Isern recalls that he left with Muñoz Marín in December, 1949, the last of the many drafts on the projected constitution bill that he had been working on since his speech of July 4, 1946. The governor was to consult his legal advisors about it and report changes to Fernós-Isern when he arrived in Washington.[60] Meanwhile, the resident commissioner, now back in Washington, worked to secure the passage of bills that would complement the proposed constitution bill. He happily reported White House support of a bill (H.R.3848) he had sponsored ten months earlier. The measure provided that, unless specifically stated to the contrary, federal laws would not apply to Puerto Rico.[61] Soon thereafter, Fernós-Isern appeared before the Senate Finance Committee to argue in favor of extending the Social Security Act to Puerto Rico.[62]

At the beginning of February, 1950, the resident commissioner announced his intention of introducing a bill providing for the constitution early in the session. In an effort to inform and engender support for the proposed bill, Puerto Rico's Washington office published 15,000 copies of its monthly bulletin containing information about the projected constitution plan and about the island's political status as compared with other non-United States territories whose relationships with a major power were similar.[63]

On February 21, 1950, DTIP's legal counsel Silverman wrote to Fernós-Isern, referring to him in the salutation as "My dear Tony." There was reference in the communication to an earlier discussion of the proposed measure by the two. Silverman said that laws that were going to remain in force after the bill's passage should be mentioned in the measure. He was opposed to using "enabling" in the proposed bill because of its statehood connotation, and suggested that the word be omitted. Instead he preferred "authorizing." Silverman requested a conference among Fernós-Isern, James Davis, and himself when Governor Muñoz Marín arrived in Washington.[64]

Muñoz Marín arrived in the United States on February 27, 1950.[65] Sometime thereafter the governor met DTIP's director Davis and Silverman. The *Popular* leader told the two administration officials that he envisaged the introduction of a simple bill in Congress authorizing the calling of a constitutional convention to draft a constitution. He listed two absolute conditions that the Puerto Ricans had to honor in writing such a document, namely, that the form of government be republican and that it include a bill of rights. The governor hoped that the proposed measure would contain a provision to exempt federal laws, or parts thereof, from applying to Puerto Rico whenever circumstances warranted it. Such a provision, it was Muñoz Marín's contention, would further the principle of self-government, especially as Puerto Rico did not have voting rights in Congress. The *Popular* leader was careful to point out that the provision was not intended to usurp Congress' power since it would still have the authority of re-enacting laws considered invalid for Puerto Rico by the president.[66]

The governor confided in Davis and Silverman that he preferred to see the bill being presented as an administration measure so as "to preclude any embarrassment in Puerto Rico should it fail of enactment or be passed in some form unacceptable to the Puerto Ricans." The request seems inconsistent with the facts of the entire matter. The constitution project had been advanced by the PPD as part of its program in the 1948 elections. It had received wide publicity. It would appear, therefore, that the governor's position had been misinterpreted or that the memorandum had misstated Muñoz Marín's position. In any event, Muñoz Marín made that request and expressed his intention of conferring with the president and Chapman (who had been promoted from an undersecretary to secretary in place of Krug) and of canvassing for support among majority and minority leaders in Congress.[67]

The governor met with Congressional leaders in the next few days. He visited Representatives Crawford of Michigan, John W. Byrnes of Wisconsin, Stephen M. Young of Ohio, and A. Sidney Camp of Georgia, thanking them for their help in the past and bidding for their support in the constitution matter.[68] Later he conferred with Senator Butler of Nebraska.[69] On March 5, 1950, the House Public Lands Committee chairman, J. Hardin Peterson, announced his promise to hold hearings on the proposed measure within twenty-four hours of its introduction.[70]

A day later the *Popular* leader conferred for thirty minutes with President Truman in the company of Secretary Chapman. Although no details of the meeting were announced, Muñoz Marín was said to be pleased about its outcome.[71] Sometime during the governor's visit, he conferred with Fernós-Isern about the draft measure that the resident commissioner had left behind in Puerto Rico. The changes of style as recommended by the governor's legal advisors were agreed to.[72] Both the governor and the resident commissioner believed there was no cause for confusion about their plan, despite criticism to the contrary about it by other Puerto Ricans.[73]

Senators O'Mahoney and Butler, who had agreed to be bipartisan co-sponsors of the proposed measure in the Senate, received a draft of the legislation from the governor and the resident commissioner. The draft bill was examined by Stewart French, an aide to Senator O'Mahoney. The memorandum prepared by French found at least three technical defects, one of which was that there was no clearly expressed enabling clause to authorize the election of delegates to the constitutional convention. Even though Puerto Rico was an unincorporated territory, an "enabling or resolving clause" was necessary, much as in the case of incorporated territories that wrote their constitutions preparatory to their becoming states in the Union.[74]

The draft bill represented, according to French's memorandum, all the changes that Governor Muñoz Marín was prepared to accept. For political reasons, the governor wanted the bill introduced without giving the impression that the constitution was a "gift from On High." He wanted it believed that it was Puerto Rico's own idea and that acceptance of the idea of "Associated Statehood" was an independet act freely expressed by the people of Puerto Rico. Furthermore, if the bill was introduced in the present form, Silverman had told French, it would have "the greatest propaganda value in Latin America." French advised the senator to discuss the proposed changes with the governor and the resident commissioner.[75]

An aide to Senator Butler also prepared a memorandum on

the proposed bill. The memorandum stated that the bill, if approved, would not alter the island's status as an incorporated territory. Nor would it deprive Congress of its power to legislate over Puerto Rican matters. "The Congress," the memorandum continued, "can still make any Federal law applicable or inapplicable to Puerto Rico as it sees fit, or pass laws affecting Puerto Rico alone when it is desirable. It can also nullify the Puerto Rican constitution if it wishes, since, technically, Puerto Rico is still a territory subject to the rules and regulations of Congress under the Constitution."[76]

On March 13, 1950, Governor Muñoz Marín appeared before the Senate Committee on Interior and Insular Affairs. The governor reported to the committee the economic progress Puerto Rico had made, much as he had done over a year ago before the House Public Lands Committee. In addition, he elaborated upon his constitution project. Muñoz Marín argued that Congress' authorization of Puerto Ricans to write their own constitution was in practice a "shorter step" than the permission it gave to the islanders in 1947 to elect their own governor, yet more "deeply important . . . morally and spiritually." He continued, "It will put them politically and morally on the level with their great democratic practice and their great effort to continue solving the difficult economic problems of Puerto Rico."[77] The senators raised few questions, presumably because by this time most of them had been personally briefed by Muñoz Marín or Fernós-Isern, or otherwise informed by the governor's team of advisors. Indeed, the committee members were so thoroughly impressed by the governor that they gave him a standing ovation at the end of the proceedings.[78]

In this cordial atmosphere, Resident Commissioner Fernós-Isern introduced the constitution bill (H.R.7674) on March 13, 1950.[79] The bill recognized the principle of government by "consent," and its passage would be regarded as having been adopted "in the nature of a compact." It further provided for Congress to authorize the drafting and adopting of a constitution by Puerto Rico, which was to be republican and was to contain a bill of rights. Once the bill passed Congress to become an act, it would be submitted to Puerto Ricans for their approval. The completed constitution was then to be transmitted by the president to Congress. If the transmittal occurred ninety days before the adjournment of the session, and if Congress should fail to act upon the constitution before the session's termination, the document was to be deemed approved.[80]

Sections 4 and 5 provided that those sections of the Organic Act of 1917 dealing with Puerto Rico–United States relations would be continued under the "Puerto Rican Federal Relations Act." The "Puerto Rican Federal Relations Act" in effect guaranteed the continuance of the fiscal and political relations between the island and the mainland. Section 6 of H.R.7674 incorporated the provisions of a bill that Fernós-Isern had sponsored on March 28, 1949. It stipulated that upon the request of the insular legislature the president might except Puerto Rico from the application of any federal law that did not specifically apply to the island.[81]

In short, the constitution bill sought to separate the dual functions of the Organic Act of 1917. That part of the Organic Act that dealt with Puerto Rico's internal matters was to be embodied in a constitution drawn up by the island. If the bill should become law, the governor was guaranteed the right of naming his own auditor and justices of the Supreme Court. That part of the Organic Act that was concerned with insular-mainland relations was to be known as the Puerto Rican Federal Relations Act. In this connection, the phrase "in the nature of a compact" was important because, as Muñoz Marín and Fernós-Isern interpreted it, there could be no further changes in the Federal Relations Act except with mutual agreement. The phrase was to become a bone of contention two years later.

True to the promise he made a week earlier, House Public Lands Committee chairman Peterson held the first hearing on the constitution bill the day after it was introduced. Governor Muñoz Marín was the only witness to testify on that day. The constitution bill, the governor insisted, did not represent a step either to independence or statehood, and Congress' passage of the measure did not imply its commitment in the future to grant either one of the two. Muñoz Marín believed that the Puerto Ricans should have full right to amend the constitution except in areas where the bill stipulated that they could not. "I would hope," he added, "that only basic exceptions of principles should be made, in order to recognize the dignity of the Puerto Rican people in the exercise of their democratic wisdom."[82]

Leading backers of the constitution bill worked to win support for the measure. At the request of Arnold Miles, director of the Bureau of the Budget, DTIP's director Davis wrote on March 16, 1950, explaining details of the bill. Davis explained the distinction between incorporated and unincorporated territories and reassured Miles that the bill's passage would not change Puerto Rico's status as an unincorporated territory and that the island's political and financial arrangement *vis à vis* the United States would remain unchanged. Davis described Puerto Rico's new status as "much akin" to that of a state in the Union.[83] Ten days later, Secretary Chapman explained the constitution bill and expressed his support for it over the National Broadcasting Company.[84]

Meanwhile, Stewart French submitted to Senators O'Mahoney and Butler a memorandum on his discussion with Fernós-Isern, preparatory to the senators' co-sponsoring the constitution bill. There were disagreements of points of view between French and Fernós-Isern. French believed that a joint resolution instead of a bill might be better to get Congress to approve the constitution project. In the end, however, he accepted Fernós-Isern's argument in favor of a bill. In the matter of "compact," the resident commissioner insisted upon retaining it because of the "desirability of such language." French apparently agreed because he found precedent of the "compact" idea in the Enabling Act of the Northwestern Territory. On another matter, namely, the delegation of legislative power to the president in case Congress failed to act upon the constitution within a specified period of time, French registered his opposition, "in theory" at least. But Senator O'Mahoney's aide was sympathetic to Fernós-Isern's argument that it would not be wise to allow the islanders to complete the constitution only to have Congress, pressed by "more immediately momentous matters," fail to act upon it.[85]

A revised draft of the bill, presumably prepared by French, accompanied the memorandum. It incorporated at least two important changes. The first was that the constitution had to be "accepted freely by a majority of the people of Puerto Rico." The second change concerned the length of time after which the constitution would become effective if Congress should fail to act upon it. French's revised draft stipulated that if the constitution was transmitted to Congress within thirty days of a legislative session, and if after one year of such transmittal Congress had still not taken action, the constitution would be deemed approved.[86]

If Senators O'Mahoney and Butler had any doubt as to whether the constitution bill had popular insular support, it was in part allayed by a joint resolution adopted by the Puerto Rican legislature on March 30, 1950. The resolution fully endorsed the measure.[87] The following day, eighteen days after Fernós-Isern had sponsored H.R.7674, Senators O'Mahoney and Butler introduced a companion bill designated as S.3336.[88] The Senate version of the constitution bill did not differ significantly from its counterpart in the House. S.3336 had added to it two "whereas" clauses concerning Congressional recognition of Puerto Rico's right of self-government. Section 2 of the Senate bill also added a provision not present in the House version. The Puerto Rican people were specifically authorized to call a constitutional convention. Other provisions dealing with the transmittal of the constitution to Congress, its fate should that body not take action within the legislative session, and the applicability of federal laws in Puerto Rico were left very much as they were in Fernós-Isern's bill.[89] The senators accepted Stewart French's recommendation with respect to the "whereas" clauses and the insertion of an "enabling" clause but rejected the recommendation concerning the extension to one year of the time in which Congress could take action on the constitution.[90]

In a statement released to the press by the two senators, it was pointed out that the bill had popular insular backing and that it was a significant step in the advancement of self-government. The senators cautioned, however, against interpreting the measure as a step in the direction of either independence or statehood. They maintained that the bill would not affect Puerto Rico's relationship with the United States.[91]

The administration indicated its support for the bill. President Truman directed the Department of the Interior and the Bureau of the Budget to forward favorable reports to Congress.[92] Secretary Chapman wrote a letter on April 28, 1950, to Congressman Peterson strongly endorsing the constitution bill. Congress, he argued, would continue to have the power to determine the island's ultimate status in the future. The bill's passage, the secretary continued, would not commit Congress to statehood legislation in the future. In a memorandum that accompanied the letter, Chapman concurred with the proposed amendments to H.R. 7674 as incorporated in the Senate companion bill.[93]

On May 16, 1950, the House Public Lands Committee conducted for the second time hearings on the constitution measure. All those who appeared before the committee endorsed the bill, although the memoranda, letters, and telegrams of those who opposed the measure were inserted in the records. The witnesses who appeared in person, furthermore, were connected in one way or another with the administrations of President Truman and Governor Muñoz Marín. Edward G. Miller, Jr., assistant secretary of State for Inter-American Affairs, endorsed the measure because it was in accordance with the United States' policy of extending greater self-government to dependent peoples. A letter from Assistant Secretary of State Jack K. McFall was read into the hearings. McFall commented on the bill's significance in an international context, saying that, "In view of the importance of 'colonialism' and 'imperialism' in anti-American propaganda, the Department of State feels that H. R. 7674 would have great value as a symbol of the basic freedom enjoyed by Puerto Rico, within the larger framework of the United States of America."[94]

Another witness was Representative Walter A. Lynch of New York, who had recently traveled to the island as one of the members of the House Ways and Means Committee to examine Puerto Rico's tax relationship with the United States. He used facts and figures to illustrate the fiscal relationship between the island and the mainland and reassured the committee that the bill would not alter it. The Department of the Interior was represented by DTIP director Davis who, in endorsing the bill, referred the committee to the April 28, 1950, letter from Secretary Chapman to Congressman Peterson, previously cited.[95]

Associate Justice A. Cecil Snyder of the Puerto Rican Supreme Court emphasized in his testimony that the bill embodied a "new, bold, unique, ingenious, creative and dynamic concept," while insular Senator Victor Gutiérrez pointed out that the bill had received the support of eighteen of the nineteen senators and thirty-eight of the thirty-nine representatives in a joint insular resolution. Fernós-Isern sought in his testimony to reassure congressmen who may have had some doubts about aspects of the bill. The phrase "in the nature of a compact," he said, was based on the principle of mutual consent in which Puerto Rico and the United States would jointly decide upon future changes in their relationship with each other. The will of Congress, Fernós-Isern continued, would prevail in whatever form and manner federal authority in Puerto Rico would be exercised. The constitution bill would not alter the powers of sovereignty acquired by the United States in 1898 by the Treaty of Paris. Then he reiterated a point, which, judging by the number of times it was repeated, must have bothered many congressmen: passage of the measure would not commit Congress to be either for or against any specific form of political formula for Puerto Rico in the future.[96]

After Fernós-Isern's appearance, no more witnesses were heard. In the communications that appear in the text, several persons opposed the bill for one reason or another. Juan B. Soto, professor of law at the University of Puerto Rico, questioned the essential premise upon which the constitution plan was based in a memorandum he had prepared at the request of the PEP. He said that a constitution was derived from the original sovereignty of the people, and as such it could be revoked only by the authority that made it. If the United States approved the bill, it would in effect be recognizing the inherent sovereignty of the people of Puerto Rico and relinquishing the rights and powers of sovereignty it acquired in 1898. If this indeed was so, the professor continued, the United States was not obliged to grant financial aid to Puerto Rico. It might even lead Puerto Rico, Soto implied, to an undefined legal status from which statehood might not be possible.[97]

Independentista leader Gilberto Concepción de Gracia stated his objection more strongly. He said, "We vehemently repudiate any constitution subject to amendment, repeal, suspension, control, or alteration by Congress or by any other power foreign to the people of Puerto Rico themselves." He argued that neither Congress nor Muñoz Marín had ever been entrusted with the power of constitution-making, which belongs "historically, juridically, and politically" only to the people of Puerto Rico. All opponents of the bill argued that the committee should hold hearings in Puerto Rico to give those persons unable to travel to Washington an opportunity to be heard.[98]

The following day a subcommittee of the Interior and Insular Affairs Committee conducted hearings on S.3336. The same persons who had appeared the previous day at the House Public Lands Committee hearings presented their arguments to the Senate subcommittee. Much of what they said was essentially if not exactly the same as their testimonies the day before.[99] The Senate subcommittee was aware of the criticism that many opponents of the bill could not come to Washington to testify for a variety of good reasons. But Senator O'Mahoney did not think it possible to hold hearings in Puerto Rico because it would cause delay and probably also kill all chance of the bill's passage.[100]

Secretary Chapman dispatched a memorandum to Senator O'Mahoney analyzing the constitution bill and urging its passage. Since it appears as if the senator was already persuaded about the merits of the bill at that stage, the secretary's memorandum was presumably intended to clarify aspects not yet clear or to emphasize the importance he attached to its passage.[101] In any event, the Senate Committee on Interior and Insular Affairs approved the bill with amendments on May 26, 1950.[102] The committee altered the language of the bill as introduced by Fernós-Isern to provide specifically for a referendum among Puerto Ricans to accept or reject the act authorizing the writing of the constitution.[103] This clarification appears to be in deference to legitimate criticism that opponents of the bill had not been given sufficient opportunity to be heard. It did not wish to be open to a charge later that the bill had been railroaded by committee members.

The Senate committee struck out section 3, which had provided that if Congress failed to take action after the president had transmitted the constitution it would be deemed approved. Congress would not agree, it would appear, to a move that implied blanket endorsement and thereby would undermine its claim of authority over insular affairs. The committee was probably similarly motivated in eliminating section 5. This section concerned federal laws specifically applicable to Puerto Rico. Despite these amendments, the Senate committee's approval of the bill was a major breakthrough. The committee gave a number of reasons in its appraisal for its favorable consideration. The first group of factors concerned the popular support for Governor Muñoz Marín and the strong endorsement given the bill by the departments of Interior and State. The second group of factors was that the bill did not envisage substantive changes in insular-mainland relations and that it did not seek to bind Congress to a final political status. The third group of factors was that the bill was in agreement with the principle of extending self-government, as embodied in the United Nations Charter, and that its enactment would enhance the prestige of the United States in the eyes of the dependent peoples of the world.[104]

The chairman of the House Public Lands Committee, Representative Peterson, did not express an opinion on the Senate amendments, but said he would hear opponents of the bill in the week of June 5, most notably Representative Marcantonio of New York.[105] On June 8, 1950, the Senate passed the constitution bill as reported to it by the Senate Committee on Interior and Insular Affairs. The bill was one of the 229 measures passed without objection.[106]

On the same day that the Senate passed the constitution bill, the House Committee on Public Lands held hearings to give the measure's opponents an opportunity to express their views. Congressman Marcantonio, who had introduced a bill on March 16, 1950, to make Puerto Rico a sovereign state, was the first to testify. His testimony consisted of two parts. The first was a speech he had made in Congress on March 16, 1950, and which he had printed in the hearings. In it, the member of the American Labor party charged that the bill was a "snare" and a "delusion" intended to continue the system of "imperialism." The measure, he explained, evaded the real issue of Puerto Rico's ultimate status and continued to give the United States veto power and exclusive jurisdiction in a number of areas. Marcantonio said that Muñoz Marín had falsely built a reputation of being a champion of the *jíbaros* when in fact he connived with the "Wall Street Crowd" in implementing "Operation Bootstrap," which he called "Operation Booby Trap."[107]

In the second part of his testimony, Marcantonio charged Muñoz Marín and Fernós-Isern of having deceived the Puerto Rican people in the November, 1948, elections. He based his assertion on a comparison of speeches made by Muñoz Marín in July, 1948, and by Fernós-Isern in October, 1948, with the promises contained in the 1948 PPD platform. Representative Marcantonio said that there were two constitutional steps involved in the bill, when in fact the PPD platform had given the impression that only one was necessary to resolve Puerto Rico's ultimate status. Fernós-Isern contested this point in a lively debate with Marcantonio. The New York congressman was the only opponent to appear in person.[108]

Other opponents of the constitution bill made their positions clear by communications to the committee. PIP leader Concepción de Gracia lamented the haste with which the committee sought to pass the bill. Celestino Iriarte, president of the PEP, desired to see a provision inserted in the bill that stated that nothing in it implied a denial of Puerto Rico's right to statehood in the future. He also hoped that the phrase "in the nature of a compact" would not be interpreted to mean that future Congresses could not act favorably on statehood. *Independentistas* Rafael Arjona-Siaca and Rafael Pérez-Marchand submitted a long memorandum about legal aspects of the measure. They argued that the bill was juridically deceptive because the "compact" idea was meant to give the impression that Puerto Ricans voluntarily accepted their "colonial" position, when in fact the powers of Congress could not be "in the least compacted, convenanted, contracted, bargained, or in any way affected by this legislation." They argued that the bill sheltered a hidden motive, "No matter what the efforts to conceal the facts, the present relations between the Puerto Ricans and the United States will continue as they are, not by the consent of the people of Puerto Rico but because in the bill Congress had expressly decreed their permanence." All those opposed to the bill's passage requested that hearings be held in Puerto Rico.[109]

Congressman Peterson appeared to believe that opponents of the constitution measure should be given further opportunity to be heard.[110] But on June 14, 1950, three days after he expressed such sentiments, the Public Lands Committee approved the bill in an executive session behind closed doors.[111] The measure as reported out by the House committee incorporated the amendments made by the Senate commitee two weeks earlier.[112] On June 19, 1950, the bill was referred to the Committee of the Whole House on the State of the Union.[113] At this point it was generally believed that the measure would pass Congress before July 4.[114] Indeed, Muñoz Marín hoped that this would happen, because its passage would give the insular government the opportunity "to add local significance to national celebration [Fourth of July], and would also lend itself to wider publication throughout the world."[115]

On June 28, 1950, the House Rules Committee placed the bill on the calendar for debate lasting for one hour on the House floor.[116] Two days later the House debated the constitution bill. There was "unusually strong" support, as Silverman wrote Muñoz Marín.[117] Among those congressmen who expressed support for the bill was one group that based its confidence in Puerto Ricans in general and Muñoz Marín in particular. Another group that endorsed the measure did so in the knowledge that Congress retained the right to decide on Puerto Rico's final political status.

Still another group that voted affirmatively was moved by a sense of paternalism towards Puerto Rico. Said Republican Congressman Walter H. Judd of Minnesota, ". . . you cannot expect to take a child in the third grade or sixth grade and move him up into a postgraduate school without the various grades between."[118]

Another Republican, Congressman Jacob K. Javits of New York, had some reservations about the bill. The measure, in his opinion, restricted Puerto Ricans to only one alternative, namely, the present status, and even that only with prior Congressional approval. If Puerto Rico could frame its own constitution, he added, it could also decide on whether it desired independence or statehood. He was, therefore, in favor of recommitting the bill for striking out sections 4 and 5. The strongest opposition came from Representative Marcantonio, who charged that the measure was a deliberate attempt by Muñoz Marín to mislead the islanders. But his motion to recommit the bill to the committee failed decisively: 1 in favor, 260 opposed, and 169 not voting. Thereafter the bill was passed by a voice vote. Both Republicans and Democrats supported the measure, which suggests that Puerto Rican autonomy was a bipartisan concern of United States legislators.[119]

On the first day of July both the Senate and the House, having reached agreement on the constitution bill, presented it to the president for his signature. On the same day that the House debated the bill, the Department of the Interior requested the Budget Bureau to recommend to the president the acceptance of the bill.[120] On July 3, 1950, President Truman signed the bill into Public Law 600, despite appeals by *independentistas* and *estadistas* that he should not.[121] Public Law 600 stipulated that it be submitted to the Puerto Ricans for their acceptance or rejection. If accepted, the government of Puerto Rico was authorized to call a constitutional convention to draft a constitution that had to provide a republican form of government and include a bill of rights. Upon the Puerto Ricans' adopting the constitution, the president of the United States was authorized to transmit it to Congress. If Congress should approve the constitution, the provisions of the act were to go into effect: the constitution was to become effective in internal matters, while that part of the Organic Act of 1917 that concerned Puerto Rico–United States relations was to continue in force as the "Puerto Rican Federal Relations Act," as provided by section 4 of Public Law 600. The law did not set a time limit for the entire procedure.[122]

Muñoz Marín and Fernós-Isern regarded the act as a victory for all Puerto Ricans. They both pointed out its great significance at the Fourth of July celebrations in San Juan. The resident commissioner urged the *independentistas* and *estadistas* among the islanders to take the opportunity of hanging their "hammocks" of independence and statehood, instead, "under the shade of the tree which sprouts into this new concept of life of liberty in confederation." Who knows, he continued, the natural evolution of this "new federative formula" might make the old dilemma disappear from everybody's mind.[123]

The striking fact about the implementation of the first portion of Puerto Rico's Commonwealth project was the relative ease with which the insular leaders secured the passage of Public Law 600. A congeries of reasons persuaded the United States that it was in her interest to enact such a law. The law offered her the opportunity to respond to charges that Puerto Rico was a colony of the Colossus of the North. Congress retained the phrase "in the nature of a compact," despite its legal vagueness, as evidence of its good faith, because such language created the impression that Puerto Rico was by her own choice entering into a relationship with the United States. The comments of at least two mainland newspapers might have reflected the exaggerated significance attached to Public Law 600 by some congressmen and administration officials. The *Boston Globe* believed that the Puerto Rican story was one that the "Voice of America should trumpet throughout Asia." The *Washington Post* argued that in the island's political progress "a more effective riposte to Soviet yelpings about American imperialism could scarcely be presented to the world."[124]

The more important consideration that went into resolving Congress' mind, however, was the nature and extent of the change envisaged by Public Law 600. The United States was not called upon to make a substantive change in Puerto Rico's existing status but merely to improve upon it and to formalize it in a brilliantly conceived constitutional scheme. Puerto Rico gained complete control of its internal affairs within a federal relationship that was unique because of its fiscal and tax relationship with the United States. The envisaged status did not undermine the United States' role in maintaining the island's position as a strategic outpost nor its supremacy in Puerto Rico's foreign affairs. And the administrations of President Truman and Governor

Muñoz Marín repeatedly stressed the fact that Congress was not relinquishing its hegemony on the matter of Puerto Rico's ultimate political status.

A factor of considerable importance was the personality and politics of Muñoz Marín. The governor's innovativeness inspired among United States lawmakers a kind of enthusiastic confidence in Puerto Rico's future that paved the way for Public Law 600. Of no less importance was the dedicated and intelligent efficiency of Resident Commissioner Fernós-Isern, who worked assiduously to see the realization of a concept that had germinated in his mind. He it was who appeared before committees, conferred and consulted with Congressional leaders and administration officials, and piloted the measure through Congress. The resident commissioner worked closely with administration officials whose help was vital to the passage of the constitution. They were, among others, Chapman, Davis, Barr, Silverman, Philleo Nash, and Stephen J. Spingarn. The help of Congressional leaders too was invaluable. Congressman Peterson, Senators O'Mahoney, Butler, and Herbert H. Lehman of New York were among the many who shared in the aspirations of Muñoz Marín and Fernós-Isern. Together they established a solution, which in the words of the *New York Times* was a "notable example of enlightened control from a governing power and energetic, intelligent progress on the part of the governed."[125]

CHAPTER EIGHT

Commonwealth of Puerto Rico, July, 1952

In securing the passage of Public Law 600, the Puerto Rican administration had succeeded in persuading the Congress of the United States of the wisdom of the plan for a Commonwealth of Puerto Rico. Then it had to be officially endorsed by the Puerto Rican people in a series of carefully planned constitutional steps. Muñoz Marín was reasonably certain of receiving the support of the bulk of the islanders. The *Popular* leader, therefore, took great pains to maintain procedural propriety, lest he should be accused of fraud later on. Any instance of malpractice would tarnish or even shatter his claim that the Puerto Rican people were establishing a promising experiment in democracy. In this his patience and resourcefulness were severely tried: firstly, by those among his compatriots who launched a rebellion and by others who labeled the entire process fraudulent; and, secondly, by Congress, which threatened to renege on its promises made in Public Law 600, to the extent of discrediting his claim of victory for the principle of self-government. That he succeeded was a measure of the man's political skill.

One of the first steps was taken at the end of August, 1950. The Joint Insular Election Committee established dates for the procedure involved in the drafting, adopting, and approving of the constitution. Referendum on Public Law 600 was set for June 4, 1951, and elections for members to the constitutional convention were to be held on August 27, 1951. The constitution to emerge out of the convention was to be submitted to the Puerto Rican people for their acceptance or rejection on January 21, 1952. The date for the registration of voters for the last two constitutional steps was originally fixed for August 14, 1950, but later moved to November 4 and 5, 1950.[1] The dates were confirmed at a special session of the Puerto Rican legislature on September 27, 1950.[2]

Muñoz Marín desired to have observers present from the State Department and the United Nations. He wanted "to render ineffective the [possible] Nationalist and Communist" charges that the entire electoral procedure was rigged.[3] But he changed his mind upon the advice of DTIP director Davis, who thought that to follow the governor's suggestion would be "dignifying" the activities of the Nationalists and the Communists. The presence of the observers, Davis continued, "would have an effect opposite to that which [the governor] wish[ed]."[4] However, Muñoz Marín and the insular authorities were "leaning over backwards" to make sure that complaints by the radical groups would have no basis.[5] The Federal Bureau of Investigations (FBI), too, was keeping a close watch on the Nationalist party in Puerto Rico. A twenty-five page report was filed by the organization on October 12, 1950, covering the party's activities for the first nine months of 1950.[6]

The campaign over Public Law 600 began in earnest in October, 1950. Muñoz Marín started with an address in Ponce, a port city in the southern part of the island, whose mayor, incidentally, was opposed to the constitution.[7] Later in the month the governor responded to the opponents of the projected constitution.[8] PEP leader Iriarte opposed the constitution plan on the ground that it was really not a PPD program but part of the foreign policy of the United States being implemented to counter charges of imperialism.[9]

But even as this debate was proceeding, the radical element in Puerto Rico was readying itself for what looked like an attempt to overthrow the insular government. On October 27, 1950, police found a cache of arms and dynamite in San Juan. The heightened vigilance of the insular police may possibly have caused the Nationalists to advance the day of the attempted coup. On October

28, 1950, there was a riot in Rio Piedras prison in San Juan in which two guards were killed and 111 prisoners escaped. This appeared to be related to the revolt that flared up two days later. Violence and arson accompanied the uprisings in eight towns. In San Juan five Nationalists boldly invaded the grounds of the governor's residential palace, the *Fortaleza,* in an attempt to kill Muñoz Marín. Four of the rebels were killed in the abortive attempt. From there the uprisings rapidly spread to other parts of the island. The towns of Utuado and Jayuya were seized by the Nationalists. The rebels burned twenty-one houses in Jayuya. In Mayaguez, Ponce, and San Juan bloody clashes occurred between the police and the insurgents.[10]

On the mainland two Nationalists attempted on November 1, 1950, to enter forcibly Blair House in the complex of the president's residence in Washington in an apparent bid to kill Truman. One of the Puerto Ricans and a White House guard were killed in the firing that followed. The other Puerto Rican, Oscar Collazo, and two of the White House guards were wounded. The president's life was not directly threatened in all this. The dead Nationalist was associated with Pedro Albizu Campos, for in his pocket was found a memorandum bearing the name and signature of the Nationalist leader. Oscar Collazo, the wounded man, was the treasurer of the New York branch of the Nationalist party.[11]

Since the Nationalists numbered no more than 500 by Muñoz Marín's calculations, he was sure that he could control the uprisings on the island with little trouble. The day after the revolt broke out he mobilized the National Guard, who used planes, tanks, machine guns, and bazookas to dislodge the rebels from their stronghold in Jayuya.[12] Elsewhere the police had succeeded in subduing the rebels. Some 400 Nationalists were forced to surrender in this massive crackdown, of whom 244 were placed under arrest.[13]

The administrations of Governor Muñoz Marín and President Truman recognized that the uprising, even though it had failed in its prime objectives, could disrupt and discredit the entire scheduled constitutional procedure. They were careful, therefore, not to overreact, despite the fact that thirty-three persons in Puerto Rico and two in the United States had lost their lives. The governor went on the air to reassure the Puerto Ricans that the rebellion was simply part of a "lunatic movement" and that the proclamation of martial law was not necessary.[14] On November 2, 1950, the governor cabled President Truman, saying that the people of Puerto Rico were "shocked and offended" by the attempt on his life but that the incident had not affected "the bonds of friendship, association, and mutual trust" between the island and the mainland.[15]

Presumably referring to the possibility of federal intervention that might have arisen, Secretary Chapman insisted that he saw no evidence of "general unrest" or "serious disturbances" affecting the economic, social, and political life of the islanders. He believed that the situation could be handled by the Puerto Rican government.[16] President Truman was of the same opinion. In a message to the governor on November 2, 1950, he complimented the insular authorities for their handling of the situation. At a news conference on the same day, the president reaffirmed his faith in the Puerto Ricans and declined to discuss the possible attempt on his life.[17]

Two days later Secretary Chapman dwelt at length on Puerto Rico in an interview over a Washington radio station. He said that the Nationalists and the Communists in Puerto Rico numbered 700 and 400 strong, respectively. The "great majority" of the islanders preferred, Chapman insisted, "the gradual development of their land under the system of Democracy" then prevailing. He believed that Puerto Rico had a great role to play in the better understanding of Latin America and the United States because it was "a synthesis of Latin American and North American beliefs." The secretary described the Puerto Rican people as "patriotic and peace-loving" and hoped that continental Americans would not judge them harshly for the acts of the two would-be assassins.[18]

Both the insular and mainland governments successfully conveyed the feeling that the uprising was the work of an inconsequentially small group of extremists and that the situation was well under control. There was no immediately noticeable impact upon United States private business activities with the island.[19] Meanwhile, the insular authorities moved to quash the power of the Nationalists. Twenty-one of the diehard *independentistas* were sentenced to life imprisonment in May, 1951,[20] while their 59-year-old ailing leader, Albizu Campos, was sentenced from twelve to fifty-four years in jail.[21] There was no evidence of a conspiracy to kill President Truman. Oscar Collazo was, however, found guilty of the murder of the White House guard.[22]

The uprising failed to prevent the registration of voters on November 4 and 5. To emphasize that things had returned to normal, Governor Muñoz Marín ordered the removal of the National Guard from the San Juan area. Indeed, the PPD leader believed that the disturbances had caused the various parties to unite, and he predicted that 95 percent of the people would approve Public Law 600.[23] The governor reported after November 5, 1950, that an additional 157,902 persons since 1948 had registered. That number largely reflected persons who had turned twenty-one years of age since 1948, and who, as it turned out, represented 30 percent of the number of persons who participated in the June 4, 1951, referendum.[24] Furthermore, at least one member of the House Public Lands Committee in Puerto Rican matters did not think that the disturbances would adversely affect the Congressional position on the constitution. He was Fred Crawford of Michigan, who in fact urged the committee to visit the island to reaffirm its faith in Puerto Rico.[25]

Much of the debate between November, 1950, and June, 1951, centered around the definition and interpretation of Puerto Rico's envisaged new status. The position taken by the Muñoz Marín administration left considerable room as to the implications of the new status. Early in December, 1950, for instance, Muñoz Marín described to an *El Mundo* reporter the position of Puerto Rico as being "part of the independence of United States."[26] PEP leader Iriarte felt that the governor's position was a permanent repudiation of insular independence and was an indication of his desire to see Puerto Rico eventually become a state.[27] PIP head Concepción de Gracia, on the other hand, stuck to his original contention that Public Law 600 was fraudulent since it perpetuated Puerto Rico's status as a colony of the United States.[28]

In the February issue of the *United Nations World*, however, Muñoz Marín termed the island's status a "new type of statehood, a statehood, which [was] related by citizenship and law to the other states of the Union." But like independent nations, the governor continued, Puerto Rico had the right to proclaim its own constitution. The Puerto Rican people alone had the right of electing their officials, and these officials were in "no way responsible to any authority of the United States." The *Popular* leader wrote, "Our autonomy is further vividly demonstrated by the fact that no official of the United States—not even the President—has authority over the Governor."[29]

A memorandum from Resident Commissioner Fernós-Isern to DTIP chief counsel Silverman suggests, however, that the insular administration was not quite clear what Puerto Rico's legal status would be. The resident commissioner defined for the division's future reference such terms as "territory," "dominion," "dependency," and "possession." The terms were defined clearly in relation to Puerto Rico's relationship with the United States, and did not have universal applicability. A "territory," according to Fernós-Isern, referred to "any area subject to the sovereignty of the United States and incorporated into the United States as an integral part thereof, but not a State." A "dominion" was described as "any area subject to the sovereignty of the United States but not incorporated into the United States as an integral part thereof, whose people shall have organized themselves under a constitution of their own adoption, into a free body politic in accordance with a law adopted by Congress in the nature of a compact with said people." "Dependency" was defined as "any area subject to the sovereignty of the United States but not incorporated to the United States as an integral part thereof, and formed into a political unit of government, which has not attained the political status of a United States Dominion as herein defined." Finally, a "possession" was said not "to describe, apply or refer to any Territory, United States Dominion or United States Dependency."[30]

It was partly as a result of the confusion and vagueness of the terms used to describe what the island's status was going to be that opposition parties were divided as to what their official position on Public Law 600 should be. The PEP had met on August 19 and 20, 1950, but the assembly was forced to adjourn without taking a vote because of disagreement among various factions. The meeting was marked by a lively and even violent disagreement between two factions. The faction headed by Miguel Angel García Méndez and Luis A. Ferré opposed Public Law 600. Its opposition was based, according to García Méndez, on the alleged contention of the law's supporters that "it would authorize a self-government status as a permanent compact or treaty" when no such "treaty" or "compact" existed within the meaning of the phrase "in the nature of a compact." García Méndez and Ferré were prepared to accept "any advantageous reforms with a temporary character but never as a final solution" to Puerto Rico's status.[31] The faction led by PEP leader Iriarte was not opposed to Public Law 600, because it did not consider its approval as foreclosing statehood as an ultimate status. The assembly sustained Iriarte's position in a hard-fought battle in which the vote was 156 to 97. Individual party members were left free to vote for or against the law, which in effect spelled endorsement.[32]

The PIP, too, was unable to reach a decision in its meeting early in 1951. In the end it resolved to let the voters decide for themselves. The resolution was approved by an extraordinary meeting in February, 1951. But PIP leader Concepción de Gracia refuted Public Law 600 in a twenty-seven–point program and challenged Muñoz Marín to a public debate, which the *Popular* leader turned down.[33] The *Independentista* leader continued to call the law a fraud, an opinion he conveyed in a letter to Secretary of State Dean Acheson. He based his charge on the ground that Public Law 600 did not grant sovereignty to the Puerto Rican people but merely approved an amendment to the Organic Act of 1917. Congress, he continued, would still retain final authority on insular affairs. The party chief also charged that insular government employees were being forced to contribute 2 percent of their salaries to defer the costs of the PPD campaign.[34] A few days before the referendum the PIP leader announced his personal decision to vote against Public Law 600.[35]

The debate on the projected constitution continued in the weeks ahead. One facet of this debate was in the form of a series of leading articles in *El Mundo* written by prominent men representing different points of view. These articles appeared in the newspaper from April to June 4, 1951, and beyond.

Juan B. Soto, a professor of law at the University of Puerto Rico, and an *estadista,* was the first to contribute a series of articles. He examined all aspects of the projected dominion status and arrived at two general conclusions, namely, that the PPD's "Associated Free State" promised more than it could fulfill and that statehood was the real solution to Puerto Rico's problems. The envisaged dominion status, Soto argued, was legally ambiguous and in effect left Puerto Rico in a state of semi-sovereign dependency. The professor pointed out that the "Associated Free State" did not carry with it legal pledges of continued economic aid from the United States. Hence, the Federal Relations Act would contain the same uncertainties that were present in the

Tydings independence bills, which the PPD had consistently opposed. He disagreed that the "Associated Free State" was equal or superior, because for one thing it did not involve the rights and responsibilities that would go with Puerto Rico's becoming a state and, for another, the economic goals sought by the PPD could better be attained under statehood. For instance, American capital would be drawn to the island more readily. He was well aware of the disadvantages that would accompany statehood, but he was convinced that they could be offset by its benefits. The payment of federal taxation, for instance, would be countered by federal grants-in-aid. He did not think that members of the Congress would always remain opposed to statehood for Puerto Rico. They could be persuaded to think otherwise.[36]

Resident Commissioner Fernós-Isern responded to the articles by Juan B. Soto. He maintained that statehood was not the issue in the acceptance or rejection of Public Law 600, even though the voters had clearly rejected it in the 1948 elections. The "Associated Free State" did not preclude statehood in the future. Puerto Rico could become a state, provided, of course, Congress and the Puerto Rican people were both willing. Fernós-Isern also pointed out that the position with regard to grants-in-aid and the retention of military bases would not alter with the implementation of the "Associated Free State." The new status would institute dual sovereignties in Puerto Rico, one United States and the other Puerto Rican. The two sovereignties were subject to certain conditions by mutual agreement. Hence, they were not conflicting but complementary. Similarly, Puerto Rico's economic union complemented its political affiliation with the United States. Fernós-Isern categorized the island's relationship as a new type of federation in which Puerto Rico was neither an independent state nor a dependency.[37]

Independentista Vicente Geigel Polanco followed with a series of articles under the heading "Neither a Constitution nor a Compact." He challenged the resident commissioner's contention that the act of drafting and adopting the constitution would make Puerto Rico sovereign in any sense. The constitution had to be approved by Congress, and the idea of a "compact" was meaningless because Congress retained final authority in the matter of insular-continental relations. Geigel Polanco backed his assertion by quoting certain United States administration officials and congressmen who had testified at the House Public Lands Committee on the constitution bill. He quoted, for instance, Representative William Lemke of North Dakota: "You know of course that if the people of Puerto Rico should go crazy Congress would be able to legislate another time." The *Independentista* concluded, therefore, that the projected constitution was being explained by the PPD in deceiving terms and that the Puerto Rican Federal Relations Act imposed inflexible provisions upon the island no different from those contained in the Organic Act of 1917. Geigel Polanco conceded the economic benefits Puerto Rico was enjoying as a result of its relationship with the United States but pointed to restrictions and limitations that were being continued: strict compliance with United States shipping laws, prohibition of commercial treaties with other countries, and federal restrictions on such agricultural products as sugar. He advised Puerto Ricans not to accept Public Law 600 because it was calling for the approval of the constitution project *and* the Puerto Rican Federal Relations Act, which he maintained were distinctly two separate questions.[38]

El Mundo ran other articles by other leading Puerto Ricans. They included articles by Jaime Benítez, chancellor of the University of Puerto Rico;[39] Socialist leader Bolívar Pagán;[40] José Trias Monge, Muñoz Marín's legal advisor;[41] and Fernós-Isern, responding to Geigel Polanco.[42]

In spite of the several legitimate points raised against the envisaged Commonwealth status by critics, it was generally believed that the islanders would overwhelmingly vote in favor of Public Law 600.[43] On June 4, 1951, 65 percent of the registered voters went to the polls. A total of 387,016 Puerto Ricans (76.5 percent of those voting) voted in favor of Public Law 600, while 119,169 persons (23.5 percent) voted against it. Secretary Chapman congratulated a pleased Muñoz Marín for managing the campaign so well and added, "Substantial minority vote further strengthens the favorable decision by showing that [the] opposition was fully and freely presented and [the] people made their own choice."[44] The secretary followed up his cablegram message with a letter addressing the governor as "My dear Don Luis." In it Chapman said that the acceptance of the law removed "the last vestigial remnants of so-called colonialism." But the secretary did not consider the constitution as a final solution: "It seems to me, in fairness to the people of Puerto Rico, that only when the economic and social goals are clearly in sight can they decide as to what ultimate relationship with the United States they desire."[45]

The PIP, however, charged that there had been polling irregularities and called for the nullification of the referendum.[46] In anticipation of such charges, Muñoz Marín had invited as observers Representatives Frank T. Bow, a Republican from Ohio, and Chester B. McMullen, a Democrat from Florida. Congressman Bow said that he had not found any fraudulent practice.[47]

On June 21, 1951, Governor Muñoz Marín called a special session of the insular legislature. The extraordinary session laid the ground rules for the election on August 27, 1951, of the delegates to the constitutional convention.[48] In compliance with these rules, the various parties met to nominate candidates to the constitutional convention. The Socialist party met on July 1, 1951, to select candidates who were to participate in the elections for constitutional convention delegates. Bolívar Pagán resigned his leadership at the meeting, although it is not known why. The party, however, affirmed its belief in statehood and instructed candidates to seek a provision in the preamble to leave open the door for that status. The PEP convened a month later on August 5 to nominate its delegates. An attempt was made at the meeting to smooth out differences between the two rival factions. A fifteen-member directorate was instituted to assume all party affairs, and two of the seats were given to García Méndez and Luis Ferré, both of whom had challenged Iriarte's leadership. In addition, nominees to the forthcoming convention were chosen from among both factions. The PEP, like the Socialist party, advised its candidates to work for a provision in the preamble to insure that statehood as an alternative was not foreclosed in the future.[49] In contrast to the Socialist party and the PEP, the PPD nominated its candidates without acrimony and accepted the unquestioned leadership of Muñoz Marín.[50]

The PIP, on the other hand, refused to participate in the constitutional procedure. Its position was that the projected constitution was a *Popular* perpetration of fraud upon the Puerto Rican people. The party instead promised to send its poll watchers to the voting centers. Its leader Concepción de Gracia insisted, ". . . we are not going to the colonial election of the 27th of August, nor to the false Constitutional Assembly, but we will participate in the registrations and elections of 1952, in order to obtain a mandate from the people." The PIP's declared non-participation in the August elections afforded the PPD with the opportunity to identify the *Independentistas* with the Nationalists. In this matter, the *Populares* effectively used the PIP's November, 1950, statement concerning the Nationalist uprising. The statement had denounced the Puerto Rican government's alleged violation of civil liberties and praised the rebels as "fellow countrymen" who had gallantly sacrificed their lives for the cause of insular independence. The PPD platform of August, 1951, declared, "The PIP, . . . postulating political separation from the American Union, solemnly declares . . . that it admires and respects those who want to destroy the force of votes by the criminal force of bullets."[51]

The elections for the delegates to the constitutional convention were held on August 27, 1951. A total of 431,828 persons voted, and, as expected, the PPD received the largest number of votes. Of the total of 92 seats contested, the PPD won 70, while the PEP and the Socialist party won 15 and 7, respectively.[52] Resident Commissioner Fernós-Isern was chosen to preside over the convention for its anticipated duration of six weeks.[53] President Truman sent a message to the convention. The president considered the meeting as a step of the "greatest importance in the development of full self-government in Puerto Rico." He continued, "It is with profound satisfaction that I contemplate the approaching task of this assembly, for I welcome Puerto Rico's association with the Federal Union on terms based solely upon consent and esteem." Secretary Chapman sent a similar message.[54]

The delegates worked for nearly five months on the preamble and completed it for the assembly's vote in the first week of February, 1952. A disputed clause held up the voting for a while. It stated that one of the purposes of the constitution was "to form a more perfect union with the United States." The word "union" was replaced by "association," but this displeased the *Estadistas*. Eventually the clause was dropped entirely.[55] On February 6, 1952, the constitution was approved by the convention by a vote of 88 to 3, with one delegate absent.[56]

On the same day Governor Muñoz Marín addressed the assembly. He characterized the new Puerto Rican status as partly "Federal" and partly "Confederal." He continued, "Within these two factors are enclosed the possibility of its development within the American union." By "Federal" he meant that there were two governments, Puerto Rican and United States, "with jurisdiction over different matters with respect to the same groups of citizens." By "Confederal" he meant that there was a "union, more or less on the basis of states that seek union, than on the basis of two governments that have jurisdiction over the same people but in different matters." The Commonwealth status was dynamic, and therefore held out several possibilities for the future. He expressed it thus, "It may be that the development of Puerto Rico will take another aspect, and that it will move toward a 'Confederal' form of government, in which there will be no area of Federal authority. . . .'' The governor insisted that in the final instance the development would be decided upon by the Puerto Rican people and not by the Congress of the United States. For the time being, however, the Commonwealth status in his opinion would remove "every trace of colonialism" because it would be based on a "compact" and the "principle of mutual consent." In the governor's estimation the status would reach "the highest possible level of political equality and political dignity."[57]

DTIP director Davis wrote to Muñoz Marín on February 14, 1952, informing him of his plans to publicize the constitution. He said he was having prepared a two-page summary of the most important features of the document for distribution. Davis said he had already spoken to Alan Barth and Herb Block of the editorial staff of the *Washington Post* about doing a piece on the constitution. The director said he planned to approach the *New York Times* and the *Herald Tribune* (New York) with similar requests. He also suggested counteracting the anti-constitution activities of L. D. Long, a continental businessman in Puerto Rico whose relations with the insular government had soured over tax problems. Davis urged the governor to come to Washington for a short visit.[58] Several days later DTIP legal counsel Silverman wrote to Alan Barth, acquainting him with background information about the constitution.[59]

Meanwhile, several other mainland citizens joined Long in leveling charges of dictatorship against Muñoz Marín. Chester M. Wright, president of the TIES organization, a Miami (Florida) group of business and professional men, accused the governor of having passed "urgent" and "gag" laws and of having converted the insular legislature into a "rubber stamp." The Puerto Rican government was a one-man affair run by a man who was authoritarian, the charge went.[60] The charges were echoed by Senators Olin D. Johnston of South Carolina and Owen Brewster of Maine, who proposed an investigation of the allegations. Senator Johnston accused the governor of having ignored a 1947 Congressional directive that a coordinator of federal agencies be established in Puerto Rico. The senator told his colleagues that he had addressed a communication to Secretary Chapman to that effect. The letter said in part, "They [the Puerto Ricans] don't want a Federal coordinator who will know what goes on, who is bound by law, for instance to advise the Congress with respect to all appropriation estimates submitted by any civilian department or agency of the Federal Government to be expended in or for the benefit of Puerto Rico."[61]

Secretary Chapman defended the governor in a news conference on February 13, 1952, saying that he thought Muñoz Marín was doing an "excellent job." On the specific charge about the federal coordinator, the secretary pointed out that Congress had on two occasions turned down appropriations to finance the staff of one. Besides, if the constitution was approved by Congress, the post in question would probably be eliminated.[62]

On March 3, 1952, in spite of the charges, the people of Puerto Rico once again went to polls to register their positions on the constitution. (The original date for the referendum was January 21, 1952, but it had to be moved back because the constitutional convention took longer than expected.)[63] Representatives Bow of Ohio and McMullen of Florida came once more as observers on behalf of the House Committee on Interior and Insular Affairs.[64] In view of the charges against Muñoz Marín, the Truman administration probably welcomed their presence.[65] A total of 373,418, or over 80 percent of the voters, balloted in favor of the constitution, while 82,473 of their compatriots voted against it.[66]

Muñoz Marín commented that the acceptance of the constitution was a source of pride for both Puerto Rico and the United States, since what was created was a "new manner of freedom in the relationship between peoples that have different cultural origins and both have equal democratic rights."[67] At least two continental newspapers shared the governor's enthusiastic optimism. The *New York Times* editorialized, "From our point of view this result ought to have good effects throughout Latin America. We are disproving the Communist and Nationalist charges of 'Yankee imperialism.' The United States has always been accused by these elements of exploiting Puerto Rico as a colony. It will be hard to sustain that propaganda effectively after what happened."[68] The *Washington Post* believed that Puerto Rico's becoming "vigorous, self-respecting, completely democratic, loyal, and friendly to the United States of America" was an instance of pride for the "so-called damn Yankees of the North." Indeed, the newspaper saw the advantage of extending the commonwealth concept to countries such as Cuba, Panama, Central America, and Venezuela to bind them in some form of loose federation.[69]

On March 12, 1952, Governor Muñoz Marín transmitted the English and Spanish enactments of the constitution of the Commonwealth of Puerto Rico to President Truman. Muñoz Marín believed that the process by which the constitution had been adopted was of great significance for both Puerto Rico and the "democratic world leadership of the United States." It had done the Puerto Ricans "a deep spiritual good" and had added to the "prestige of the institutions of the free world in their [insular and mainland Americans] moral fight against the rulers of the captive world." The governor stressed the fact that the document was based on "bilateral action through free agreement." He continued, "No doubt opinions may differ as to the details of the relationship, from both the Puerto Rican and the general American points of view, but the principle that the relationship is from now on one of consent through free government, wipes out all traces of colonialism."[70]

The same day that he wrote to the president, Muñoz Marín addressed a letter to Secretary Chapman. He said he was fully aware of the constitution's international significance and requested the secretary to publicize the official ceremony at which Resident Commissioner Fernós-Isern was to present the constitution to the president. The governor repeated the request on April 4, 1952.[71] Chapman wasted no time in having prepared a draft message for the president to send to Congress, together with the constitution.[72]

The Interior secretary's draft message was essentially retained as the president's message to Congress when the constitution was officially transmitted on April 22, 1952, to the legislative body. President Truman stated, "I do find and declare that the Constitution of the Commonwealth of Puerto Rico conforms with the applicable provisions of the act of July 3, 1950, and of our own Constitution." The message briefly described the provisions of the insular constitution and pointed out that with the document's approval "full authority and responsibility for local self-government will be vested in the people of Puerto Rico . . . . No government can be invested with a higher dignity and greater worth than one based upon the principle of consent."[73]

The constitution of the Commonwealth of Puerto Rico was completed after the convention had carefully studied the constitutions of the various mainland states in the Union, the Constitution of the United States, and the United Nations Charter. It contained nine articles. Article I established that the island was to be officially designated as the Commonwealth of Puerto Rico. The term "Commonwealth" was adopted on February 4, 1952, by Resolution 22 in the plenary session of the convention. It was the closest equivalent to the Spanish term "Estado Libre Asociado" and was defined as "the status of the body politic created under the terms of the compact existing between the people of Puerto Rico and the United States, i.e., that of a state which is free of superior authority in the management of its own local affairs but which is linked to the United States of America and hence is a part of its political system in a manner compatible with its federal structure."[74]

Article II contained the bill of rights. The opposition in Congress in the months ahead centered around two sections of this article. Section 5 guaranteed every Puerto Rican citizen the right to an education. It continued, "Instruction in the elementary and secondary schools shall be free and shall be compulsory in the elementary schools to the extent permitted by the facilities of the state. No public property or public funds shall be used for the support of the schools, or educational institutions other than those of the state. . . ."[75]

Section 20 was to cause considerable controversy. It borrowed ideas from the United Nations Declaration of Human Rights. The section recognized human rights in the following areas: to receive free elementary and secondary education; to obtain work; to attain an adequate living standard "for the health and well-being of [every person] and of his family, and especially to food, clothing, housing, and medical care and necessary social services"; to provide social protection in the event of unemployment, ill health, age, or disability; to give special care and assistance for motherhood and childhood. An explanation as to why these rights had to be guaranteed in the constitution read as follows:

"The rights set forth in this section are closely connected with the progressive development of the economy of the Common-wealth and require, for their full effectiveness, sufficient resources and an agricultural and industrial development not yet attained by the Puerto Rican community." In other words, they were intended as goals for which the Puerto Ricans were to strive.[76]

The legislative power of the Commonwealth of Puerto Rico was vested, according to article III, in the legislative assembly, consisting of 27 senators and 51 representatives in the two Houses. Minority parties were guaranteed representation. Section 22 provided that the governor was to appoint a controller with the advice and consent of the insular Senate. The person filling this post was still being appointed by the president at the time. The next article dealt with the powers and duties of the executive, while the article following was concerned with the powers and responsibilities of the island's judiciary. There were to be five justices of the Supreme Court, and under the new constitution their appointments were to be made by the governor instead of the president as was then the case.[77]

Article VI provided, among other things, for the general elections to take place every four years, with no restrictions as to how many terms a governor may hold office. All persons over twenty-one years of age, irrespective of literacy or property-holding, were to be eligible to participate in the elections. The procedure for amending the constitution was provided for in article VII. The insular legislature could propose amendments to the constitution. If there was a two-thirds majority for the proposed amendment in both Houses, it was to be submitted to the qualified electors in a special referendum. If, however, the proposed amendment had a three-fourths majority in both Houses, the legislature could provide for a referendum to be held at the same time as the next general elections. It should be emphasized that United States approval was not necessary in the ratification of an amendment. Section 3, however, stipulated that no amendment purporting to alter the republican form of government or to abolish the constitution was admissible.[78] Article VIII dealt with senatorial and representative districts.

Among the provisions laid down in the ninth and last article was one calling for the constitution to take effect when the governor proclaimed it, which must be within sixty days of Congress' ratifying it. No provision was made for procedure in the event

Congress changed parts of the constitution, which suggests at least two things: first, that the convention felt the document complied with the conditions established by Public Law 600, and therefore Congress would agree with it entirely; second, since the document reflected the popular will of the Puerto Rican people on domestic matters, the constitutional delegates felt that Congress would not change any aspect, even if it disagreed with it, for the sake of the principle of self-government.[79]

Indeed, Resident Commissioner Fernós-Isern argued that the constitution met the four conditions necessary for its acceptance by Congress: it provided for a republican form of government with three separate branches, it contained a bill of rights, it conformed with the applicable provisions of the United States Constitution, and it was in agreement with Public Law 600.[80]

On April 22, 1952, Senator O'Mahoney sponsored Senate Joint Resolution (S.J.Res.) 151, while the companion resolution in the House was designated as House Joint Resolution (H.J.Res.) 430.[81] The two resolutions provided for the approval by Congress of the constitution, inasmuch as the document conformed "fully with the provisions of [Public Law 600] of July 3, 1950, and of the Constitution of the United States."[82]

The House Committee on Interior and Insular Affairs held a hearing on April 25, 1952. Resident Commissioner Fernós-Isern was the first person to testify. He reviewed the provisions of the Puerto Rican Federal Relations Act and reassured the congressmen that the Commonwealth of Puerto Rico would operate within their framework. He stressed the fact that the political and economic union had been democratically endorsed by a majority of the Puerto Rican people. Fernós-Isern appealed to the legislators to approve the document on the additional ground that its meaning transcended "the horizons of Puerto Rico and . . . of the United States."[83]

The resident commissioner's testimony was well received. Committee members generally asked questions to drive home the fact that the constitution was a popular document approved in elections that were free from any kind of electoral malpractice. Representatives Bow of Ohio and McMullen of Florida testified to the last fact, as they had observed the referendum. Clair Engle, congressman from California, was one of the few committee members, however, who had doubts about aspects of the constitution. He drew attention to section 20 of the bill of rights and expressed his puzzlement as to how such rights could be incorporated into a constitution without the legislature's obligation of implementing them. The congressman also raised similar doubts about the right to education as expressed in section 5 of the bill of rights. Furthermore, he believed that the outlawing of wiretapping was more correctly a legislative function. Representative Monroe M. Redden of North Carolina agreed with his California colleague, saying that the rights guaranteeing social protection might lead the Puerto Ricans to expect too much from their government.[84]

Despite the reservations about the bill of rights, most committee members appeared to agree with the statement inserted into the hearing by Congressman Crawford of Michigan, who was unable to attend the session. He expressed his support for the constitution on two general grounds. First, Puerto Ricans deserved the protection of the United States as American citizens. After all, the islanders had adopted the ideals and institutions of the United States and had generally cooperated in the same way that continental citizens had. Second, the United States had a friend in Governor Muñoz Marín. Crawford said, ". . . I think it will be found that the administration of the present Governor of Puerto Rico is just about as constructive and helpful and cooperative as between and with everybody concerned, as any appointee, military or civilian, who has been sent from the United States to Puerto Rico." If Congress believed that changes were necessary, he hoped that it would resubmit the constitution to the Puerto Ricans to make such changes but that it would not reject it out of hand. Except for Dr. Jaime Benítez of the University of Puerto Rico, no more witnesses were heard.[85] The House committee, according to the *New York Times,* gave quick and unanimous approval of the constitution.[86]

The Senate Committee on Interior and Insular Affairs conducted the first of its two hearing sessions on April 29, 1952. Governor Muñoz Marín, who was in Washington at the time, came to testify before the committee. He asserted in a prepared statement that Congress' approval of the constitution would signify that "the last juridical vestiges of colonialism [had] been abolished in the relationship between the United States and Puerto Rico." The principle of compact as contained in Public Law 600, the governor continued, added the "basic moral element of freedom" that had hitherto been absent. He was quick to point out, however, that the relationship could be improved in its details, although not in its essence. Muñoz Marín rejected the notion among some Puerto Ricans that any solution outside of independence or statehood was "colonialism."[87]

The governor characterized the Commonwealth status as one that was not "federated statehood," but neither was it "less than federated statehood." Because it was not like "federated statehood," many erroneously concluded that the Commonwealth status was based on inequality. This was not so. He based his judgment on the merits of the constitution produced by the convention. The procedure involving referenda and elections over a period of about eighteen months had strictly adhered to the principle of democracy and legality. Muñoz Marín described the essential features of the constitution: it had little in it that was strictly legislative because the PPD sought to give the legislature of Puerto Rico the greatest possible freedom to act upon matters concerning policy.[88]

There was, the governor said, continuing his argument, a bill of rights guaranteeing essential freedoms, and the government of Puerto Rico was republican with the powers of its three branches separated. Indeed, the powers of the executive were reduced in favor of the legislature and the judiciary. This to Muñoz Marín was clear evidence of a "magnificent democratic spirit" among the Puerto Rican people. He gave several other examples of this: the practice of vote-buying had disappeared; the government had sold four of its plants to private business, as evidence that politics should not interfere with business; and an anti-government newspaper, *El Imparcial* (San Juan), was able to secure through public auction valuable printing contracts from the insular government.[89]

To drive home his argument the PPD leader pointed out that the Commonwealth status offered the people of Puerto Rico an opportunity to free themselves from a "deadening anguish" that accompanied the continued debate over political status. He said, ". . . the alternative to the dilemma is not colonialism, but that a new alternative, equal in dignity, although different in nature to independence or statehood, can be conceived and is in fact being created by the joint action, on the highest moral level, of the Congress of the United States and the people of Puerto Rico."[90]

The committee members were mainly interested in having the governor respond to charges of fraud made against the PPD.

Few questions directly concerned the constitution. The main charge was about electoral fraud. The governor replied to the charge to the apparent satisfaction of the committee members. The persistent nature of these charges persuaded DTIP legal counsel Silverman to prepare later a memorandum on a specific allegation that between 3000 to 5000 additional voters had been prevented from voting in the referendum in March, 1952. Most of the persons involved here had turned twenty-one between January 21, 1952, and March 3, 1952, the time span between the old and the new dates. A specific law would have been necessary to accommodate the eligibility of these persons, and so the government of Puerto Rico decided to count them as ineligible except if the margin of acceptance or rejection of the constitution should be between 3000 and 5000. As it turned out, the margin of acceptance was 290,945.[91]

Resident Commissioner Fernós-Isern and DTIP director Davis testified briefly. No opponents of the constitution were heard. A letter from *Independentista* leader Concepción de Gracia appeared in the appendix of the hearings. One point raised in the letter, not taken up by the committee but featured prominently in the debates in the Senate later, was whether Congress would have sole and final authority on matters concerning Puerto Rico once it approved the constitution.[92] Both the House and Senate hearings reflected little opposition to the constitution among committee members. It was this which probably led Secretary Chapman to tell newsmen on April 29, 1952, that he believed Congress would endorse the constitution.[93]

Some senators were, however, raising questions about the constitution, which was presumably the reason why the Senate Committee on Interior and Insular Affairs held a second round of hearings on May 6, 1952. Nine senators were present at this session, in contrast to only four in the April 29 session. Apparently a need was felt to refute charges of electoral fraud more strongly, because Congressmen McMullen of Florida and Bow of Ohio testified at length on their roles as observers in the March 3, 1952, referendum. They insisted that the referendum was free from any kind of corruption. The committee refused to pursue a charge of another kind. Senator Johnston of South Carolina had raised in the April 29 hearing an incident that had occurred about twenty years ago in which Muñoz Marín, then a fiery *independentista,* had demanded the removal of the American flag when he stepped on an auditorium platform to address a crowd of people. The senator was not satisfied with Muñoz Marín's reply at the first hearing, and he requested the committee to pursue the matter further. The committee refused because it felt it was concerned with the merits and demerits of the constitution and not with the governor's qualifications.[94]

A substantive issue was raised at the hearing by Senator George W. Malone of Nevada. He desired to know whether there was a provision in the constitution that prohibited Congress from making any change in the relationship between the United States and Puerto Rico. DTIP legal counsel Silverman replied no, saying that even though Public Law 600 used the word "compact" the relationship between the two would be "in the nature of contractual obligations." Silverman continued, "It is our hope and it is the hope of the Government, I think, not to interfere with the relationship but nevertheless the basic power inherent in the Congress of the United States, which no one can take away, is in Congress . . . ." Congress had the power to annul any law in any one of the territories, according to the United States Constitution. Senator Malone remained doubtful, because he had seen in the United States how many of the powers that rightly belonged to Congress had been assumed by the president. He wondered, in effect, whether a general constitutional guarantee was sufficient to permit Congressional action regarding Puerto Rico, if and when the question arose. "Suppose," he asked, "these internal matters become a question of great interest to this country, the way they are being administered. Do we have the right to go in at all? . . . Suppose they become obnoxious to the Congress of the United States. What happens then?"[95]

Senator Guy Cordon of Oregon continued with the line of questioning initiated by his colleague from Nevada. He quoted from an article written by Muñoz Marín's legal advisor, José Trias Monge. Trias Monge had written that the pact was legally binding and that it could not be revoked except by mutual consent. Senator Cordon quoted from the article, " 'Once the compact is formalized, the constitution of Puerto Rico may not be amended except in the manner provided for by the constitution of Puerto Rico itself, the local laws shall not be subject to derogation by Congress, neither the Statute of Federal Relations nor law 600 may be amended without the consent of the people of Puerto Rico.' "[96]

Senator O'Mahoney, who had co-sponsored Public Law 600 in 1950, disagreed with Trias Monge's position. He argued that the law had not been adopted as a compact *per se* but "in the nature of a compact." He continued, ". . . an agreement in the nature of a compact . . . was one under which the Congress was reserving to itself, the sections of the Organic Act which were set out in Public Law 600 as the Federal Relations Act, and under which it undertakes to delegate to the people of Puerto Rico the authority to adopt their own laws with respect to local administration, and that this local administration is within the scope of a free self-governing, democratic republic similar to that of the United States, but had nothing to do with those subjects covered by the provisions we have called the Federal Relations Act." The Wyoming senator told a doubting Senator Cordon, ". . . if the people of Puerto Rico should step outside, if an attempt should be made to change the constitution and deal with these matters outside the scope of the grant, I think that the authority of the Congress of the United States, under the [United States] Constitution, could not be impaired or reduced."[97]

Another part of the constitution, section 20 of the bill of rights, also came briefly under attack by Senator Malone when chancellor Jaime Benítez testified. Furthermore, the Nevada senator did not believe that the government to be established under the constitution would be strictly republican. He saw elements of democracy in the constitution.[98]

Although no Puerto Rican directly opposed to the constitution appeared before the committee to testify, several communications from opponents of S.J.Res.151 were inserted in the appendix of the hearings. These communications raised similar, if not the same, questions of constitutional ambiguity and vagueness raised by the senators. Indeed, the quotation of Trias Monge's article used by Senator Cordon was part of a memorandum prepared by *independentista* Arjona-Siaca and *estadista* Carlos H. Julia, Jr.[99]

In view of the many questions raised in the Senate hearing, it was not surprising that H.J.Res.430 should have met some opposition when it was debated on the House floor on May 13, 1952. Section 20 of the bill of rights expectedly came under heavy attack from several congressmen. Representative Charles A. Halleck of Indiana, a Republican, saw in it the hand of former Governor Tugwell. In his opinion the section did not conform with the United States Constitution. Another Republican congressman, Carl T. Curtis of Nebraska, believed that the section called for a "totalitarian government" and could lead to "slavery." Idaho Representative Hamer H. Budge read into the debate remarks he had made on a previous occasion. "The Constitution of the Commonwealth of Puerto Rico," he said, "in quite different fashion attempts not only to protect the citizens from an autocratic government but to set up a government not for protection of rights but for affirmative dispensation of rights in the form of economic benefits." Another Idaho representative, John T. Wood, warned, ". . . if we grant this constitution, with its Socialist bill of rights, we have practically doomed the islanders to economic destruction. We know they cannot operate under it. Then why give it to them? I am firmly opposed to giving a child stone when it asks for bread."[100] Both Representatives Budge and Wood were Republicans.

There were, however, congressmen who agreed with Fernós-Isern that the constitution fulfilled the conditions established by Public Law 600 and conformed with the Constitution of the United States. Democratic Representative Isodore Dollinger of New York urged passage of H.J.Res.430 without amendments. Republican Congressman Javits of New York criticized legislators who in effect insisted that the constitution should be inhibited in terms of what they saw as right or wrong in their respective state constitutions or the federal Constitution. He reminded his colleagues that the insular constitution reflected the will of the Puerto Rican people. Majority leader John W. McCormack of Massachusetts agreed and pointed to the constitution's wider implications in Latin America. If the people of Puerto Rico wanted section 20, Congress should oblige, whether or not it complied with Public Law 600 and the United States Constitution. Samuel Yorty of California said that congressmen should consider the fact that Puerto Rico was a "showcase of the United States" and that everybody was watching to see what Congress did.[101] House leaders had planned to obtain the chamber's approval without a roll call; but when it became apparent that opponents would demand one, further consideration was postponed until a later date.[102]

On May 27, 1952, the Senate Committee on Interior and Insular Affairs recommended to the Senate the conditional approval of the constitution. Its amendments were confined to article II, the bill of rights. Section 5 was amended so as to guarantee that the provision about "free and wholly nonsectarian education" did not prohibit private educational institutions. The added declaration read, "Compulsory attendance at elementary public schools to the extent permitted by the facilities of the state as herein provided, shall not be construed as applicable to those who receive elementary education in schools established under nongovernmental auspices." The committee struck out section 20 entirely. The reason it gave was as follows: "Corresponding enforceable duties to the rights asserted cannot be determined and fixed under section 20, and therefore it is unrealistic, confusing, and misleading to assert such rights in a constitution which is intended to be fundamental and clear statement of matters which are enforceable and of the limitations on the exercise of power."[103]

The committee report further stipulated that wherever the words "democratic" and "democracy" appear in the preamble the references were in no way to be construed to mean the changing of a republican form of government. It also clarified in its report the status of federal authority in Puerto Rico: "The enforcement of the Puerto Rican Federal Relations Act and the exercise of Federal authority in Puerto Rico under its provisions are in no way impaired by the Constitution of Puerto Rico, and may not be affected by future amendment to the constitution, or by any law of Puerto Rico adopted under its constitution." The report stated also that the approval of the constitution did not imply any promise of statehood. It characterized the new status as neither independence nor statehood. "It is," the report explained, "a self-governing community bound by the common loyalties and obligations of American citizens living under the American flag and the American Constitution and enjoying a republican form of government of their own choosing." The insular constitutional convention was authorized to accept the amendments on behalf of the Puerto Rican people, and the constitution was to go into effect as soon as the governor proclaimed its operation.[104] The Senate committee accommodated its members' criticism concerning the bill of rights, but its declaration concerning federal authority in Puerto Rico fell short of claiming Congressional jurisdiction in the island's internal matters directly. Puerto Rico could amend its constitution, except with respect to the bill of rights and republican form of government, without Congressional authorization.

On May 28, a day after the Senate committee's action, the House of Representatives debated H.J.Res.430. Early in the debate it was made known that the House Committee on Interior and Insular Affairs had met that morning before the scheduled debate and had decided to eliminate section 20 and amend section 5, as the Senate committee had done the day before. Fernós-Isern announced his acceptance of the amendments, when he spoke halfway through the debate. At least two members of the House, Representatives Halleck of Indiana and George Meader of Michigan, both Republicans, wanted it clearly understood, however, that the constitution would not supersede the Puerto Rican Federal Relations Act. Congressman Meader had consulted the American Law Section and was satisfied that, in approving H.J.Res.430, Congress would not "in any way make an irrevocable delegation of its constitutional authority." Judging from the amount of time spent in the debate on this aspect, however, this was not a contested point.[105]

The debate centered mainly around the merit or demerit of section 20 as part of the constitution, and whether Congress had the right to tell the Puerto Ricans that it should be eliminated. After all, the islanders had overwhelmingly endorsed the section, and it was in compliance with Public Law 600. Those congressmen who supported the retention of section 20 argued that many states within the Union had such provisions written into their constitutions. Besides, if rejected, the impact upon Latin American countries may be serious, and it would afford the Soviet Union the opportunity to discredit the United States. Congressman Javits of New York said for instance, "If we should deny to them [Puerto Ricans] as elemental a right as self-determination, what respect could they have for all our protestations that we want people to make up their own minds as to how they will be governed?" Those who desired the exclusion of section 20 based their opposition upon arguments ranging from its binding nature to the notion that it was socialistic and would destroy republicanism. Congressman Wood of Idaho said, for example, "They are setting up a people's democracy which is foreign to our idea of a representative republic."[106]

When it seemed as if congressmen would approve H.J.Res. 430 with the amendments recommended by the House committee, Representative Meader of Michigan introduced late in the debate a major amendment. It read, "That nothing herein contained shall be construed as an irrevocable delegation, transfer or release of the power of the Congress granted by article IV, section 3, of the Constitution of the United States." (The reference here was apparently to the territorial clause of the Constitution.) Meader said that he was not clear whether a future Congressional law inconsistent with the island's constitution and laws by its legislature would take precedence over the latter. He asked, "Can the Congress, if it so desires, either pass inconsistent laws or repeal or amend laws that Puerto Rico passes? Clearly under the present situation we can. If this Puerto Rican Constitution is approved, can we?" The Michigan congressman had consulted lawyers who had told him that Congress could, but he wanted to eliminate any doubt in simple language.[107]

Congressman Wayne N. Aspinall of Colorado protested that the Michigan representative had not deemed it proper to suggest the amendment in the committee. He continued, "I believe the amendment is too far reaching for discussion at this time, and I suggest that we oppose it and defeat it." There was general objection to the Meader amendment, and it was rejected after Representative Clair Engle of California made an eloquent appeal for the passage of H.J.Res.430.[108] A roll call having failed to show an absence of a quorum, a vote was taken and the joint resolution was passed.[109]

The unexpected Meader amendment indicated the kind of opposition that the constitution might possibly run into in the Senate. The Senate committee leaders who hoped to steer the passage of S.J.Res.151 were possibly aware that some senators might raise objections. The articles that two of them had had printed in the appendix of the *Congressional Record* gave some indication of this. Senator Owen Brewster of Maine complained that the tax exemption laws of Puerto Rico were a misuse of the tax structure because the island was enticing away textile and other companies. Senator Johnston of South Carolina did not share some of his colleagues' admiration for Muñoz Marín, as evidenced in the senator's insistent allusion to the flag incident referred to earlier involving the Puerto Rican leader in his young radical days. On May 15, 1952, he had had printed in the record an editorial from a Tulsa, Oklahoma, newspaper, which stated that Puerto Rico was really a burden because it had proved to be a "gigantic incubator of people who often do not understand American traditions or ideals but who are glad to qualify for

American residence or American charity." The South Carolinian was responsible also for printing in the record an article that appeared in the *New York Daily News*. It objected to section 20 and suggested that the islanders should be made to write another constitution, or else "socialism, or fascism, unwanted by the great majority of Americans will have crawled in at our back door."[110]

Amid this kind of uncertainty, the Senate debated the constitution on June 23, 1952. Senator Johnston early introduced the first of his two amendments. It desired to limit the term of office of the governor to only one four-year period. The senator said that the amendment was not directed against Muñoz Marín; but, he argued, it was Congress' duty "to throw as many safeguards as possible around the constitution so as to protect the people of Puerto Rico as well as the people of the United States." The amendment was aimed against the "tendency in some countries for certain individuals to obtain control of the government and keep control." The opposition to the amendment was spearheaded by Senator O'Mahoney, who argued that such a limitation should have been written into Public Law 600 in 1950 and that, in states where no such limits were placed, governors did not automatically become dictators. He argued, furthermore, that Governor Muñoz Marín was a "remarkable man" with an exemplary record, whose concern for constitutional propriety was evidenced by the fact that the constitution guaranteed representation for minorities. The argument of the opponents prevailed and the amendment was rejected."[111]

The South Carolina senator's second amendment provided, ". . . that no amendment to or revision of the constitution of the Commonwealth of Puerto Rico shall be effective until approved by the Congress of the United States." His argument was that as a "possession" of the United States, Puerto Rico "should stay all the way under our control and not be permitted to rewrite [its] constitution." The senator was concerned that after disapproving section 20 Congress had no guarantee that the Puerto Ricans would not reintroduce it later. There appeared to be greater sympathy for this amendment than was the case for the first amendment, presumably because the issue was one which directly concerned the Senate, namely, the affirmation of Congressional authority over Puerto Rico. Senator O'Mahoney, chairman of the Senate Committee on Interior and Insular Affairs, agreed to accept it.[112]

A third amendment sponsored by Senator John C. Stennis of Mississippi was defeated. The Stennis amendment provided for jury trial in the area of misdemeanors. The constitution had already made provision for trial by jury in the case of felony. The opponents believed that this was unnecessarily imposing the Anglo-Saxon system of jurisprudence and law upon a Latin American system, which would involve costs and other adjustments on the part of the insular government. Besides, if at any time in the future the Puerto Rican government decided to provide for jury trial in misdemeanors, the constitution would not prohibit it from doing so.[113]

The Senate agreed to the amendments made to H.J.Res.430 but insisted upon its own amendment concerning Congressional prerogative to oversee changes to the Puerto Rican constitution. Senator O'Mahoney requested a conference of the two chambers in the event that the House of Representatives should disagree with the Johnston amendment.[114] The House disagreed two days later and arranged to send conferees.[115]

Governor Muñoz Marín was understandably perturbed about the Senate amendment, because it undermined his claim that the constitution's approval would grant Puerto Rico complete freedom in internal matters. He sent a radiogram to Davis saying that if the Johnston amendment prevailed it would destroy "the whole spirit of the constitutional process" and would inflict "untold mental and moral harm" on the Puerto Rican people. Acting director Dan H. Wheeler cabled a reply the same day saying that the DTIP would do "everything possible" to have the amendment eliminated in the conference.[116]

The Senate and House conferees met on June 28, 1952, and agreed to eliminate the Johnston amendment. They believed that "in keeping with the spirit of Public Law 600, Eighty-first Congress, and the purposes of the Puerto Rican Constitution, the people of Puerto Rico should have freedom to change their constitution within the limits of applicable provisions of the United States Constitution, the Puerto Rican Federal Relations Act, Eighty-first Congress, and House Joint Resolution 430." In accordance with this sentiment the following amendment was substituted for the Johnston amendment: "Any amendment or revision of this constitution shall be consistent with the resolution enacted by the Congress of the United States approving this constitution, with the applicable provisions of the Constitution of the United States, with the Puerto Rican Federal Relations Act, and with Public Law 600, Eighty-first Congress, adopted in the nature of a compact." The conferees eliminated section 20 of the bill of rights and, except for minor changes, retained section 5 as amended by the House in May, 1952. The constitution was to become effective upon the constitutional convention's formally accepting the amendments made by Congress and the governor's officially proclaiming its operation.[117]

The conference report was submitted to the Senate on July 1, 1952. Senator Johnston was unhappy that his amendment had been dropped but was willing to support the adoption of the constitution as amended. The Senate accepted the report.[118] On July 2, 1952, H.J.Res.430 was examined and signed by the Senate and the House. On the same day the Department of the Interior responded to the Bureau of the Budget by requesting that it recommend to the president the approval of H.J.Res.430. It regretted the amendments but felt that the great efforts of Muñoz Marín, Fernós-Isern, and other delegates of the constitutional convention should not be allowed to go in vain.[119] A similar request was sent by assistant secretary of State Jack K. McFall to the Budget Bureau.[120]

On July 3, 1952, the joint resolution was presented to the president, who signed it late in the afternoon. He hailed it as indicative of United States dedication to the "principle of self-determination and to the ideals of freedom and democracy." The statement released to the press said that "with the approval of H.J.Res.430, the people of the United States and the people of Puerto Rico [were] about to enter into a relationship based on mutual consent and esteem." The joint resolution was signed into Public Law 447 on July 7, 1952.[121]

Muñoz Marín, who had on previous occasions used the Fourth of July to appeal to high idealism, did not miss the opportunity on July 4, 1952. He told the Puerto Ricans that the new Commonwealth status was "dynamic and full of vitality, carrying in itself the energy for growth." The governor continued, "We should repose politically in this status for a time so that our people can direct all their energy toward the great effort of resolving their hard economic problems . . . ." On July 11, 1952, the constitutional assembly approved the amendments made by Congress, and decided to submit them to an insular referendum at the next general election in November. Eighteen days later, the

Puerto Rican legislature adopted a resolution ratifying in effect the action by the constitutional assembly.[122]

The climactic event, however, took place on July 25, 1952, when Governor Muñoz Marín pronounced the date as Commonwealth Day. In the presence of 35,000 people, among them distinguished guests from the United States and other neighboring countries, the governor raised the new Commonwealth flag. The flag was significant, for it was originally designed by Puerto Rican revolutionaries in 1895: five red and vertical stripes with a white star enclosed in a blue triangle. An action by President Truman intended to convey his good will towards the Puerto Rican people was announced on that day: the death sentence of the would-be assassin Oscar Collazo was commuted to a life sentence.[123]

The Puerto Ricans established in the Commonwealth status an experiment that was new and unique in constitutional history. Muñoz Marín defined it differently at different times. He described the status as one in which Puerto Rico was part of "the independence of the United States." At another time he said that Puerto Rico had not become a state in the Union but that it had acquired a status "equal to statehood" in which the island enjoyed a "new kind of freedom." The PPD chief described the insular-mainland relationship as being embodied in two kinds of government, "Federal" and "Confederal," while Resident Commissioner Fernós-Isern spoke of dual sovereignty, one Puerto Rican and the other United States, neither one in conflict. There is in every one of these descriptions an element of truth, but they are also ambiguous and constitutionally vague. In practical terms such definitions would, and indeed did, lead to a divergence of interpretation between the insular government and the mainland Congress. And yet, despite the ambiguity of the descriptions and the vagueness of constitutional definitions, both the Puerto Ricans and the United States Congress endorsed the Commonwealth status. There are a number of possible reasons.

Insular opponents did not have positive programs with which to counter the Commonwealth status. Advocates of independence and statehood pointed to the legitimate weaknesses of the status but failed to offer the Puerto Rican electorate a clear alternative program of their own. Admittedly, they were at a political disadvantage, because the insular voters were not called upon to choose from several status positions but were asked to either endorse or reject the Commonwealth status. Under these circumstances, the *Populares* presented themselves as offering a positive plan that would give the Puerto Ricans a respite from the "mental anguish," as Muñoz Marín explained it, that had accompanied fifty years of debate on the question of political status.

Besides, the political opponents of the PPD had nobody to match the charisma and reputation of Muñoz Marín. *Personalismo* is a factor of considerable importance in insular politics. If the people had doubts about the Commonwealth status, those doubts were dissipated by their faith in the PPD leader. He was their first elected governor, enormously popular in the United States and parts of Latin America, and they were proud of the kind of political skill and resourcefulness he had demonstrated. No doubt many Puerto Ricans would have considered a vote against the Commonwealth status as a vote against Muñoz Marín.

The same kind of confidence that the United States administration and Congress had in Muñoz Marín was responsible for the acceptance of the constitution. Furthermore, the United States desired to dispel charges by Communist and non-Communist countries that Puerto Rico was a "colony" being controlled against the will of the people of the island. Beyond this, however, the continental power's acceptance of the Commonwealth status was based on more sober grounds. It was the administration's understanding as expressed by Secretary Chapman in one of his communications to Muñoz Marín that the dominion status was not a permanent one and that sometime in the future, when conditions permitted it, Puerto Rico would choose between independence and statehood. The Congress of the United States, on the other hand, agreed to accept the Commonwealth status on the understanding that the phrase "in the nature of a compact" did not mean that Congress was irrevocably giving up its jurisdiction over Puerto Rican matters, internal and external. Congress, however, did not wish to state this as strongly as was suggested by the Johnston amendment. Instead, it sought to reassure the Puerto Ricans that it would exercise its jurisdiction over the island within the limits of the promise it was undertaking in accepting the new relationship between Puerto Rico and the United States. And future Congresses were under the moral obligation of not reneging on the promise made by the Eighty-first and Eighty-second Congresses.

CHAPTER NINE

The Commonwealth, 1952-1968

There is no exact parallel to the Commonwealth status of Puerto Rico. It differs considerably from the status of countries within the British Commonwealth, because the basis of the association is the political independence of the member nations. Puerto Rico's status had more in common with the position of small British Caribbean island territories when the United Kingdom organized in the late 1950s the Federation of British West Indies on the principles of federation and mutual consent. There were also some common features in at least two of the categories of possessions established by the French government in 1946. These two groups were "associated states" (Vietnam, Laos, and Cambodia) and "associated territories" (French Togoland and Cameroons). They were partly integrated with the French central government by means of their limited participation in the French National Assembly, and partly independent of the central authority in France because of their relative freedom in local matters.[1]

In endorsing a unique constitutional formula in the form of the Puerto Rican Commonwealth, the United States departed from its traditional territorial policy of permitting either full statehood or complete independence. The new constitutional pattern might conceivably have been extended to at least two other unincorporated territories, namely, Guam and the Virgin Islands. However, two general factors have prevented this from happening: one, the arrangement was born largely out of the long-term development of the peculiar relationship between Puerto Rico and the United States; two, the Commonwealth status has from the very beginning faced problems of definition. Since these problems are related with the significance of the Commonwealth, it is necessary to examine their development in detail.

The difficulties centered around the interpretation of the nature of the relationship between the United States and Puerto Rico. Muñoz Marín and Fernós-Isern saw in the Commonwealth arrangement more than a mere extension of autonomy by Congress. Whether or not they regarded in 1952 the Commonwealth status as permanent or transitory, they considered the relationship as having been conceived in a compact, and therefore it was not subject to changes except by mutual consent. It was on the basis of this principle that Puerto Rican leaders attempted on several occasions in the next sixteen years to improve and clarify the relationship. These attempts failed in their objective, and revived the debate on political status.

Although the debate came up in all its details only in 1959, the matter of the relationship was discussed by insular and continental authorities when the United States presented in 1953 Puerto Rico's case before the United Nations to cease reporting on the island to the world body. The presentation will be discussed here in some detail because the argument used by the United States before the international organization was incorporated by Puerto Rico in 1959 in building a case for the existence of a compact.

The United States had since June of 1947 submitted reports to the United Nations concerning Puerto Rico. Article 73 (e) of the Charter of the United Nations called upon members responsible for administering territories whose people had not yet attained "full measure of self-government" to submit such reports. In the five years since 1947, Puerto Rico had attained almost complete autonomy in domestic matters. There was no common definition of the phrase "full measure of self-government," and, therefore, presumably each member nation was left to decide for itself whether a particular territory, within its constitutional and governmental frame of reference, had reached the status. DTIP's legal counsel Silverman believed that Puerto Rico had been transformed from a "non–self-governing territory" to a "self-governing territory," and therefore it was no longer necessary for the United States to continue submitting reports on the island.[2]

Resident Commissioner Fernós-Isern initially proposed to President Truman to discontinue reporting to the United Nations.[3] Governor Muñoz Marín agreed with the idea, probably to prove by a deed to the Puerto Ricans and the rest of the world that the Commonwealth's inception had in effect ended the island's colonial status. It would be a gesture of great symbolic import and psychological advantage. In September, 1952, Muñoz Marín sent to Washington two of his aides to discuss with the departments of the Interior and of State the procedure to follow in notifying the United Nations of United States intention of ceasing to report on Puerto Rico.[4]

The two aides came prepared with a draft letter that Muñoz Marín was to send to the president. The Department of the Interior suggested changes, the most important of which was the deletion of the statement that Puerto Rico had "ceased to be a territory of the United States." It felt that the statement was a conclusion of law "probably not correct," and might cause controversy. It was also unhappy about the statements in the draft that maintained that insular laws could not be repealed or modified by "external authority" and that Puerto Rico's status and the terms of association with the United States could not be altered without the island's full consent. The Interior department was not certain whether this was correct or not. It agreed to the retention of the statement, however, provided it was made clear that this was Muñoz Marín's opinion, and not a settled point in law.[5] The State department, too, recommended a change. It suggested that the references to "vestiges of colonialism" be dropped from the draft letter because it had "certain psychological disadvantages."[6]

A day later, September 26, 1952, Davis informed Interior Secretary Chapman that the DTIP had agreed to discontinue notifying the United Nations, but that the details of how to do this had not yet been worked out. Apparently the trip by the two aides had not been entirely successful in clearing up differences in interpretation over what Puerto Rico's new status meant.[7] To iron out the disagreements, Muñoz Marín invited Davis and Silverman to come to Puerto Rico. Davis said he was unable to come, but agreed to send Silverman.[8] It is not known whether Silverman made the trip or not.

The disagreement over whether Puerto Rico was still a territory or not had not been resolved by October 9, 1952. In a six-page memorandum prepared by Acting Secretary of the Interior Vernon D. Northrop to Secretary of State Dean Acheson, there were frequent references to Puerto Rico as a "territory."[9] Muñoz Marín took strong exception to this. He said the Commonwealth could not be abolished by Congress alone because "the form, content, and continued existence of the Commonwealth, as well as its origin, depend not on the unilateral power of Congress, but upon the bilateral will of the people of Puerto Rico and the Government of the United States . . . ." Puerto Ricans would be, he continued, "profoundly disturbed if the terms 'territory,' 'dependency,' or 'possession' were applied to the Commonwealth because none of them appropriately connote[d] the spirit or the substance of our political situation."[10] Secretary Chapman complied with the governor's request, for he dispatched an amended memorandum to Secretary Acheson—it presumably superseded the October 9, 1952, version—in which all references to Puerto Rico as a "territory" were dropped. Chapman said that it would be preferable to emphasize the uniqueness of the Commonwealth.[11]

Muñoz Marín amended a draft letter intended for him to send to the president in accordance with the governor's interpretation of the Commonwealth status. The draft letter was prepared by Davis. Muñoz Marín objected to the phrase "our view" in the following sentence, "It is our view that laws cannot be repealed or modified by external authority." It detracted from the import of the point being made here because, he insisted, Congress could not repeal insular laws. Only the courts were in a position to say whether a Puerto Rican law was valid or invalid. The whole paragraph, as amended by Muñoz Marín, read as follows: "The legislative power of the Commonwealth under the compact and the Constitution essentially parallels that of the state governments. The laws enacted by the Government of Puerto Rico pursuant to the compact cannot be repealed or modified by external authority. Their effect and validity are subject to the adjudication of the courts. Our status and the terms of our association with the United States cannot be changed without our full consent."[12] The changes were incorporated by Muñoz Marín in a letter to the president on January 17, 1953.[13]

The governor's letter to the president (see Appendix B for the complete text) was intended for transmittal to the United Nations. Consequently, it dwelt at length on the progress that Puerto Rico had made toward autonomy since 1898. It stressed, first, the United States' willingness to grant the Puerto Ricans complete self-government. Muñoz Marín wished to convey the impression that United States rule was never harsh. Second, the letter emphasized that the two-year constitutional procedure, which culminated in the Commonwealth of Puerto Rico in July, 1952, had popular insular support. The following sums up the message the governor wanted to transmit to the United Nations: "The Commonwealth of Puerto Rico . . . represents the government that the people of Puerto Rico have freely adopted. It reflects our own decision as to the type of institutions and the kind of relationship to the United States which we desire. There can be no doubt that in the full sense of the term, in form as well as in fact, the people of Puerto Rico are now self-governing." Above all, he wanted the world body to know that the relationship between the island and the continent was in effect a "compact" and that Puerto Rico had become a Commonwealth in "free and voluntary association" with the United States.[14]

It soon became apparent that neither the Interior department nor the State department completely agreed with the idea of compact as understood by Muñoz Marín. A draft memorandum, dated January 27, 1953, was prepared by the Interior department. The memorandum was to be submitted to the United Nations concerning the cessation of information on Puerto Rico. The draft memorandum was reviewed a couple of days later by Resident Commissioner Fernós-Isern and Abe Fortas, who was serving as counsel to the Puerto Rican government. It is apparent from the revisions proposed by Fernós-Isern and Fortas that most of the difficulty centered around the difference in points of view over the concept of the Commonwealth and its relationship to Congress. Specifically, the divergence of opinion was over the term "compact." The insular representatives believed that Congress had endorsed the compact idea, since Public Law 600 had been adopted "in the nature of a compact." They therefore inserted the term "compact" in at least three paragraphs. Paragraph two as revised by Fernós-Isern and Fortas, for instance, read as follows: "In view of the attainment of full measure of self-government under the Constitution formulated and adopted by the people of

Puerto Rico within a compact with the United States . . . the Government of the United States has decided that it is no longer appropriate for it to submit information on Puerto Rico pursuant to Article 73 (e) of the Charter." They revised, to take another example, paragraph twelve, which in part read, "Four political parties participated in the campaign preceding the referendum; two advocated approval of the compact embodied in the Act of Congress . . . ."[15]

A Mrs. Fleming of the Department of State (?) analyzed the proposed revisions by Fernós-Isern and Fortas. She saw serious objection to the inclusion of "compact," because it was "an unsettled, fundamental question of American constitutional law." Congress had differentiated between "compact" and "in the nature of a compact" because it had established various conditions of approval of the constitution. She continued, "Neither the federal legislation nor the legislative history of these laws support [the claim] that there is a 'compact' between the United States and Puerto Rico . . . ."[16] Fernós-Isern disagreed with this position in a memorandum he dispatched to the legal counsel for the state department. He cited at length from the Senate and House hearings on H.J.Res.430, and from the Congressional debates on it that followed during the second session of the Eighty-second Congress to prove that Congress had intended to recognize the existence of a compact. Indeed, he argued, Congress was so careful about it that it did not lay down stipulations when Congress finally approved the constitution. Fernós-Isern said he did not understand why the State department raised such questions when neither the Interior department nor Congress had raised any.[17]

Mrs. Fleming's advice prevailed, however, for in the memorandum that was officially transmitted to the secretary general of the United Nations on March 23, 1953, all references to "compact" as interpreted by the insular government were omitted. Governor Muñoz Marín's previously cited letter to the president on January 17, 1953, and a copy of the text of the Puerto Rican constitution accompanied the memorandum.[18]

The memorandum reporting the cessation of United States reports on Puerto Rico was divided into four parts, each aiming to show that Puerto Rico had attained a "full measure of self-government" and that it was therefore no longer necessary to continue submitting reports on the island. The first part described in brief the "steady progression of self-government" in

Puerto Rico since the island became United States territory in 1898, and pointed out that the Commonwealth status was a culmination of fifty-four years of that progression. The second part concerned itself with the origin and development of the Commonwealth status between 1948 and 1952. This section emphasized the principle of government by consent. Public Law 600 had declared that it was " 'adopted in the nature of a compact,' " but had also stated that the constitution would become effective only "if approved by Congress."[19]

The memorandum's third section dwelt on the features of the Commonwealth status. The most important features discussed were the separation of the three branches of the government, a bill of rights assuring essential freedoms, the guaranteeing of representation of minority parties, and so on. The last section spoke about the present status of the Commonwealth. It pointed out that the island had entered into "voluntary association" with the United States and that its status was different from the territories of Hawaii, Alaska, Guam, and the Virgin Islands, where the chief executives and the judges of the highest courts were still appointed by the president. Puerto Rico's relationship with the United States was a matter of "mutual consent." The following sentence sought, however, to highlight the island's relative independence in its affairs: "By the various actions taken by the Congress and the people of Puerto Rico, Congress has agreed that Puerto Rico shall have, under that Constitution freedom from control or interference by the Congress in respect of internal government and administration, subject only to compliance with applicable provisions of the Federal Constitution, the Puerto Rican Federal Relations Act and the acts of Congress authorizing and approving the Constitution as may be interpreted by judicial decision."[20]

Presumably to iron out some of the differences and to coordinate the presentation of the Puerto Rican matter before the United Nations, Muñoz Marín invited Benjamin Gerig of the Department of the Interior (?) to San Juan. Gerig was in Puerto Rico from June 19 to 23, 1953, during which time he had two meetings with the governor, Fernós-Isern, and legal advisor José Trias Monge. They discussed at great length the way in which the case should be presented and the kind of responses to make to anticipated questions. Agreements were reached in the following matters: one, the United States delegation should include a high-ranking Puerto Rican; two, the aim of the delegation was to explain Puerto Rico's status in a manner so as to achieve "the fullest possible understanding"; three, the delegation was to make clear that the decision to cease reporting was not obligatory; four, the matter should be disposed of in the forthcoming General Assembly and not be allowed to drag out into the next session; five, the delegation was to oppose any effort to grant oral hearings to any of the minority groups in Puerto Rico.[21]

But they could not agree on a question of fundamental importance: could Puerto Rico unilaterally alter the new status? No clear agreement was reached on this point. Gerig realized, however, that the position of the United States delegation on the matter should be "very clear." He pointed out a decision given by the Federal District Court in Puerto Rico that might possibly be utilized by the United States delegation. The Court ruled on a case that in effect said that the agreement could not be changed unilaterally.[22]

The United States delegation decided to use the Federal District Court's opinion in its presentation. The delegation freely referred to the idea of compact, even though the March 23, 1953, memorandum had avoided all reference to it. On August 27, 1953, Mason Sears, United States delegate to the United Nations, told the General Assembly's Committee on Information from Non–Self-Governing Territories that the Commonwealth was conceived "in the nature of a compact." He continued, "A compact, as you know, is far stronger than a treaty. A treaty usually can be denounced by either side, whereas, a compact cannot be denounced by either party unless it has the permission of the other." Sears referred to the Federal District Court ruling. The resident commissioner, a member of the United States delegation, echoed Sear's argument: "As of July 25, 1952, the jurisdiction of the Federal Government in Puerto Rico is based on a bilateral compact to which it is a party and into which the people of Puerto Rico have entered of their own volition." Frances P. Bolton, another member of the United States team, told the Fourth Committee of the Trusteeship that since a bilateral compact existed between the island and the continent mutual consent was necessary to make any changes.[23]

The United States delegation succeeded in doing what it had set out to do. It blocked attempts by *independentistas*, who sought to present their cases in oral hearings. (The PIP, however, sub-

mitted lengthy memoranda.)[24] The delegation was able to respond satisfactorily to the questions raised by delegates from
other countries skeptical about the claim that Puerto Rico had
ceased being a dependency. The delegates from the Soviet Union,
India, Mexico, and Guatemala were especially critical. The
United Nations committee approved on November 5, 1953, however, a draft resolution to accept the request by the United
States.[25] By the time the draft resolution was debated by a plenary
session of the General Assembly on November 27, 1953, sufficient
groundwork had been laid by the United States delegation to ensure success. United States Ambassador to the United Nations,
Henry Cabot Lodge, Jr., assured the assembly that he had been
authorized by his government to say that if at any time the insular
legislature requested "more complete and even absolute independence," the president would recommend that Congress grant
it.[26] The resolution was adopted by the assembly by a vote of
26 to 16, with 18 member nations abstaining. Among those countries voting affirmatively, incidentally, were fifteen Latin American states. Only Guatemala and Mexico from among the American nations voted against the resolution, while Venezuela and
Argentina abstained.[27]

The language of the resolution as adopted appears to be
more than was anticipated in the March 23, 1953, memorandum.
The idea of a compact was explicitly recognized in the resolution.
The resolution read, "Recognized that, in the framework of their
Constitution and of the compact agreed upon with the United
States of America, the people of the Commonwealth of Puerto
Rico have been invested with the attributes of political sov-
ereignty which clearly identify the status of self-government at-
tained by the Puerto Rican people as that of an autonomous
political entity."[28]

The endorsement by the United Nations, as significant as it
was within an international context, did not contribute directly
to clarifying the nature of the relationship between the island and
the mainland. The Puerto Rican government was to argue later,
however, that the United States action had confirmed the general
principle that the relationship could not be unilaterally changed.
The difficulty arose when attempts were made to translate the
principle into reality in specific areas of relationship between
Puerto Rico and the United States. Two major attempts were

made in the next fifteen years, and on neither occasion was the matter resolved.

Although Muñoz Marín had earlier expressed a desire to improve and clarify the relationship between Puerto Rico and the United States, it was only in 1959 that he made the first real effort towards this end.[29] On March 19, 1959, the Puerto Rican legislature adopted a joint resolution requesting Congress to implement several proposals in order to clarify insular-continental relations.[30] The proposals were incorporated in a bill (H.R.5926) introduced on March 23, 1959, by Fernós-Isern. A companion measure (S.2023) was sponsored by Senator James E. Murray of Montana a couple of months later. The legislation is generally referred to as the Fernós-Murray bill.[31]

The Fernós-Murray bill sought to replace the Federal Relations Act, whose language was described as "anachronistic," with the "Articles of Permanent Association of the People of Puerto Rico with the United States." The "Articles of Permanent Association" contained fifteen articles, which were divided into three groups in Muñoz Marín's summary of them. The first group was described as "self-executing modifications." There were several important provisions in this section. One was for the transfer of debt-incurring limit of the Commonwealth and municipal governments from the Federal Relations Act to the Puerto Rican constitution. Another sought to have appeals to go direct from the insular Supreme Court to the United States Supreme Court of Appeals. A third provision concerned the resumption of sharing in the common burdens of the Union. It provided that the difference between the United States Internal Revenue tax on liquors and the Puerto Rican Internal Revenue tax on rum shipped to the United States would go to the federal treasury as an insular tax.[32]

The second group of articles consisted of "non–self-executing modifications." The first of the two most important provisions in this group concerned Puerto Rico's paying the costs of federal functions on the island and in some cases taking over the responsibility for these functions. The second provision sought to establish machinery to work out a special rate of tariff on articles imported into Puerto Rico from other countries. The example cited by Muñoz Marín was the importation of codfish, a staple food in Puerto Rico, from Canada. A third group of articles was listed as "miscellaneous modifications." This category included a provision for mutually exempting insular and mainland bonds from taxation, another for guaranteeing the resident commissioner's seat in Congress in the "compact" itself, a third for establishing procedures in turning over federal property in Puerto Rico to the Commonwealth government, and a fourth for allowing the Federal District Court of Puerto Rico to conduct trials in Spanish whenever necessary.[33]

In effect the bill sought to attain explicitly moral and legal recognition to the Puerto Rican concept of a "compact," one which could not be altered without Puerto Rican concurrence. This is the way the Washington administration interpreted it, as reflected in the memorandum by assistant director of DTIP Sylvester I. Olson. The bill was intended to give, the memorandum continued, a few more "perquisites" of a state that Puerto Rico did not have, while at the same time liberalizing the fiscal arrangement between the island and the mainland. Indeed, the measure sought to transfer to the Commonwealth government substantial powers then exercised by the federal government.[34]

A hearing scheduled on June 9, 1959, revealed considerable opposition to aspects of the measure from members of Congress, and the various executive departments of the federal government. Senator Henry Jackson of Washington questioned Governor Muñoz Marín on a substantive issue, one on which the entire Puerto Rican attempt rested. The senator was concerned that the Commonwealth concept of compact meant Congressional compliance with the thesis of bilateral action. If this was so, it would mean that Congress could not legislate for the island without the express consent of the insular government. In such an arrangement, Congress would be restricted in its powers to a point where Puerto Rico could resist federal authority. Approval of the measure, Senator Jackson concluded, would compromise Congressional power indefinitely. The various executive departments, too, raised questions in matters concerning their respective jurisdictions in their written observations. These questions generally dealt with specific aspects of the Fernós-Murray bill. The consensus was that serious practical difficulties would arise if the constitutional aspects of the insular-continental relationship remained unresolved.[35]

Since many changes were necessary to meet the criticism of Congress and the administration, Fernós-Isern decided to introduce a "clean bill" instead of making amendments. Meanwhile,

Muñoz Marín made a major policy statement in September, 1959, known as the Cidra Declaration. The governor declared that Puerto Ricans would be permitted to vote on a political status of their choice sometime in the future when their per capita income reached a certain level. He limited the status alternatives to only Commonwealth and statehood. The Cidra Declaration was officially approved by the central committee of the PPD.[36] Whatever reasons impelled Muñoz Marín to make such a declaration in the midst of the Puerto Rican effort to improve the Commonwealth status in Congress,[37] it was significant from at least three points of reference. First, it was a tacit admission on the part of Muñoz Marín that the Commonwealth in its present form was not intended to be a permanent solution. Two, the PPD was no longer considering electoral victories every four years as continued endorsement of the status. Three, the party of Muñoz Marín appeared to have moved away more than ever from independence.

A new version of the Fernós-Murray bill was introduced in September, 1959. The latest version softened the idea of "irrevocable concept." Article IV (a) was changed so as to eliminate any possible interference with the quota system as established by the Sugar Act. Section (f) of the same article deleted language that had placed the burden of proof upon the president in claiming that the "general interest of the United States" required him to reject an insular request to exclude Puerto Rico from a trade agreement. Article VIII was rewritten in order to preserve the supreme authority of the United States over navigation on island waters, harbors, and inlets. A new article, article XVI, was added in response to the Interior department's criticism that the old version of the bill seemed designed to freeze the status question. The article provided that at some future date, when the per capita income of the people of Puerto Rico reached the level equal to the lowest state in the Union, the entire terms of association would be reviewed.[38]

A special subcommittee of the Committee on Interior and Insular Affairs decided to hold hearings in Puerto Rico. Apparently the committee desired to hear a wider variety of Puerto Rican sentiments before deciding on the bill. The hearings were conducted in the first ten days of December, 1959. *Estadistas* and *independentistas* were given the opportunity to testify at the hearings. The *estadistas,* encouraged by the admission of Alaska and Hawaii as states in the Union and by their growing electoral strength, insisted that the PPD plan would foreclose statehood, and was in fact a clever and devious scheme to make the island independent eventually. The *independentistas,* on the other hand, accused the governor of having abandoned independence and of moving towards statehood. They insisted that independence was the only logical solution to the status issue.[39]

At least three points of view emerged in the hearings on the nature of the relationship between the United States and Puerto Rico. In the end these will probably help to clarify the association, and presumably form the basis of the eventual settlement of a vexing question.

The first view was that of the Commonwealth government as reflected in a lengthy memorandum submitted jointly by Puerto Rico's Attorney General, Hiram Cancio; the governor's legal advisor, Trias Monge; and the Washington law firm of Arnold, Fortas, and Porter, which was retained by the insular government. The memorandum reviewed the constitutional procedure up to 1952 and concluded that a compact had been created. Beyond 1952 two specific instances confirmed its existence: first, the argument used by the United States government when it presented in 1953 Puerto Rico's case before the United Nations; second, the decision by the Court of Appeals for the First Circuit in *Figueroa* v. *People of Puerto Rico* (232 F. 2d 615, 620, 1st Cir. 1956), which stated that Public Law 600 had indeed offered a compact. The court had concluded, "We find no reason to impute to the Congress the perpetration of such a monumental hoax." The Fernós-Murray bill, the memorandum continued, did not challenge Congressional powers and federal sovereignty over Puerto Rico in areas closely analogous to those of the states within the Union. But this point did not alter the fact that a compact existed.[40]

A second position was referred to in a memorandum prepared by Robert Kramer, assistant attorney general of the United States. The memorandum was submitted at the request of the Senate Committee on Interior and Insular Affairs. Kramer discussed the second position as one of the two theories (the other being Puerto Rico's, just reviewed above) being espoused by some people, but was careful not to impute it to either the administration or Congress. According to this theory, the compact involved no more than an agreement on the part of Congress to repeal most of those portions of the Organic Act dealing with internal matters. Congress, however, continued to exercise plenary authority under the territorial clause of the United States Constitution. Hence, the compact was not intended to effectuate a total or even partial divestiture of that authority. Congress still retained the power to nullify insular acts. The memorandum concluded, ". . . if the compact were construed to prevent Congress from amending it unilaterally, Congress would be limited in its legislative authority over some matters about which it may legislate with respect to the States."[41]

A position that might be termed intermediate was advanced by David M. Helfeld, a professor of law at the University of Puerto Rico. He was concerned less with legality and constitutionality and more with morality and political reality. Or as he himself explained it in his testimony, his approach was an attempt to harmonize legal theory with political reality. Public Law 600, the professor argued, had to be viewed as embodying a political understanding that rested "on morality, on the good faith and the good will of the participants." In view of this, and in view of the realities under which insular-continental relationship operated between 1952 and 1959, it was not likely that Congress would take a regressive step concerning the association. To support his argument, Helfeld pointed out that Congressional action since 1947 had been to advance progressively Puerto Rico's political freedom. His argument implied that even though in theory one Congress could not bind future Congresses, in practice it was not likely that future Congresses would renege on decisions made by earlier Congresses.[42]

Fernós-Isern relates that the Senate committee was not expected to report out the bill. The House committee, however, continued to consider the bill. It hired a special counsel, Judge Shriver, to make recommendations. The special counsel consulted with Fernós-Isern in several conferences to agree upon a bill and reported favorably to the committee in May, 1960. However, further consideration of the bill was postponed until the following year because it was thought to be too late in the session for the bill to pass both chambers. The bill was to be reintroduced in 1961 but was abandoned by Muñoz Marín in early January of 1961 "in a surprise move."[43]

The difficulty that the 1959 attempt ran into in Congress persuaded Muñoz Marín to try out what Fernós-Isern calls the "Presidential approach."[44] In July, 1962, he wrote a letter to

President John F. Kennedy in which he called for clarification of the Commonwealth in its "moral and juridical basis" to prove false the charge that the status was not a "free choice of the people of Puerto Rico in their sovereign capacity." The relationship could be strengthened on the basis of "permanent association," provided that aspects that were not "indispensable" were eliminated. He ended by suggesting that the Puerto Ricans register their preference in a referendum from among three alternatives: Commonwealth, statehood, and independence. President Kennedy endorsed the governor's sentiments and indicated the propriety of consulting the people of Puerto Rico concerning their status preference.[45]

Following this exchange, the Muñoz Marín administration sponsored a bill in the insular legislature calling for a plebiscite. Hearings were conducted in which some eighty witnesses testified. The opposition to the bill centered around the need to define "Commonwealth" before submitting the status to referendum, and the absence of any guarantee that Congress would be willing to act upon the results of the referendum.[46]

On December 31, 1962, the Puerto Rican legislature incorporated the provisions of the bill into a joint resolution and passed it. The joint resolution proposed the "prompt settlement" of the island's status in a "democratic manner." The preamble of the resolution defined statehood as "the way enjoyed by the 50 states of the Union," and independence as "the form already known in other countries of America." Commonwealth was defined as a "permanent union with the United States," according to the following principles: first, the affirmation of the sovereignty of the people of Puerto Rico and their right to enter a compact with the United States as a "juridical equal"; second, the establishment of a permanent and irrevocable union based on "common citizenship, common defense, common currency, [and] free market"; third, a clear delineation of United States powers with respect to Puerto Rico, and the reservation of all other powers to the island; fourth, participation by the people of Puerto Rico in certain federal processes, e.g., Puerto Ricans taking part in the election of the president and vice president; fifth, adoption of a formula to provide for insular contribution to the United States treasury. Section 2 of the resolution requested Congress to indicate the form of Commonwealth it was willing to accept before a referendum was conducted.[47]

In accordance with section 2 of the joint resolution, H.R.5945 and other similar bills were introduced in Congress providing for the creation of a United States–Puerto Rico Compact Commission. The commission was to consist of twelve members, four appointed by the president of the United States, four by the governor of Puerto Rico, and two each by the Senate president and the House speaker of the United States. Its task was to draft a compact along the lines of the definition of the Commonwealth in the joint resolution. The president was specifically authorized to enter into a compact with Puerto Rico, after which the islanders would choose from among an adequately defined Commonwealth and the other two alternatives.[48]

Independentista and *estadista* opponents of the bill criticized it sharply at the hearings that followed. They contended that the plan proposed in the bill was not in accordance with the insular joint resolution and was intended to endorse the Commonwealth status. They pointed out that the commission's task would be limited to defining only the Commonwealth status, and not the other two, and that the president would be authorized to enter into a compact only with respect to the status favored by Muñoz Marín. Furthermore, they objected to including on the referendum ballot the Commonwealth status, which they regarded as temporary, side by side with two permanent alternatives. Some Congressional critics, too, were unhappy with aspects of the bill, and insisted that the commission's recommendations not be made obligatory for Congress to act upon.[49]

When it became apparent that the measure would not pass Congress, it was abandoned. In its place a new bill was introduced that was acceptable to *independentistas* and *estadistas*.[50] It finally became law in February, 1964. This act created a United States–Puerto Rico Commission on the Status of Puerto Rico, whose function was limited to examining all facets of insular-mainland relationship and submitting its findings to the president, Congress, and the Puerto Rican legislature. The original bill contained a provision that stated that Congress had to act upon the commission's recommendations concerning a plebiscite. This act had no such provision. The commission's membership, too, was changed. Its thirteen members as finally apportioned were as follows: a chairman, and two persons appointed by the president, four members of Congress, six Puerto Ricans of whom three were *Populares*, two *Estadistas*, and one *Independentista*.[51]

The commission worked from June, 1964, to August, 1966, under the chairmanship of James H. Rowe, Jr., a Washington attorney who had also headed the 1949 Commission on the Reorganization of the Puerto Rican government. Using the services of advisors and experts in all fields, the commission conducted the most thorough and balanced study of Puerto Rican views on the question of status. Exhaustive hearings were held in San Juan in both Spanish and English. Between May 14 and 18, 1965, the commission heard witnesses on legal-constitutional aspects, while for four days during July and August, 1965, its attention was focused on socio-cultural factors. Finally, between November 27 and December 1, 1965, testimonies concerning economic aspects of insular-continental relationship were heard. Impressed by the scope and breadth of the study, the legislative bodies of the United States and Puerto Rico ordered the printing of an additional 4500 copies of the three separate volumes and the commission report so that its findings might reach a wider reading public.[52]

The report of the commission arrived at conclusions that in themselves were not new. But the commission's thoroughness and relative impartiality gave them a ring of authority. The report stated that all three alternatives were equally valid morally and that any one would confer upon the islanders "equal dignity." Moreover, no legal or constitutional reasons would bar the people of Puerto Rico from choosing any status position. The commission insisted that Puerto Rico had to maintain absolutely the economic growth rate established since 1940, whatever its status. Here, the commission grappled with the problem of extrapolating existing Commonwealth growth patterns upon those advocated by statehood and independence supporters to arrive at some conclusions. It warned that any abrupt change in the direction of either statehood or independence would cause serious economic dislocation. In the commission's judgment, a transition period of at least fifteen years would be necessary in the case of statehood, and a longer unspecified period in that of independence. Whatever status alternative the Puerto Ricans chose, the commission pointed out, it would require "mutual agreement and full cooperation" of the two governments to implement it. The commission's position implied that the Commonwealth status could operate on a permanent basis.[53]

However, the commission's conclusions on the specific questions of compact and the dual operation of insular and continental powers in Puerto Rico were somewhat circumlocutory. And it was precisely in these areas that the Commonwealth status had showed weaknesses. The report stated, ". . . the precise allocation of powers between the Puerto Rican Government and the Federal Government is a matter subject to determination only on the basis of the individual analysis of each area of governmental activity." The commission apparently did not wish to decide upon a matter that could be resolved only by the two respective governments. But it did emphasize the bilateral character of the Commonwealth status insofar as "the basic governmental structure" was concerned. Neither government was free to act unilaterally with respect to certain specific areas. Or as the report stated the matter, ". . . there are in effect two spheres of power: the congressional power and the power of the Government of Puerto Rico. Within each sphere there are areas in which each government is free to act without consultation of the other government and without impinging on the principle against unilateral amendment where the fundamental government character of commonwealth is concerned."[54]

The commission believed that a referendum would be helpful in establishing the "will of the citizens of Puerto Rico." Consequently, it recommended that a plebiscite be held in which all three alternatives would be presented. Following the plebiscite, the commission continued, *ad hoc* advisory groups should be established to recommend to the president, Congress, and the governor of Puerto Rico the "appropriate transition measures" to be taken.[55]

Muñoz Marín, no longer a governor but still wielding enormous influence on the PPD as a senator, was delighted at the commission's conclusion that the Commonwealth status was equally valid. The *Populares* sponsored a bill calling for a plebiscite on July 23, 1967. Despite the opposition of the PER and PIP members, who argued that a transitory status should not be placed on the ballot next to two permanent alternatives, the measure became law on December 23, 1966. The act called for a referendum on July 23, 1967, for the Puerto Rican people to choose from among the three alternatives. A majority of over 50 percent for any one position was to be construed as representing the will of the people. If either independence or statehood was chosen, Congress would be asked to extend to the island the desired status. A majority vote for the Commonwealth status was to mean the following: first, reaffirmation of Puerto Rico's existing status of permanent association with the United States; second, common citizenship was to be the absolute basis for the continued association; third, the government of Puerto Rico would undertake to improve the Commonwealth relationship; fourth, no change was to take place in United States–Puerto Rico relationship without prior approval of the Puerto Rican people.[56]

The proposed plebiscite caused division in the ranks of the PER and the PIP. The PER decision to boycott the referendum led the party's vice president, Luis A. Ferré, to organize an opposition of United Statehooders advocating participation in the plebiscite for statehood. Similarly, the PIP's decision to boycott the polls caused a rift within its ranks. Dissident *Populares,* too, registered their opposition to their party's official endorsement of the Commonwealth status and decided to join the Anti-Plebiscite Sovereignty Fund. Muñoz Marín was reasonably certain, however, that the electorate would endorse the Commonwealth status. Indeed, this was probably why he decided on a referendum. He was fully aware of his popularity and of the fact that the Commonwealth had become identified with his leadership. The 69-year-old founder of the PPD, therefore, campaigned hard, traveling to each one of the 76 districts in the island.[57]

On July 23, 1967, 703,000 (65.8 percent) of the 1,067,000 registered voters went to the polls. The abstention was 30 percent higher than in general elections. The Commonwealth status was endorsed by 60.5 percent of those voting. Statehood registered 38.9 percent of the votes, while independence was supported by a mere 0.6 percent of the voters. Muñoz Marín claimed two days later that the referendum had ended "the century-long debate about political status." That exaggerated claim was pardonable, given the fact that the Commonwealth status, the creation of Muñoz Marín, Fernós-Isern, and other *Populares,* had been directly and specifically endorsed for the first time by the Puerto Rican people. The victory also meant that Muñoz Marín could leave politics on a triumphant note.[58]

It is highly probable that the debate on political status will continue for as long as the question of Commonwealth status does not culminate in a final and permanent solution. Had the 1959 attempt succeeded in improving its terms[59] before it was postponed "by agreement,"[60] it might have transcended the essentially economic rationale upon which it had been conceived. To be sure, Congress did not deny that the status was a new and unique experiment in federalism in which Puerto Rico was somewhere between a sovereign country and a state within the Union. The 1959 attempt, however, did not help to define more clearly in practical terms what the experiment was. Consequently it revived a debate that Muñoz Marín had hoped had disappeared. There is no telling whether the debate would end if the island became a state in the Union or an independent country. But politicians in the future might profit from Muñoz Marín's lesson: it is not enough to have a status that accommodates economic realities—it is imperative that a sensitive part of the Puerto Rican personality make-up, known, for want of a better term, as "dignidad," be accommodated too. It will probably take another politician with a bit of poetry in his make-up to harmonize the two. Yet, it is clear that the Commonwealth status has been an acceptable and successful vehicle for the majority of the Puerto Rican people. Whether it would stay as transitional or be declared permanent lies with the future.

CHAPTER TEN

"Operation Bootstrap": The Economic Dimensions of the Commonwealth Status

Although references to Puerto Rico's economic realities have been made earlier in the study, a full discussion of the systematic insular response to them has been reserved for this chapter.* Economic aspects of Puerto Rico's relationship with the United States also shaped the island's political and constitutional ties with the mainland. Indeed, they figure very prominently in giving rise to the Commonwealth concept.

Puerto Rico's economic dependence upon the United States was a fact well recognized by *Popular* leader Muñoz Marín and others. Muñoz Marín had at one time believed that political independence for the island could be arranged within the framework of this dependence. He gradually abandoned the hope that Puerto Rico could achieve political sovereignty and still retain the economic benefits of its continued relationship with the United States. His expulsion of *independentistas* from the *Popu-*

---

* The economic program began in the second half of the 1940s. Its discussion might have preceded the chapters dealing with the formulation and implementation of the Commonwealth status, but at the expense of narrative continuity. Hence, its placement here.

lar party in 1946 was symptomatic of this realization.[1] A year later, the *Popular* leader embarked upon a policy evocatively known as "Operation Bootstrap" in an effort to industrialize Puerto Rico. The new economic program in effect acknowledged the island's dependence on the United States and energetically sought to use continental resources in a way that increased Puerto Rico's ties with the mainland. In Muñoz Marín's pragmatic way of thinking, political formulas had to accommodate economic realities.[2]

The beginnings of the new economically realistic policy can be traced at least two years before its official commencement of 1947. The man at the center of this approach was Moscoso, who had been general manager of PRIDCO since its inception in 1942. Moscoso explored the possibilities of offering inducements to private capital in 1945, but he was prevented from openly advocating such a program because the then governor, Tugwell, was opposed to enlisting the facilities of private capital in what was a public corporation venture. It was only after Governor Tugwell's departure that Moscoso could more fully and openly reorient Puerto Rico's industrialization drive.[3]

There were a number of reasons for the shift in policy. Perhaps the most important was that the early ventures of PRIDCO failed to live up to their expectations. Four of the five subsidiaries established by the Development company were far from being successful operations. The Puerto Rico Glass Corporation was contracted to be built in February, 1943, but began its operation in June, 1945, months behind schedule. Financially it faced a dim future in 1947, although it later proved to be a success under private supervision. PRIDCO's second project, the Puerto Rico Pulp and Paper Corporation, encountered similar problems, along with difficulties with respect to personnel, management, litigation, and substandard machinery, to name a few.[4]

The Puerto Rico Shoe and Leather Corporation was formed in January, 1946, but it took over a year to begin operations. The corporation spent another year training its personnel, so that it really only began functioning in January, 1948. Although the plant was said to have good prospects at that time, it ran into difficulties later on. The fourth of the Development company's project, the Puerto Rico Clay Products Corporation, was afflicted with problems of one sort or another from its inception. It was organized in November, 1944, but did not begin operations until

August, 1947, because of the difficulty resulting from wartime and postwar conditions of obtaining the necessary equipment. Soon after starting operations, its sanitary ware section experienced serious marketing and other difficulties and had to be discontinued.[5]

By May, 1948, PRIDCO had invested over $22 million in its industrial program, of which $10,700,000 was invested in its subsidiaries.[6] Only one of its ventures, the Puerto Rico Cement Company, organized in 1939 by PRRA, was an unqualified success, and its heavy profits substantially made up for the losses on the remaining four subsidiaries.[7] But the overall performance of the subsidiaries was dismal, especially when measured against their own objectives. Their difficulties were widely covered in the insular press, so that the economic program failed to attract local private capital as it was originally intended. The program fell far short of its goal of self-sufficiency by 1947.[8] Moreover, Moscoso and his staff became involved in labor contracts and problems of material allocations and industrial bottlenecks instead of concentrating on planning and administering the economic development program.[9]

The employment openings offered by the Development company's activities fell far short of its anticipated goal of 10,000. By 1947 the number of employees in PRIDCO's operations reached a mere 1500.[10] According to Moscoso's calculations, employment in the government plants cost approximately $10,000 per job in capital expenditure. Even if this were halved, the cost of providing full employment would exceed $300 million.[11] At this pace, Puerto Rico could not achieve a level of employment commensurate with an acceptable rate of unemployment, nor could it balance employment between agricultural and industrial sectors. And one of the program's goals was to make employment less dependent upon seasonal labor.[12]

Moscoso realized, too, that growing mainland competition and changing marketing trends in the postwar period would put further strain on the island's economic program. The sanitary ware section of the Puerto Rico Clay Corporation had to be closed mainly because of this reason. In the case of the glass plant, the drop in the sale of rum in the United States made it necessary to reduce the production of bottles. The island's shoe plant could not meet local demands for greater variety in the styles of footware manufactured.[13] Besides, most manufacturing units experienced difficulties of production establishment and marketing because they were small undertakings organized under individual ownership rather than corporations and relied heavily upon the United States for raw material and machinery. Over 72 percent of the total of 2077 plants in 1946 depended wholly or partly upon the United States for raw material and markets. And such manufacturing industries that were developed—sugar, tobacco, needlework, and canned fruit—were largely aided by United States capital.[14]

By 1947, then, the problems that beset the insular industrialization program suggested a need for reorientation. The program's early emphasis upon local capital and self-sufficiency had failed because of the scarcity of adequately trained labor and managerial personnel, market restrictions, shipping costs, competition of highly developed, low-cost, continental industries, the absence of risk-taking funds on the island, and so on.[15]

The policy shift that occurred officially in 1947 was in evidence as early as 1945. Moscoso, who was going to become a central figure in the new approach to industrialize Puerto Rico, conceived some of his new ideas after reading ads that were being run by some southern states in leading magazines and newspapers in 1945. One such ad that caught the general manager's special attention was the promotional campaign sponsored by the state of Mississippi to attract investment. The program was known as the "Balance Agriculture with Industry" Plan. In September, 1945, Moscoso persuaded the board of directors of PRDCO (known as Puerto Rico Industrial Development Company, PRIDCO, after 1946) to undertake in its newly established "Aid to Industrial Development" (AID) program an advertising campaign in the United States to promote Puerto Rico as a good place for investors. In addition, he prevailed upon the directors to open an office in New York City, ostensibly to help the Development company's subsidiaries in marketing and procuring their products. But Moscoso intended the office to be used also as an industrial promoter, and gradually it shifted its energies more and more towards this end.[16]

Upon Moscoso's recommendation, the board of directors appropriated a total of $53,000 to be used in the preparation of a booklet describing the locational and other advantages of opening industries in Puerto Rico. A leading New York advertising agency owned by McCann-Erickson was hired to help in preparing and placing an ad about Puerto Rico in the February, 1946, issue of *Fortune* magazine. A booklet along similar lines was published in 1946, and numerous ads were run in well-established magazines such as *Business Week* and *Nation's Business*. Direct contacts by mail, too, were made.[17]

A total of 726 enquiries were received from firms that were interested in investing in Puerto Rico, but none appeared to the Development company as really worthwhile. Moscoso apparently wanted to attract prestigious firms that would lend a great boost in the promotional effort. At least one reason why the early advertising campaign was not successful was because it was wanting in modesty in the claims it made for Puerto Rico as a good location for industries.[18] But it failed mainly because the incentives the Development company offered were not sufficient in themselves to attract mainland industries to open branches in Puerto Rico. The AID program had an allotment of $0.5 million to construct factory buildings to be sold or leased to prospective private firms. About ten small concerns were established before 1947 under this incentive. Obviously the Development company would have to offer larger incentives to attract capital from the continental United States.[19]

The new program that was developed by the insular government between 1946 and 1948 attempted to do just that. It sought to take advantage of the special tariff and tax relationship between the United States and Puerto Rico, and the provisions of the Internal Revenue Code of the United States. If, for instance, a mainland industrial firm opened a branch in Puerto Rico, these exemptions could permit its goods to enter the mainland markets free from tariffs. The problem was to offer an additional incentive large enough for a mainland industrial establishment to take the risks involved in transferring in whole or in part its operation to a new location. The Puerto Rican government offered this incentive in the form of industrial tax-exemption, together with other incentives, already existing, such as provision of factory buildings and low-cost labor.

Attempts had been made earlier in Puerto Rico to pass a tax-exemption law. Efforts in 1919, 1925, 1930, 1936, and 1944 did not prove successful. In the 1944 attempt Moscoso personally lobbied for a tax-exemption measure, but the bill was vetoed by Governor Tugwell. Moscoso was successful in 1947 and 1948 when the Puerto Rican legislature, with Piñero as the governor, passed two laws, Act No. 346, May, 1947, and Act No. 184, May, 1948, known as the Industrial Tax-Exemption Acts. The tax-exemption legislation provided for a twelve-year period (July 1, 1947, to June 30, 1959) during which the existing and newly established firms from the United States were to operate free from most of the taxes that they were held liable to pay on the continent, and an extra three years during which they were partially exempted. The acts exempted industries from three major tax levies: first, taxes on individual, corporate, and partnership incomes; second, municipal and central government taxes levied on the property used by an exempted firm and on property leased to such a firm; third, local levies such as license fees and excises.[20]

In addition, the Puerto Rican government provided by separate legislation several relief measures that exempted firms participating in the program from insular excise taxes on machinery, apparatus, raw material used by them, and on goods transferred from one manufacturer to another or to an agent for shipment outside of the island. There were, however, limited categories of incomes and taxes from which the industrial establishments were not exempt. They were: investment income, interest payment accrued on loans made to an exempted firm, and such minor taxes as federal social security, workmen's compensation premiums, fees on motor vehicles, and *ad valorem* excise taxes on "luxury" products such as radios and cigarettes, and so on.[21]

The economic program was revamped in three related areas in accordance with the new policy: a drive to build up the tourist industry, the disposal of PRIDCO's five subsidiaries to private interests, and a systematic campaign to promote continental private investments. In its drive to develop tourism, PRIDCO pursued its original intention to contract with a private hotel company to operate facilities built by the Development company. The hotel to be built was to serve the needs of potential businessmen visiting the island as well as tourists willing to exchange dollars for Caribbean sunshine and hospitality. PRIDCO negotiated with the Hilton company in 1947 a settlement that in part stipulated that two-thirds of the profits were to go to the Development company. The Caribe Hilton Hotel was completed at a cost of $7 million to PRIDCO and opened its doors to visitors in December, 1949.[22]

The Puerto Rican government believed that the moment was

opportune to sell PRIDCO's five subsidiaries to private interests. The failure of the subsidiaries had caused Muñoz Marín's *Popular* party considerable embarrassment, as its opponents leveled unsparing criticism at government policy. Muñoz Marín did not have to admit complete failure—and indeed, he did not—and he salvaged as much political credibility out of the situation as he could by claiming that the transfer was an anticipated phase of the economic program. Despite Muñoz Marín's and Moscoso's desire to dispose of the subsidiaries, neither was willing to sell them in haste or at less than the best possible price. PRIDCO made known its desire to sell the government plants as a package deal and waited for the offers. It was subsequently decided, however, to separate the Puerto Rico Shoe and Leather Corporation for sale to a reputable continental firm. Such a firm, it was PRIDCO's feeling, would have the skill and the facility to broaden the variety of the plant's products and would lend the former government corporation's products the prestige and popularity that the United States firm enjoyed on the continent. In December, 1949, the shoe plant was transferred to Joyce Inc.[23]

PRIDCO had to wait considerably longer to sell its remaining four subsidiaries (cement, glass, paperboard, and clay products). It was about to sell them to a New York businessman, Karl F. Landegger, when it received a considerably better offer of $10.5 million from the island's Ferré Enterprises. Besides, Muñoz Marín saw political advantage in selling the plants to the Ferré family because it represented influential leadership in the island's Republican party, which was in political opposition to the *Popular* party. The transfer to the Ferré family would partly still criticism of government failure in its industrialization program, and would demonstrate by a sale to private investors that they had nothing to fear from a government that accepted opposition within the limits of democratic processes. The sale to the Ferré Enterprises was contracted in September, 1950, although the actual transfer of the four plants took place in April, 1951.[24]

The major aspect of the Puerto Rican government's economic program was to attract United States investments. Mainland companies were now invited to open new ventures or branches in Puerto Rico to produce either finished products or parts to be shipped to the United States for use in parent firms. PRIDCO preferred to promote mainland firms with established reputations. First, such firms would generate an all-round confidence in the island's program and would help in the promotional effort. Second, such businesses were more likely to have greater depth in management skill and other industrial resources to accommodate whatever problems that might arise in operating newly located industries.

Following 1947, the insular government mounted a concerted promotional campaign. It opened offices in major cities on the mainland and advertised its program widely in such magazines as *Time, Newsweek,* and the *New Yorker.*[25] The government periodically supplied statistics to the press and interested manufacturers to show the progress made. PRIDCO released, for instance, its fifth annual report to the press in 1948, showing, among other things, that it had appropriated nearly $2 million to build twenty-three new factories sold or leased to prospective businessmen.[26] In addition, businessmen and bankers were taken on inspection tours of new facilities and were given considerable prominence and attention at official occasions.[27] There was, for instance, a goodly representation of business executives and financiers at Muñoz Marín's inauguration as governor in January, 1949.[28]

In an open letter to mainland industries in July, 1948, Governor Piñero enumerated the advantages of investing in Puerto Rico, especially for those that were labor-oriented. He stressed wage differentials and a ready labor force of 675,000 that could be recruited and trained for the industries' use by the insular government under its AID program. Piñero reassured businessmen that there were few strikes in Puerto Rico, and those that did occur were usually resolved by arbitration. There was also available, the governor continued, cheap transportation facilities. Some of the other benefits he listed were: tax-exemption, absence of tariff barriers and federal taxation, government's aid in finding suitable sites for building factories at its own expense, and the ready supply of electric power from the government hydrolectric plant at cheap rates.[29]

In addition to such promotional efforts, several Puerto Rican leaders spoke directly to business groups. An insular representative addressed the American Marketing Association on the way in which the tax moratorium on industries worked.[30] Muñoz Marín stressed at a press conference the importance of the economic program for the island's well-being,[31] and later spoke to about eighty executives of investment and commercial banking institutions at a luncheon in New York City.[32]

The first of a series of major industries to be drawn to Puerto Rico was the Textron textile plant. Moscoso was pleased with their relocation to Puerto Rico because the textile plant would allow PRIDCO to consider developing a whole series of other products related to textiles, including the development of a finishing and printing mill and the establishment of an apparel industry. Originally, a textile plant had been planned in 1945 as a subsidiary corporation of PRIDCO, known as *Telares de Puerto Rico*, but it was abandoned by mid-1947. The Development company invested $4.3 million in building the plant for the new venture, and the Textron firm organized a Puerto Rican corporation with an initial investment of $0.5 million worth of stock.[33]

Textron's experience in Puerto Rico, however, proved to be an unhappy and controversial one. Its transference from New England to Puerto Rico caused anxiety among the New England residents. Its announced closing of six mills meant retiring 3500 workers, and caused Republican Senator Charles Tobey of New Hampshire to launch an investigation. As chairman of the Senate Subcommittee on Interstate and Foreign Commerce, the senator said, "The United States has been acting as a wet nurse for Puerto Rico for years. It is robbing United States workers of their livelihood to subsidize companies like Textron in the territory by granting Federal tax exemptions. We are killing off things here to build in Puerto Rico."[34] It was directly as a result of this unfavorable turn of events that Muñoz Marín adopted a new rule of not exempting industries that shut down their plants entirely in the United States so as to relocate them in Puerto Rico. "It is not," he told a joint session of the insular legislature, "the philosophy of the Government over which I preside to seek the closing of factories in order to have them open in Puerto Rico."[35] In response to a letter in March, 1949, by Congressman Thomas J. Lane of Massachusetts, Muñoz Marín reassured the legislator in a question-answer format that he was opposed to "industry-stealing." The letter dealt with other pertinent issues, and Representative Lane had it inserted in the *Congressional Record* for the benefit of other congressmen.[36]

If the charges of "industry-stealing" helped the Puerto Rican government in policy clarification, Textron's experience as an industrial operation was potentially harmful to the island's industrialization program. By mid-1950 the textile plant management had become disillusioned because of its mounting difficulties with labor, management, and so on. Indeed, by 1954 Textron was pressing for the closing of its tricot plant and was spreading among mainland manufacturers unfavorable reports on Puerto Rico as a suitable industrial location. This forced Moscoso in 1956 to appeal to top Textron management officials to stop undermining the development program. In 1957 the Textron plant transferred its management to Indian Head Mills in the United States, which was formerly part of the Textron empire.[37]

Despite the adverse publicity emerging out of the Textron affair, there were, by fiscal year 1950, 114 old and new industries in operation, 34 of which had been opened in that year, and an additional 12 were in the process of being established.[38] PRIDCO's function over the previous two years had changed from being a corporation directly managing industrial enterprises to a regulatory and guiding agency operating as a regular department of the government. Its role with the private sector, too, had changed. Hence, a need was felt to reorganize the administration of the industrial program.[39]

— Muñoz Marín had coincidentally appointed in 1949 the Commission on Reorganization of the Executive Branch of the Puerto Rican government to recommend to him the necessary administrative changes in anticipation of the adjustments envisaged under the new political status of Commonwealth. The commission recommended, *inter alia,* the creation of a new executive Department of Commerce and Industry under which were to be placed PRIDCO, the Transportation Authority, the Communication Authority, Office of Industrial Tax-Exemption, Office of Rent Control, and General Supplies Administration.[40]

However, since the Puerto Rican government did not have the power to create new executive departments, Muñoz Marín established in 1950, partly on the commission's recommendations, the Economic Development Administration (EDA), placing PRIDCO and the Transportation Authority under its control. Teodoro Moscoso was named as the administrator of the new agency, in which capacity he acted as the "board of directors" of the Development company. The promotional and research functions of PRIDCO, as well as labor recruitment and training, were transferred to EDA. PRIDCO retained, however, functions normally performed by a corporation, such as making loans and renting industrial buildings. In effect, EDA (more popularly known as *Fomento*) operated as an executive department, and its administrator had as much freedom in the running of PRIDCO as a cabinet member would have had.[41]

The reorganization of the economic program in 1950 set the stage for the development under "Operation Bootstrap." There were problems, to be sure, and the insular government modified aspects of the program where changes were deemed necessary. But statistics show that the program's essential goal of promoting continental capital had succeeded. The *Fomento* was fairly liberal in approving petitions from businesses that sought to participate in the program. Petitions were accepted or rejected on grounds of policy rather than strict legal eligibility, and the chief criterion that appears to have been used by the EDA was the desirability or nondesirability of industries in terms of the Development administration's economic objectives. As of June, 1952, 350 petitions were accepted and only 35 were refused.[42] The success of the program is apparent from figures given by H. C. Barton (see Table 1).[43]

TABLE 1. INDUSTRIAL STATISTICS UNDER "OPERATION BOOTSTRAP"

Year ending June 30	Number of Industries				
	Opened	Closed	Existing	Operating	Being established
1943–1948	24	0	24	24	9
1949	28	0	52	50	9
1950	34	3	83	80	12
1951	36	5	114	108	17
1952	63	11	166	157	28
1953	75	12	229	223	31
1954	74	21	282	264	30
1955	52	31	303	292	35
1956	88	27	364	354	49
1957	90	25	429	422	91
1958	96	45	480	464	84
1959	111	28	563*	530	91

* Of this total 113 were locally operated.

As of June, 1952, the firms attracted to Puerto Rico were largely light industries with concentrations in seven major categories: food, textiles, apparel, chemicals, fabricated metals, electrical equipment, and miscellaneous manufacturing.[44] In 184 new firms operating as of July 1, 1952, the sum of $68 million in capital was invested. Of this total $20 million (29 percent) represented government funds in the form of buildings and loans provided by PRIDCO and the Government Development Bank. The remaining amount of $48 million was the contribution of private investors, of which $28 million was from the United States and $20 million from Puerto Rico.[45] The total investment of over $500 million between 1947 and 1958 represented an increase of 35 percent.[46]

Tax-exemption was the most important factor in attracting mainland capital. Ninety-five percent of the fourty-four industries polled attributed tax-exemption as the most powerful incentive in their operating in Puerto Rico. Three other factors that were considered as the next most important trailed far behind: low wages, 70 percent; efficiency of machinery and equipment, 69 percent; and the attitude of the community, 65 percent.[47] The Development administration calculated that a corporation earning an income of $100,000 before paying taxes would pay $46,500 in federal taxation, leaving a profit in the amount of $53,500. Tax-exemption in Puerto Rico would increase the corporation's profit by 87 percent. In the case of an individual owner with a profit of $100,000, federal income tax in the sum of $67,320 would reduce it to $32,680. Under Puerto Rico's tax benefits, the owner's profits would be catapulted by 206 percent.[48] The total tax benefit reaped by mainland businesses between 1947 and 1951 reached close to $5.3 million.[49] The long-term annual capital flows from the mainland between 1947 and 1958 increased from $18 million to $161 million.[50] The net income originating in tax-exempt manufacturing businesses rose from zero in 1947 to $1.8 million in 1950, $4.2 million in 1951, $7.0 million in 1952, $23.4 million in 1953, and $46.5 million in 1954.[51] By contrast, the net income arising out of both tax-exempt and non–tax-exempt manufacturers increased from $27 million in 1940 to $115 million in 1952.[52]

Puerto Rico benefited enormously from the increased economic activities. Product series statistics as well as the net income by industrial origin reflect this. Table 2 shows figures randomly selected from tables prepared by the Puerto Rico Planning Board.[53]

Table 2. Product Series and Net Income by Industrial Origin

| | Current Dollars, in Millions (Fiscal Years) | | | | |
	1940	1950	1960	1970	1972
Gross product	286.7	754.5	1,681.3	4,601.7	5,822.5
Manufacturing	26.7	88.7	288.8	949.1	1,139.2
Trade	26.5	101.7	236.9	670.3	819.4
Finance, insurance, real estate	24.6	51.8	140.5	442.4	558.1
Contract construction	2.6	26.8	87.3	344.7	478.9
Agriculture	70.5	149.4	180.2	184.4	210.6

There was a corresponding upward trend in the island's per capita income and in the number of employed. The per capita figures were $121 in 1940, $279 in 1950, $582 in 1960, $1,417 in 1970, and $1,713 in 1972.[54] The number of workers in Puerto Rican factories climbed from 31,000 in 1939 to 59,700 in 1953, 70 percent of whom were employed in businesses that were assisted by the *Fomento*.[55] Between 1950 and 1954 there was an addition of 20,000 workers in construction plants, transportation and other public services, and manufacturing. The gain, it must be admitted, was offset by the drop in employment in the home needlework industry and agriculture.[56]

The fact most noteworthy from the point of view of this chapter is that Puerto Rico's industrial program, from 1947 to 1952 and beyond, more firmly integrated the island's economy with that of the United States. Harvey Perloff lists six criteria to measure economic integration of one geographic region to another. First, the bulk of the trade of one is with the other, and is of vital importance to the economy of the first. Second, there is a common tariff structure. Third, the credit needs of one are supplied by the banks of the other, and the currencies of the two are identical. Fourth, the public finances of one make an important contribution to the fiscal revenues of the other. Fifth, the investments of one make up a substantial part of the total investments in the other. Sixth, the mobility of labor and the shifts of industry characterize the relationship of the two regions.[57]

Before the six criteria are illustrated by statistics, it would be useful to point out the unique features in the fiscal relationship between Puerto Rico and the United States that have added new and intricate dimensions to the issue of economic integration. This fiscal arrangement, which had been in operation since 1900, provides for all federal customs duties collected in Puerto Rico and for federal excise taxes on rum and tobacco shipped to the United States to be returned to the insular treasury. In 1917 the Puerto Ricans were also made United States citizens without their having to pay federal taxes collected from all Americans under the internal revenue laws. Furthermore, Puerto Rico receives federal grants-in-aid even though it is not a state within the union. These factors have helped the insular leaders in planning their economic program. The extent to which this program, however, has further integrated the insular economy is revealed in the discussion of Perloff's formula.

Puerto Rico imports most of its products from the United States and, indeed, exports most insular goods to the mainland. In fiscal 1947–48 the percentage of Puerto Rico's exports and imports amounted to 97 percent and 94 percent respectively. The export and import percentage for fiscal 1951–52 was 92 percent, while imports decreased to 89 percent.[58] In fiscal 1950–51 the excess of imports over exports was over $115 million.[59] The bulk of Puerto Rico's imports consisted of manufactured articles, but even in 1958 more than half the meat, nearly half of the eggs, and about one-third of the milk consumed on the island came from the mainland.[60] It was only heavy, long-term capital investments that helped to finance the growing deficit in goods and services in the balance of payments.[61]

A common tariff structure has permitted United States manufacturers to take advantage of tax-exemption and low-cost labor secure in the knowledge that their produce would be marketed on the mainland without tariff barriers. Of the total sale outside of Puerto Rico, more than two-thirds were contributed by EDA-promoted mainland industries (in addition to sugar, rum, and tobacco sales), almost all of it to the United States.[62] (Only in the case of sugar were restrictions on imports to the mainland imposed. The United States placed a quota limitation of 900,000 tons of raw sugar per year from the island, which allegedly cost Puerto Rico $25 million in retired acreage and reduced refining, in addition to laid-off workers.)[63] Moreover, in terms of the fiscal arrangement, excise taxes and customs duties were returned to the Puerto Rican treasury. Excise taxes have amounted to between 8 and 10 percent of the Commonwealth government's total net recurrent revenues for every fiscal year between 1950 and 1972, and customs duties have amounted to between 1 and 3 percent.[64]

Puerto Rico's access to United States credit has helped the island to finance its deficits in a variety of ways. In 1950 the insular government issued $18 million worth of Commonwealth bonds in the United States. The number of such bonds decreased sharply the following year, but it has steadily increased thereafter. Furthermore, the availability of mainland credit facilities tied the island's banking system to that of the United States through the association of domestic banks to their correspondents and the relationship of foreign banks with their head offices. Both the head offices and correspondents have supplied credit to insular banks.[65]

As a result of Puerto Rico's unique political status, it has received federal contributions in the form of grants-in-aid, direct expenditure of regular federal civilian agencies, emergency federal expenditures, payments and services to insular veterans, and expenditure by the Social Security Administration. The figures in Table 3 underscore this close fiscal relationship with the United States.[66]

TABLE 3. COMMONWEALTH GOVERNMENT NET RECURRENT REVENUES

| | *Selected Fiscal Years, in Thousands* | | | | |
	1940	1950	1960	1970	1972
Commonwealth sources	20,970	90,406	193,462	562,488	752,434
Non-Commonwealth sources (customs duties, U.S. excises, federal grants-in-aid)	5,340	18,867	57,854	260,839	390,741
Total	26,310	109,273	251,316	823,327	1,143,175

The federal contribution of $390,741,000 for fiscal 1972 represents more than one-third of the total recurrent revenues for the Commonwealth government.[67] In addition, United States defense spendings have made an enormous contribution to the island's economy. Federal defense expenditures in Puerto Rico for the ten-year period from 1942 through 1951 amounted to $570 million. In contrast, the nondefense expenditures for the same period totaled $114 million. The wages, salaries, and supplements paid by the federal government between fiscal 1960 and fiscal 1970 came to $1,267 million.[68]

The disbursements by the government of the United States

play an absolutely essential role in Puerto Rico's economy. They help to balance the unfavorable trade figures between the United States and Puerto Rico.[69] They have given employment to many Puerto Ricans and have helped in financing essential measures, in addition to stabilizing basic industries. In raising the island's income, the federal disbursements have strengthened the purchasing power of consumers, which in turn has made possible industrial expansion and increased importation.[70] Muñoz Marín hoped in 1953 that eventually the island could dispense with the substantial federal aid.[71] This has remained a hope for the future.

The bulk of foreign investments in Puerto Rico was also from the United States. The long-term mainland capital invested increased from $18 million in 1948 to $161 million in 1959.[72] Two-thirds of the investments in 1957, according to the London *Economist,* were from the United States. European manufacturers had been thwarted from making large investments because of the fear on the part of American firms of "back-door imports." Hence, the EDA was forced to cut its promotional activities in Europe. In 1957, the *Economist* stated, not a single European company was established.[73]

With the island's economy so heavily dependent on United States businessmen, it would be natural for Puerto Rico to be subject to mainland economic cycles. Werner Baer studied the effects upon the Puerto Rican economy of the recessions of 1953–54 and 1957–58. The impact of the two recessions, Baer discovered, depended on whether an insular firm was a mainland plant established in its entirety or a subsidiary of a continental firm producing finished products or parts to be assembled later on the mainland into finished products. The effects of the recessions were more direct on the first rather than the second type. Generally, however, a number of factors cushioned the adverse effects of the recessions, so that Puerto Rico's industrialization program was not directly but indirectly affected. Indirectly, mainland recessions meant a reduction in migration of Puerto Ricans to the continent of the United States, which in turn meant an increase in unemployed workers on the island.[74]

Population growth and migration are two crucially important factors in Puerto Rico's economic program. The essential goal of the entire program was to raise the standard of living and cut down the rate of unemployment. The task is Himalayan in proportion. The rate of growth of an already overpopulated island—

there were 668 persons per square mile in 1945[75]—is exceptionally
high, so that the labor force increments by the natural process
of births and deaths grow far more rapidly than employment
openings can absorb them. Total employment has risen from
512,000 in 1940 to 658,000 in 1950, and from 760,000 in 1955 to
860,000 in 1960. But the population of Puerto Rico has grown,
too. It rose from 1,869,000 in 1940 to 2,275,000 in 1960.[76] While
it is to the credit of the insular government that it has been able
to reduce unemployment from 17.9 percent in 1940 to 12.8 percent in 1950,[77] the rate of unemployment did not drop below 11
percent until 1964.[78]

Migration has, therefore, acted as an escape-valve. As United
States citizens, the Puerto Ricans have freely migrated to the mainland to avail themselves of work opportunities, thus removing a
sizable percentage of the natural increase that would otherwise
swell the ranks of the unemployed and the underemployed. In
the ten-year period between 1941 and 1951, about 240,000 Puerto
Ricans left the island, reducing by half the excess of births over
deaths of 486,000 in the same period.[79] Between 1950 and 1954
some 100,000 Puerto Ricans migrated to the United States.[80]
Emigration is, therefore, essential for a healthy state of the island's
economy, even though in January, 1949, Muñoz Marín insisted
that it should not be regarded as a permanent part of the solution
to Puerto Rico's problems.[81] Indeed, the money sent back to the
island by Puerto Ricans in the United States is a considerable
boon to the insular economy. Puerto Rican agricultural workers
who migrate to the mainland seasonally alone contribute close to
$6 million per year to the general economy.[82]

The shift of mainland industries to Puerto Rico raises two
additional problems. First, would industries stay when the period
of tax-exemption expires? It was apparent that because over 90
percent of the firms were being attracted for this reason the period
of tax-exemption would have to be continued for a longer term.
Another tax-exemption law was passed in 1954, providing for the
granting of a ten-year period of exemption to successful applicants
regardless of the year in which it first received the grant. Firms
that had been exempted in 1948 could petition to have their grants
redrawn in terms of the 1954 law.[83] The insular government was
well aware that the tax-exemption law has not helped an equitable
distribution of wealth, nor have the enormous rates of profit been
reinvested in Puerto Rico. Still, the Development administration

hoped that the higher incomes for the economy as a whole would offset the inequity in the tax structure, and that in the end the Puerto Rican economy might become less dependent on tax-exemption as a permanent feature of insular economy.[84]

Second, could the Puerto Rican government continue to insist on minimum wages below federal levels established by the Fair Labor Standards Act in the face of opposition by mainland unions? The government of Muñoz Marín has insisted that any extension of mainland minima to the island would destroy Puerto Rico's economy. This argument, plus the astute handling of the whole matter by Muñoz Marín, persuaded Congress in 1954 not to pass a minimum wage law for Puerto Rico. But it was clear that low-cost labor as an incentive for mainland investors lost its original strong appeal because of its vulnerability to attacks by labor organizations.[85]

Muñoz Marín and Moscoso were fully cognizant that the revamping of the industrialization program had serious political implications. It was a well–thought-out, long-term program, which envisaged utilizing to the island's fullest advantage the neither-independence-nor-statehood political status of Puerto Rico in 1948. Both realized that the island would lose its unique tariff and tax relationship under independence or statehood, and that without the unique elements in its association with the United States their economic program could get nowhere. If Puerto Rico could attain statehood, assuming that was possible in 1948, it would lose many of the federal contributions, would not be able to grant tax-exemption, and would be burdened by federal taxation. Under independence, assuming once again that it was possible in 1948, Puerto Rico could not attract mainland industries, if only because the strong incentives of a common tariff structure and accessibility to the United States market facilities would disappear.

Businessmen wishing to invest in Puerto Rico desired to be reassured about at least two aspects of insular politics and program: first, whether Puerto Rican leadership was reliable; second, whether a substantive change of the island's political status was expected shortly. Such was the case of a potential industrialist who inquired of the firm of Arnold, Fortas, and Porter. The Washington firm was in a good position to respond to such a request, because it had been retained in 1946 by the insular government to handle legal matters that might arise in its relations with continental citizens and businesses. Arnold, Fortas, and Porter reassured the businessman on both counts. The document stated that Muñoz Marín was a highly reliable leader under whom there was no concern to fear government expropriation of private interests. Furthermore, the firm's communication continued, the recent concessions of self-government to Puerto Rico—referring to the Elective Governor Act of 1947—had weakened the sentiment for independence and strengthened that for dominion status. The letter ruled out statehood even more strongly.[86]

The firm's confidence in Muñoz Marín and the island's economic program was shared by key administration officials and congressmen. DTIP's director Davis believed that the island's industrialization program had a brilliant future.[87] Michigan's Representative Crawford expressed enthusiasm for Puerto Rico's economic program, and California's Representative Norris Poulson was convinced that the only man capable of saving the island's economy was Muñoz Marín.[88] The developmental project impressed members of the House Committee on Public Lands when Muñoz Marín unfolded it in detail on July 12, 1949. He hinted in his testimony that he was planning in the near future for a political formula that would accommodate economic realities in Puerto Rico.[89]

"Obviously, the United States could not," he recalled in 1953, "maintain its present good economic treatment of Puerto Rico, which is vital to our continued development, if we acquired a status which had all the legal paraphernalia of separate independence. It became clear that only under some form of status in which we retained our American citizenship could we preserve the economic conditions which are necessary for our survival as a people." A new political approach meant moving away from the "either/or" formula, he added. "We continued to be preoccupied as a collective group with the notion of a plebiscite in which we would be required to choose between separate independence and federated statehood—despite the fact that under either alternative the economic life of our people would be gravely threatened."[90] Economic considerations largely gave birth to the concept of the Commonwealth of Puerto Rico.

CHAPTER ELEVEN

The Status Debate Continues

The subject of Puerto Rican status has been the most persistent topic of discussion among the people of Puerto Rico. The debate has been variously described as debilitating and "futile," as an "obsession" that has caused anger and "mental anguish." A negative criticism is implied in such terms of description: why do the Puerto Ricans insist upon continuing a Sisyphus-like wrestling with a definition of themselves in relation to the people José de Diego called the "Gentlemen of the North," instead of tackling the more mundane and material matters of struggle and survival? The quest of self-identity, however, constantly urges fulfillment. It need not be harmful. On the contrary, it can lead to spiritual and moral growth. This indeed has been the case with Puerto Ricans, for they permitted Muñoz Marín to channel the quest in a constructive manner away for the time being from independence and statehood. Repose in the Commonwealth status, he told them, so that they might search fruitfully for a permanent solution *and* at the same time apply themselves to the important tasks that face them. Fernós-Isern echoed Muñoz Marín's sentiments when he told *independentistas* and *estadistas* in 1950 to hang their "hammocks . . . under the tree which sprout[ed] into this new concept." Who knows, he continued, the formula might yield a permanent settlement to an old dilemma.

That Muñoz Marín succeeded in weaning Puerto Ricans away from an "either independence or statehood" way of thinking was a measure of his leadership abilities as much as it was a reflection of the islanders' spiritual growth. He himself had started out as an *independentista* at the time the PPD was founded in 1938. But by the time the party scored a narrow electoral victory in 1940, he was beginning to have doubts about pursuing either independence or statehood for the immediate future. The economic well-being of Puerto Rico became his primary consideration. By 1946, when he had consolidated his political position, he abandoned independence as a *Popular* goal. He argued persuasively that Puerto Rico could not economically sustain either independence or statehood and convinced fellow Puerto Ricans that the continued association of the island with the United States under the most liberal terms of self-government possible was in its best interest. He separated the issues of autonomy and political status to the extent that the dichotomy of these two closely interrelated issues could be achieved.

This approach harmonized with the attitude of Congress, which, in the heightened security-conscious atmosphere of the postwar period, desired to retain control over the island in vital matters. And this 3,500-square-mile Caribbean island was strategically placed at the gate of its sister islands and the Panama Canal. There was, therefore, little sentiment in Congress to grant the island independence, even though the various bills introduced by a champion of Puerto Rico's independence, Senator Tydings of Maryland, included absolute provisions for maintaining United States military and naval bases on the island. Congress preferred instead to grant self-government in small doses. There was little opposition to the appointment of the first Puerto Rican as governor, Jesús T. Piñero, in 1946. About a year later, the United States legislators, reassured by the able governorship of Piñero, believed that the islanders should be allowed to elect their own governor. But their caution and conservatism did not yet permit the auditor and the justices of the Puerto Rican Supreme Court to be appointed or elected by the islanders. One suspects that they were fearful lest a pattern of anarchy and revolutions follow a sudden grant of self-government and thereby detract from the island's important strategic role. A few members of Congress were influenced in their thinking by such patterns in some Latin American countries and were wont to consider Puerto Rico to be Latin American in "temperament."

Congress was, however, quite impressed by the administrative abilities of Governor Muñoz Marín. Influential members of the Congressional committees concerned with Puerto Rican matters frequently praised the work of the governor, and generally did anything possible, such as print his speeches in the *Congressional Record*, to make more of their colleagues aware of the existence of a talented administrator and a reliable friend. They pointed enthusiastically to "Operation Bootstrap" and the significance Puerto Rico's economic well-being would have for the rest of Latin America. Resident Commissioner Fernós-Isern's quiet but industrious efficiency in Washington was also instrumental in projecting a favorable image of Puerto Ricans generally.

The most notable among the influential members on Puerto Rican affairs were Representative Crawford of Michigan and Senators Butler of Nebraska and O'Mahoney of Wyoming. Others were Representatives Engle of California, Taylor of New York, and Peterson of Florida and Senators Cordon of Oregon and Lehman of New York. Congressman Peterson and Senator O'Mahoney were chairmen, respectively, of the House Committee on Public Lands and the Senate Committee on Interior and Insular Affairs. Of course there is no way of telling why members of Congress showed interest in Puerto Rico. Representative Crawford came from a state that had beet sugar interests, which in theory should have made him an opponent for the increase of quotas on Puerto Rican sugar. And perhaps he was. But he did not desire to eliminate Puerto Rican competition in this area by granting the island independence. Indeed, he devised plans to utilize Puerto Rican migrant labor for farms in Michigan. New York representatives and senators generally supported the advancement of insular autonomy, which probably reflected their concern for the Puerto Rican constituents in their state. Partisanship was not seriously involved, for both Democrats and Republicans generally backed Puerto Rican self-government.

These several factors accounted for the virtual absence of opposition in 1950 when Muñoz Marín, very ably supported by Fernós-Isern, in whose mind the concept had germinated, asked Congress to permit the islanders to write their own constitution. It seemed to many members of Congress the logical step in the advancement of insular autonomy. The Puerto Ricans had demonstrated their capabilities in the exercise of responsible self-government. It is probably true that many congressmen and senators saw the step as an issue separate from the question of political status. However they interpreted the phrase "in the nature of a compact," they probably understood Public Law 600 of 1950 to give the islanders complete autonomy in internal matters, except that if things ever went out of control on the island Congress had the final authority to straighten them out.

This observation should not detract from the positive and progressive attitude of many of the United States legislators who believed that Puerto Ricans deserved the greatest possible self-government within the bounds of the United States policy of enlightened control over former dependencies and territories. Many were aware, too, that in the Commonwealth a new and unique experiment in federalism was being established. In retrospect it seems unfortunate that Congress did not define this experiment more clearly, because its vagueness was to become a source of controversy in the years ahead. But if Congress had attempted to do so, or if Fernós-Isern had been less adroit in his maneuvering, the project might have become bogged down in an endless debate over the question of political status.

Reference has been made so far only to Congress' reaction to insular autonomy. The United States administrations, especially that of President Truman, played a substantial role. The Truman administration could boast of three major developments in the short space of seven years: the appointment of a Puerto Rican as governor, the first elective governor, and the establishment of the Commonwealth. Indeed, this was by far more than the administrations from 1898 to 1945 could claim for any and all overseas possessions. The Truman administration was, however, operating in a new era when big nations felt at least a new moral obligation to extend greater and greater self-government to its colonies, dependencies, and the like. National movements in Africa and Asia, inspired by Western political ideas of sovereignty, independence, and freedom, demanded an end to the domination by Western colonial powers. The colonial revolt had built up pressure in the years after the First World War and had gained momentum in the years following the Second. In Asia, for instance, India had achieved independence by 1947; and Burma, Ceylon, Indonesia, the states of Indo-China, and Malaya were in different stages of evolution towards self-government and independence. The United States never regarded Puerto Rico as a colony and was sentitive to reference of it as one. It extended self-government to Puerto Rico as if it were a colony, however.

The Truman administration owed a great deal to its predecessor in terms of the direction that Puerto Rican development took. The personnel in the Department of the Interior under the Roosevelt administration worked for the same ends that were to be achieved under the Truman administration. Secretary Ickes, Undersecretary Fortas, and Governor Tugwell were committed to achieving an elective governorship in Puerto Rico. They were fully aware that the governor's post in the past was a position regarded as payment of partisan loyalty to some continental politician. They were convinced that Puerto Rico's administration should not be subject to partisan politics, for it was too important and too serious a task, one which involved the welfare of over two million people. But as progressive as their attitudes were, they failed to obtain even a modicum of self-government for the island, primarily because of the administration's deteriorating relationship with Congress. Secretary Ickes and the others were in no small way responsible for the failure in 1943–1944 to pass a bill intended to make the governor's post elective. Thwarted in this matter, the Roosevelt administration could not even consider resolving the status question. The dilemma is summed up in Abe Fortas' words:

> . . . I—and I believe Secretary Ickes—at all relevant times was deeply influenced by the practical limitations imposed by the Congressional situation. It was clear that Congress could not be induced to make a bold forward move as the first step toward achieving improved status for Puerto Rico. It was clear that the task had to be accomplished by successive moves.
>
> I was at all times completely in sympathy with the idea that Puerto Rico should have an elected governor and complete dominion over all of its internal affairs through locally selected officials, and that United States participation in Puerto Rico's internal government should be eliminated so far and as soon as possible.[1]

These high officials, although they were for a time members of the Truman administration, left their posts within twelve to eighteen months of Truman's taking over the presidency. It was after their departure that relations between the administration and the Congress improved. Indeed, harmonious relations with the legislative body were absolutely necessary, because the Eightieth Congress was dominated by Republicans. This pattern was continued in the Eighty-first and Eighty-second Congresses, when Democrats were in control. Some of the persons worthy of mention are undersecretary, and later secretary, of the Interior Chapman; DTIP director Davis; and head of the Caribbean Branch of the DTIP, Mason Barr. Chapman had entered the Roosevelt administration in 1933 as an assistant secretary in the Interior department. By the time he became the secretary in 1949, his grasp of the Puerto Rican question was enormous and his understanding of the workings of Congress and the government excellent. He and other Interior personnel worked closely with Fernós-Isern to coordinate their actions *vis à vis* Congressional leaders. The smooth cooperation and coordination in the passage of the 1947 Elective Governor Act and of Public Laws 600 in 1950 and 447 in 1952 are examples of the approach that was absent in the early 1940s.

Fernós-Isern played a vital role in the implementation of the Commonwealth. He represented in Congress not only the insular government but the Puerto Rican people as well, since he had been elected by them. He acquitted himself extremely well as liaison between the Puerto Rican government on the one hand and the administration and Congress on the other. Since he was intimately involved in the formulation of the Commonwealth concept, he was in a good position to explain it to legislators and administrators, and to defend it before committees, conferences, and meetings.

A factor of considerable importance was the personality and politics of Muñoz Marín. This factor has been stressed in the advancement of Puerto Rican autonomy throughout this study. His inspiring leadership won the support of the Puerto Rican people. Fernós-Isern states, ". . . without him it would have been most difficult if not impossible to move the Puerto Rican people in the direction of Commonwealth and to sustain their efforts for its achievement."[2]

Muñoz Marín used to the island's fullest advantage his familiarity with American political traditions and institutions, sometimes even to the point of exaggerated ego-building for the United

States. His excellent command of the English language, according to García Méndez,[3] was no less an advantage in his cultivating the friendship of administration officials and Congressional leaders, many of whom he came to know on a first-name basis. They in turn could not but be impressed by his charisma and knowledge of things. Congressional committees sometimes broke tradition by giving him standing ovations, and Congressional leaders saw in him a man who transcended Puerto Rico and through whom the United States could communicate with Latin America. They trusted and respected him, and his policies of close cooperation and association reassured them. Whatever reservations administration officials and Congressional leaders may have had about granting Puerto Rico greater self-government, such thoughts were partly allayed by the personality of Muñoz Marín. This was a considerable achievement for a man who up to 1937 had openly advocated political severance from the United States.

The success of the Commonwealth status was based considerably on its economic advantages. The implication of this was that neither statehood nor independence could offer similar benefits for the near future. Indeed, the United States generally accepted the argument in the 1940s and thereafter that economic disaster would follow if either of the two alternatives was hastily imposed upon the island.

In the case of statehood it was argued that it would lose customs dues and excise taxes on offshore shipments, as well as other forms of federal benefits. Besides, Puerto Ricans would need to pay federal taxes under statehood, and this might overburden their earning capacities. There would, however, be increased federal contributions: increased grants-in-aid, social security, assignments for roads, and so on. But it was difficult to calculate exactly whether the losses could be offset by the gains.

It was because of these compelling reasons largely that statehood never became an issue in Congress in the same way that it did in the cases of Hawaii and Alaska, two other important United States territories. These two territories, however, were "incorporated" and hence subject to full United States taxation even before they achieved statehood. They received no benefits from customs duties and United States excise taxes on offshore shipments, nor could they offer tax exemption as in Puerto Rico. Statehood in Hawaii and Alaska did little to change their tax relationship with the United States. Moreover, Hawaii and Alaska were rich in natural resources and promised to be self-dependent assets within the Union. In addition to all that, the people of Hawaii and Alaska had explicitly shown their preference for statehood in popular referendums. Indeed, Hawaii had even organized in 1950 a constitutional convention to draft a constitution on the basis of statehood, although it became a state only in 1959.[4]

To be sure, organized political and economic groups advocating statehood in Puerto Rico conducted vigorous campaigns for support among United States lawmakers and the insular electorate. But Congress and the Puerto Rican people remained unconvinced about statehood in the face of its apparent disadvantages. In part, statehood proponents were unable to build up momentum for their cause in Congress because an anti-statehood party dominated insular politics throughout the 1940s. In the unlikely event that the Puerto Ricans had chosen to ask Congress for statehood in 1950, they would have faced some other hurdles that confronted Hawaii and Alaska in their battles for statehood, namely, partisan politics, race, noncontiguity, and so on. But the Puerto Rican statehood movement in the 1940s never really got off the ground.

In recent years, the support for statehood among Puerto Ricans has increased. Nearly 39 percent of those voting in the 1967 referendum chose statehood. The years of successful association under the Commonwealth have probably made Puerto Ricans more receptive to permanent affiliation with the United States. The move to become a state in the Union, however, would be an irrevocable one, and Puerto Ricans are not likely to rush into it. The findings of the 1965–1966 United States–Puerto Rico commission further suggest that the transition would be a difficult one. Leading *estadista* García Méndez concedes that the phenomenal increase in yearly Puerto Rican gross income has made Puerto Rico the "metropolis" and the United States the "colony."[5]

The *independentistas* probably enjoyed some strength in the early 1940s, in part, because the PPD had not yet shed its image as a party of independence. There were many *independentistas* within the ranks of the PPD. But Muñoz Marín abandoned independence as a *Popular* goal in 1946 and expelled *independentistas* from the party. Thus spurned, the independence group formed a party of its own, the PIP. It has, however, shown no great electoral popularity and has grown weaker over the years.

The Puerto Rican people have remained unconvinced about independence. Only 0.6 percent of those voting in the 1967 referendum favored independence. To a very great extent this is because the *independentistas* failed to present effective plans and programs of how Puerto Rico might adjust to independence without suffering a drop in the growth rate and serious economic dislocation. The 1965–1966 United States–Puerto Rico commission was not persuaded that the transition to independence would require ten but not more than twenty years, as maintained by an economist representing the PIP. It felt that fundamental changes would be necessary in the institutional relationship between the island and the mainland. As an independent country, Puerto Rico would need to develop additional and alternative sources of financing capital investment and new export markets, for which an unspecified transition period, much longer than fifteen years, would be necessary.

From an economic point of view, the Commonwealth status has been extremely beneficial to Puerto Rico. It has fully exploited the unique tax and fiscal relationship between the island and the mainland to become industrialized and to upgrade the standard of living of the Puerto Rican people. Few other groups of people have achieved so much so rapidly. In the process of its achievement, however, Puerto Rico has developed a pattern of institutional relationship with the United States that has more and more come to assume a permanent structure. Puerto Rico's economic growth rate has become firmly tied to the pattern. This is why transition to statehood or independence in the future is going to be difficult. But the great merit of the Commonwealth status is that it is not irrevocable—it has left room for the Puerto Ricans to grow not only materially but spiritually as well, until a permanent solution can be found.

There are, of course, limitations to the status. The 1959 attempt to improve its terms indicated a substantial range of areas that required redefinition and refinement. Its opponents have not been slow to point out its weaknesses. *Independentista* Geigel Polanco raises a fundamental question: "The fact is that substantial powers are still exercised in Puerto Rico by the Federal Government of the United States." He denies that Puerto Rico has achieved full autonomy or that the relationship is based on the principle of bilateral "compact."[6]

García Méndez points to its legal and constitutional anomalies. The Federal Firearm Act, he says, was made applicable to the United States but not to Puerto Rico. The Taft-Hartley Act, however, is applicable to Puerto Rico as well. Furthermore, the "National Labor Board has jurisdictional priority over the Insular Labor Board in any matter where a conflict of jurisdiction might emerge." In judicial matters, too, contradictory decisions prevail. He cites several examples, two of which are: in *Mora* v. *Torres* (113 F. Supp. 309 D.P.R. 1953) it was decided that the Fifth Amendment was still in force in Puerto Rico because the island was no longer a territory but subject to a new relationship determined by a "compact" that could not be unilaterally changed. However, a similar decision by the U.S. District Federal Court of Puerto Rico in *Detrés* v. *Lions Building Corporation* was revoked by the Court of Appeals 7th Circuit (234 2d 596 1956), which stated that Puerto Rico was still a "territory" and that there was no difference between a "territory" and the "Commonwealth."[7]

In view of these weaknesses in the Commonwealth, what is the future of the status issue in Puerto Rico? It is appropriate to permit the thoughts of Fernós-Isern, the man who helped to formulate and implement the Commonwealth, to answer the question:

> My own personal belief is that statehood in the union would mean a totally anomalous situation for Puerto Rico and the United States. It is an unnatural extremely difficult accommodation. I can not conceive that the people of Puerto Rico will ever agree to it, or ask and persist asking for it, and to pay the price for it. On the other hand I believe that it is not in the interest of the United States that the association of Puerto Rico therewith be dissolved. The United States will always find it contrary to its best interest to set up an independent republic in Puerto Rico.
>
> Since the Puerto Rican people will insist on a completely self-governing commonwealth, it is obvious that the dilemma will not be "independence vs. statehood," but rather full self-government in association with United States or full self-government separated from the United States. Ultimately the decision will be made not by the Puerto Rican people themselves, but indeed directly or indirectly by the United States.[8]

Appendix

A. MEMORANDUM FROM MUÑOZ MARIN TO SECRETARY ICKES

January 5th, 1937.

MEMORANDUM FOR SECRETARY ICKES
From Luis Muñoz Marín

RE: Political status of Puerto Rico.

Statehood or Independence:

It is universally recognized in Puerto Rico that the taking of definite steps with regard to the final political status of the island should not be further delayed. It is almost as universally recognized that no form of colonial status—that is of delegated and therefore revocable powers to Puerto Rico,—will be acceptable to, or dispose of the problem in, Puerto Rico. There are only two forms of political status that remain possible: independence and statehood. Both have the quality of dignity for the Puerto Rican people, and both have the quality of juridical permanence, neither being revocable in law.

Of these two definitive solutions, statehood seems to be ruled out for reasons of a practical nature—from the viewpoint of the United States as well as from that of Puerto Rico.

217

Statehood, from Puerto Rico's viewpoint:

From the point of view of Puerto Rico, statehood would accomplish no economic change favorable to Puerto Rico but would rather tend to perpetuate the present unsound economic system based on the overwhelming preponderance of sugar. It would have the adverse economic effect of depriving Puerto Rico of its customs receipts, its income and inheritance tax receipts, of a large part of its internal revenue receipts. Therefore, the only economic change encompassed by statehood would be to convert the Federal Government into one more absentee extractor of the wealth produced by the Puerto Ricans. It can be easily seen what such a change would mean to the already miserable standard of living of the population, and to the Government services, especially Education and Public Health. Politically, it would involve minor and superficial improvements by creating a handful of additional elective offices.

Statehood, from U.S. viewpoint:

From the point of view of the United States, what advantage does statehood entail? None whatever that can be seen, save the aid and counsel in Congress of eight representatives and two senators from an unassimilated and, due to intense population and other factors, unassimilable nationality. If Puerto Rico contributed its eight or nine million dollars to the Federal Treasury as a State, the State Government would immediately collapse. If it did not contribute this money, because of instant replacement in the form of relief and other grants, then there would not even be this gain. On the other hand, the United States would be embarking on an entirely uncharted sea,—the incorporation of overseas territory thickly populated by people of a foreign culture into the perpetual Union. And whatever threats exist today in Puerto Rico to legitimate American interests, whether as taxpayers or as producers, would then be made to exist in perpetuity. This perpetual quality of statehood should be enough to terrify both the people of the United States and the people of Puerto Rico. After all, even independence can be taken back with the consent of the Puerto Ricans. Statehood cannot be taken back even if the Puerto Ricans should ardently desire to have it taken back and the American people should desire to take it back with equal ardour.

Independence: Tydings Bill

The only remaining solution, independence, was in fact accepted as the only alternative to the colonial system in the so-called Tydings independence bill. Whatever the pernicious clauses of that bill (and they were many), this recognition of the only alternative was clearly realistic. The United States could certainly not allow the Puerto Rican people to vote on statehood unless they could commit themselves to grant statehood if favored by the popular vote.

While introducing the offensive and destructive so-called Tydings Bill again would certainly not help matters in Puerto Rico, it is nevertheless true that dropping the whole subject and not presenting any legislation leading to independence,—if-the-people-want-it, would disclose the presentation of the Tydings Bill last April naked to the Puerto Rican people, divested of its only good quality (the recognition of a right) and reduce it to a gesture of political chicanery in extreme bad taste, and of economic terrorism. The fact that the bill was the fruit of Dr. Gruening's twisted and unadmirable state of mind, and that your approval and that of the President extended only to the principle involved and not to the horrible details, is known to few. To the people of Puerto Rico at large, the Tydings Bill, as drafted, is the last word, the only word, of the Roosevelt Administration on the subject.

1936 elections

The last elections in Puerto Rico cannot be considered as changing the need for decent independence legislation, because the result was clearly determined by the economic terrorism of the Tydings Bill. This is not an ex-post-facto conclusion. As soon as the Tydings Bill was introduced as an Administration measure, I informed officials of the Division of Territories (Dr. Gruening and Mrs. Hampton) that the bill was an instrument that had made absolutely certain the defeat of the forces that had been supporting the Administration against the vicious attacks of the sugar corporations and their political representatives. After the Tydings Bill was presented, I resigned, in proof of the sincerity of my conviction, my own candidacy for Resident Commissioner in Washington, to which I was nominated unanimously twice by the Convention of the Liberal Party. It was obviously impossible for a political force to win an election when the chief political plank of its platform was apparently defined by the U.S. government, which has the deciding power, as ruin and starvation. Although in spite of the economic terrorism of the Tydings Bill the Liberal forces polled 48% of the popular vote (more than I expected under the circumstances), an election held under such clear-cut economic duress cannot be considered as an expression of public opinion, unless you wish to consider the high percentage of the votes polled, in spite of the duress, as an indication of public feeling. I think I may have presented to you personally this certainty of the loss of the elections by the Liberal forces, through no fault of their own, as far back as last April or May, when I had one or two interviews with you on the subject of the Tydings Bill. However, I am not certain that I presented this to you, but I certainly did to Mr. Chapman, Dr. Gruening, and Mrs. Hampton. It definitely does not represent hind-sight.

Now, I wish to point out to you, Mr. Secretary, why independence for Puerto Rico, although certainly no utopia, is necessary from the point of view of Puerto Rico, and I believe inevitable from the point of view of the United States.

Possible motives of Empire

In the first place I think you will agree with me that, aside from military reasons, which play no part in the Puerto Rican problem,(*) there are only two motivations for the control of one people by another: one is economic exploitation; the other is the White Man's Burden. Economic exploitation is simple and straightforward. The White Man's Burden can be one of two things: a sincere desire to help another people, or a disguise to make exploitation respectable and palatable to the decent people of the exploiting country. It is historically clear that the sincere desire to help is a motivation that functions only during a very small part of the time and on very rare occasions. I believe that the Roosevelt administration is one of those rare occasions, so far as Puerto Rico is concerned. Even under the Roosevelt Administration, the state of mind of one individual, in a key position, has been enough to swamp the character of generosity of the Roosevelt–Puerto Rican policy, to place the island unnecessarily in the hands of the worst reactionary interests, poisoning the whole situation with the spirit of distrust and revenge. But even if this had not been so, the Roosevelt Administration, your own tenure as Secretary of the Interior, have only four years and fifteen days to go. To any believer in liberty such as you are, to any anti-imperialist, such as Dr. Gruening used to be, to any believer in the rights of people to control their own destiny, it seems that the historically proven reality that peoples don't control other peoples, in the long run, except for purposes of exploitation, must be the basis for any fair-minded decision as to Puerto Rico. I believe it is clear that, if the United States continue to own Puerto Rico, most of the long years that will follow the Roosevelt Administration will be devoted, as all the long years that preceeded it, mainly to protecting exploitation of the people of Puerto Rico by a few privileged interests over here and, as an incident, in Spain. On the basis of that truth it is that I lay, in terms as simple as that, the need of independence for Puerto Rico.

Practical need for Independence,
from Puerto Rico's viewpoint

However, there are more detailed reasons why independence is necessary for Puerto Rico. Under the American tariff Puerto Rico has become practically a one crop country. This crop—sugar cane—, like all crops subject to

---

(*) Puerto Rico, especially since the American flag was raised over the Virgin Islands, is said not to be of military importance to the United States. However, in any case, every sensible Puerto Rican will agree that even under independence the United States should have all the naval and military facilities in Puerto Rico that they may require for their national security. The national security of the United States will always be a primary concern of the Puerto Rican people, because of the friendly relations existing, because of the good neighbor policy, and because the security of the whole Caribbean will always be intimately involved with the national security of the United States.

complicated processing before reaching market, is of the worst for farmers and workers. It comprises 70% of the total production. It is 50% absentee-owned in the United States (in three Atlantic seaboard cities of the United States) and about 20% owned in Spain. This causes an absentee outflow of wealth produced by low-wage laborers and low-income farmers that can be estimated at some 15 to 20 million dollars a year. With the farmers constantly being driven out of the best cane lands, with this continuous extraction of wealth, with this continuous "human mining" (in the sense in which the Department of Agriculture uses the term "soil mining"), it is clearly seen that a change in this system is imperative and cannot be long delayed. The Roosevelt administration recognizes this, and were it not for Dr. Gruening's state of mind, would be doing something more or less substantial about it by keeping Reconstruction to its original aims. But I do not think that any student of history can hold that such a favorable situation could be trusted to last very much beyond the Roosevelt administration.

So long as the present system continues, Puerto Rico will not be able to produce the tropical foods that it consumes. So long as Puerto Rico is subject to dumping from the United States, all land distribution policies, unless it be for the planting of more sugar cane, will be nullified and destroyed by a dumping on the Puerto Rican market of the same products produced by the families that may receive the land. Then there is the problem of coffee, essentially the soundest crop in Puerto Rico. It is sound because land in coffee is more evenly distributed than in any other crop; because it has to grow under shade and therefore automatically protects forestation over the whole coffee-growing area; because it has a potential (formerly existent) European market at good prices without the need of tariff favors; because it is grown on the uplands where the climate is healthier, the tuberculosis rate is lower and malaria is at a minimum, where the only major health problem, outside of those arising principally from a starvation diet, is the hookworm, easily cured if effort can be concentrated upon it; because less than one per cent of it is absentee owned. Coffee was Puerto Rico's principal crop when the American regime began. Under present conditions there is no hope for the coffee industry. The quality of Puerto Rican coffee is too high priced for the American market, and only a negligible amount enters it. On the other hand, Spain, the principal natural market for Puerto Rican coffee, has given Puerto Rico a quota of only 450 hundredweights, that is, the product of about 200 acres. Other coffee-producing countries have large quotas in Spain, which does not produce coffee, because of their bargaining power in establishing reciprocity treaties. If Puerto Rico had such bargaining power, it could quickly recover the Spanish and other markets for its coffee. This would not hurt any United States producer. For instance, Puerto Rico consumes Spanish wines in quantity, and it does not consume California wines. Puerto Rico could admit Spanish wines free in exchange for a reasonable coffee quota, this being a benefit to Puerto Rico without impinging on the interests of any United States producer. Other Spanish luxury products, which hurdle the high tariff anyway because of long established Puerto Rican consumer habits, are in the same category.

With local tariff-making and treaty-making powers, Puerto Rico could:

(1) successfully recreate a class of small landholders

(2) increase food production

(3) develop its coffee industry

—all this with a negligible adverse effect on the economy of the United States.

Population problem

The population problem is of course the most serious social and economic problem that the Island has. The threat involved in this problem will not, I believe, vary very much whether the present status is continued or independence is established. It will be a tragic problem under any circumstances. Church opposition to birth control will exist under any regime, and will cease to exist or to be effective when the problem reaches a climax, under any regime. Under the present status, opposition to birth control has also a tinge of jingoistic feeling which it would lack under independence: that is, it is looked upon by some as an attempt to impose American *mores* on the Puerto Rican people. The fact that this feeling is absurd does not make it less of a reality.

Emigration is another solution that perhaps won't vary much whatever the political status. Emigration could be arranged on a large scale to the unpopulated parts of the Dominican Republic, across the Mona Channel— emigration with land distribution to the emigrants. I do not believe that the United States could afford, especially under the Good Neighbor policy, to have hundreds of thousands of Puerto Rican American citizens on Dominican soil who would surely create an unceasing stream of diplomatic problems. Probably such emigration could only be arranged on the basis of the emigrants' acquiring Dominican citizenship after a short term of residence, or return to Puerto Rico if they did not wish to acquire it. Under such terms there would be no substantial difference in the problem if the citizenship that they relinquished was the American or the Puerto Rican.

Government under independence

From the point of view of government, there is of course the danger that Puerto Ricans will establish bad governments, as there was once a danger— when Aaron Burr was almost elected President instead of Jefferson—that the young United States would establish bad governments. On this, I want to say two things:

(1) that the danger that the United States will establish bad governments in Puerto Rico is a danger already proved by the facts.

(2) that Puerto Rico has in its development certain clear-cut differences

from other Latin American countries that have established bad governments. These differences are:

(a) that there is no wilderness in which bandit revolutions can prosper;

(b) that Puerto Rico has a peaceful tradition;

(c) that Puerto Rico has never had an army and need never have one, as the model republic of Costa Rica has not;

(d) that it has had the benefit (in most ways an undoubted benefit) of 38 years of democratic practice. (It has been democratic practice so far as the electorate is concerned, although of course not democratic in so far as the power conferred by the electorate on its representatives is petty and unreal);

(e) that it would begin its independent life not in the midst of the chaotic conditions created by revolution, but under conditions of peace, friendship, mutual understanding, cultural and economic reciprocity with the United States.

In spite of all these advantages, we may still establish bad governments. It seems to me that the establishment of bad governments by the people of Puerto Rico, or the appointment of bad governments by the government of the United States, is largely in the hands of fate. We must take our chances.

Spiritual effects of the colonial system

Also the spiritual havoc brought about by a Government that is democratic in its selection but not democratic in the powers that it is allowed to exercise, should not be underestimated. Under the colonial system Puerto Ricans have nothing to fight for politically, excepting jobs under the budget —patronage and pie, in the continental vernacular. The Governor's veto power, and Congressional veto power behind that, debar Puerto Ricans from any real broad policy-making. Only when there happens to be a sympathetic administration in the United States (the present one is the only example) can any real fundamental policies be attempted. The very pettiness of the power fought for in elections makes the elections all the cruder and sets a low standard for the qualities involved in political leadership. Last, but not least, colonial government tends to develop an attitude of bootlicking, toadying, proclamation of a 100% americanism, most proclaimers of which do not understand even 10% of what americanism in the best sense means. Imagine your children brought up in that atmosphere and you will sense how I and many other Puerto Ricans feel about it. I certainly do not want my own children to grow up and live their lives out in the spiritually corrupting atmosphere of a colony.

Independence: from U.S. viewpoint

From the viewpoint of the United States, of the American people, the ownership of Puerto Rico is as bad business as it is for the mass of the Puerto Ricans. Certainly, the workers, the farmers, the over-whelming majority of businessmen of the United States, do not make one cent's profit out of ownership of Puerto Rico by the United States.(*) A few sugar corporations do make an enormous profit out of Puerto Rico. They take out so much money produced by Puerto Rico that the island is constantly on the verge of a social collapse. As a result of this a fair-minded Administration has to supply the people of Puerto Rico, through Federal agencies and from the Federal Treasury, with part of the millions that exploitation has taken out and continues to take out of Puerto Rico. Thus you have the general body of American taxpayers, who are completely blameless for the situation, paying millions as a fine for the misdeeds of a few corporations, (some of which are not even American corporations) and in order to keep going the population that produce the absentee profits. The Americans that feed the cow are not the Americans that milk it. The hit-and-run driver that runs over the people of Puerto Rico is not the innocent taxpaying bystander who pays the hospital bill so that Puerto Rico can get out on the streets again to be run over, to go to the hospital; to be run over, to go to the hospital, to be run over—endlessly.

Reconstruction might have corrected this situation substantially and permanently for both the Puerto Rican people and the American taxpayers, if Dr. Gruening's mind had not become irrevocably twisted as a result of irrelevant circumstances. But even if this had not happened there would be no guarantees of success beyond the termination of the present Administration.

Consideration of this angle of the problem cannot be concluded without mentioning certain dangers to American producers from a possible overproduction of competing products in Puerto Rico. Without ruining Puerto Rican production, decent arrangements can be arrived at under independence that, while protecting the life of Puerto Rico, will forever safeguard American producers against a contingency that they legitimately fear.

Legislation recommended

On the basis of the foregoing comments I would suggest to the Administration the presentation of a bill along the following lines: Under thorough election safeguards (including safeguards against buying the votes of a starving population) elections for a Constitutional Convention would be called. The Constitutional Convention would draft a Constitution and submit it to the President of the United States. When approved by the President the Constitution would be submitted to the people of Puerto Rico, under the

---

(*) Producers of wheat, cotton goods, textiles, metals, machinery, petroleum products, chemical products, automobiles, and many other products that Puerto Rico cannot produce, and the handlers of said products, do have a large volume of sales in Puerto Rico which should be maintained under any reciprocity agreement, as Puerto Rico should obviously give preference to U.S. products that it cannot produce, over the rest of the world.

same election safeguards. When approved by the people of Puerto Rico, the Constitutional Convention would appoint commissioners and the President of the United States would appoint commissioners to draft a commercial reciprocity agreement. When the agreement so drafted had been approved by the President and by the Constitutional Convention, it would be submitted to the Senate of the United States for its approval. When the Senate of the United States had approved it, elections would be called in Puerto Rico, under similar election safeguards, for the election of the first Puerto Rican Government. Some time after this election, the President of the United States would proclaim the independence of Puerto Rico, the elected Government would take office, and the reciprocity agreement would go into effect simultaneously. If there is a constitutional difficulty in giving such agreement the status of a treaty because of its being approved before Puerto Rico acquired the status of a sovereign nation, it could be submitted again to the Senate, (the dates can be so close so that it would be the same Senate) to make the agreement constitutional in the United States; and in the few months elapsing the statu[s] quo in trade would be maintained. In case of disagreements in the course of this process, modifications would be made according to objections presented and that step in the process repeated. The procedure of voting on the Constitution is that used in the case of the Philippines. I believe it is a great improvement on an *a priori* plebiscite because it gives the people a chance to vote on an independence the general structure of which they know beforehand. Of course if the majority of the people were against independence as such, they could make known their will by voting against the Constitution as often as it was presented, regardless of its clauses. (It is a certainty that they would not do this.) A reasonable limit would be placed on the number of submissions of the Constitution to the people. I should be grateful for the opportunity of presenting a draft of a bill embodying these principles.

Reciprocity

I have not dwelt on any particular form for the reciprocity agreement provided in the proposed legislation because such agreement, being subject to approval by both sides to the transaction, presumably would be satisfactory to both sides whatever its exact terms might be. However, I may state here briefly my own conception of what a mutually fair reciprocity agreement would embody. In such an agreement, Puerto Rico should give an airtight preference to the United States in the Puerto Rican market for all commodities (wheat, cotton, cotton manufactures, textiles, metals, machinery, automobiles, moving pictures, coal, petroleum products, chemical products, dried meats, etc.) that Puerto Rico cannot produce. In exchange for this the United States should admit into the American market under the best possible conditions such quotas of sugar, tobacco, citrus fruits and needlework as do not impinge upon the legitimate interests of U.S. producers of these commodities. A margin of freedom should be left to Puerto Rico to negotiate with European countries for reasonable coffee quotas. The articles included in this margin should be those that the United States do not sell in quantities to Puerto Rico in any case, such as wines, olive oil, and others. The principle involved would be that Puerto Rico should give U.S. products complete preference over the products of all other nations excepting the products germane to Puerto Rico itself.

Danger of a plebiscite to U.S. prestige

A plebiscite presenting merely the abstract idea of independence involves, I believe, a certain very real danger to the United States. If the plebiscite should defeat independence, whether fairly or not, no one would believe in the genuineness of the plebiscite in Puerto Rico, in Latin America, or in the world. In the first place, I do not recall a single historical example where a people were made to vote on the naked problem of their own sovereignty as against that of another people. Plebiscites such as those held in the Saar and in Tacna-Arica, have always been to give a population caught between frontiers, so to speak, a chance to decide under which of two existing sovereignties they wish to be. If an abstract plebiscite should be lost in Puerto Rico, with the forces of the insular government controlled by the United States, with the police controlled by the United States, with the judicial machinery controlled by the United States, with money spent by Federal agencies controlled by the United States, nobody in the world would believe that the plebiscite had been fair and that Puerto Ricans had freely voted against their own sovereignity over their own country. The well-known accident of Dr. Gruening's sudden ferocious opposition to independence (the author of the so-called independence bill, no less!) would merely help to make matters worse. But even assuming complete impartiality and fairness on the part of all the United States agencies in Puerto Rico, it must be clear to you that such impartiality would simply not be believed in either by Latin America or by the rest of the world, including most people in the United States.

Conclusion

In conclusion, I should like to say that if the American people are victims of the ownership of Puerto Rico, if the mass of the Puerto Rican people also are victims of that ownership, if the logic of events and interests seems to make it quite clear that the present situacion [sic] cannot go on and that independence is the only solution,—why allow obstacles to arise irrelevantly in the way of what will eventually be to the common interest of both the American people and the Puerto Rican people? Why not establish a clear-cut policy, of which the introduction of a bill as suggested is one step and the curbing of anti-independence propaganda by high Federal officials is another? Why not move conscientiously and with a clear head and a clear objective toward the intelligent discharge of responsibilities incurred in Puerto Rico and the intelligent and friendly establishment of independence—, this process to be halted only by a repeated adverse vote of the Puerto Rican people on the Constitution submitted to them?

Of course if it should be so halted I really don't know what the United States could do with this problem. That improbable bridge, however, can be crossed when and if it is reached.

B. LETTER FROM MUÑOZ MARIN TO THE PRESIDENT

COMMONWEALTH OF PUERTO RICO
La Fortaleza, San Juan
Office of the Governor

January 17, 1953

The President of the United States,
Washington, D.C.
My dear Mr. President:

On July 25, 1952, the Commonwealth of Puerto Rico was formally installed in response to the wish of an overwhelming majority of the people of Puerto Rico pursuant to a compact between them and the Government of the United States. Puerto Rico became a Commonwealth in free and voluntary association with the United States, and its people have now attained a full measure of self-government. Accordingly, I respectfully suggest on behalf of the Commonwealth of Puerto Rico that the Government of the United States take steps to notify the United Nations of the status of Puerto Rico, that it is no longer a non–self-governing area, and that reports concerning it are no longer appropriate under Article 73(e) of the Charter.

This development has climaxed fifty-four years of growth in mutual understanding and mutual good will. Democratic rights in Puerto Rico have been progressively recognized as self-government has increased. Since 1917, the people of Puerto Rico elected all members of their legislature which had comprehensive powers to enact laws for Puerto Rico. Since 1948, the people of Puerto Rico also elected their own governor, and all other officials of Puerto Rico were locally elected or appointed by elected officials except the Auditor of Puerto Rico and the Justices of the Supreme Court. Until the

Commonwealth of Puerto Rico began to function, the latter officials were appointed by the President of the United States with the advice and consent of the United States Senate. The Congress of the United States, however, retained full jurisdiction to legislate with respect to Puerto Rico without the consent of its people, to override its laws, to change its form of government and to alter its relations to the United States.

These reservations have been to a large extent formal. In the entire fifty-four years history of United States administration of Puerto Rico, Congress did not in any instance exercise its power to annul or amend an Act of the Puerto Rican legislature, nor did it modify the relations of Puerto Rico to the United States except progressively to extend self-government to its people in response to their wishes. Even before 1948, the appointed Governor of Puerto Rico was a Puerto Rican whose selection was recommended by the majority political party of the island. After 1948, the appointed Auditor and Justices of the Supreme Courts were Puerto Ricans, also appointed with the recommendation and approval of the majority party.

This political history has been accompanied by a mutually beneficial economic relationship. The people of Puerto Rico have received many services from the Government of the United States and have benefited by grants-in-aid. Puerto Ricans have not been subject to the payment of taxes and have been entirely free of imposts, duties or any form of exactions for the support of the Federal Government. At all times since the turn of the century we have enjoyed free trade with the United States, and since 1917 we have had the benefit of common citizenship. Despite the fact that our population has grown from 953,000 inhabitants in 1900 to 2,219,000 in 1950, our standard of living has substantially increased. For example, the average per capita income in 1930 was $122.00 as compared with $319.00 in 1950.

The people of Puerto Rico have been keenly aware of our basic economic problems due to the density of population and the poverty of natural resources. We are proud of the progress that we have made and are continuing to make by the utilization of our own talents and our democratic institutions. This progress would have been impossible, however, if it had not been for the sympathetic cooperation of the United States, manifested in a wide variety of ways, material and political. We have been helped in building sounder social and educational bases for the exercise of our political rights and for our own economic advancement. Our joint efforts in combatting illiteracy and improving health conditions have produced remarkable results. In 1900 the literacy rate in Puerto Rico was 20 per cent as compared to 78 per cent in 1950; and in the same period the death rate has dropped from 25.3 per thousand to 10 per thousand.

Although the relationship was one of freedom and justice in practice, the people of Puerto Rico were not satisfied to remain in a status which appeared to reflect the imposition upon a people of the will of another community. We are proud of our culture and background, and we cherish our individual dignity and our common heritage. We profoundly believe that our government should be solidly based upon our own will and our own free choice. Accordingly, for some years, as our democratic institutions developed and became firmly established, the people considered and debated the matter of their status.

Specifically, the people of Puerto Rico discussed three choices: independence, statehood within the Federal Union, or association with the United States as a free Commonwealth. At no time did we consider that our choice was restricted, or that any alternative was foreclosed to us or could not be achieved by peaceful means; and it should be said that at no time did the United States attempt, directly or indirectly, to interfere with our choice. On the contrary, President Truman said in a message to the Congress as long ago as October 1945,

> "It is the settled policy of this Government to promote the political, social, and economic development of people who have not yet attained full self-government and eventually to make it possible for them to determine their own form of government***. It is now time, in my opinion, to ascertain from the people of Puerto Rico their wishes as to the ultimate status which they prefer, and, within such limits as may be determined by the Congress, to grant to them the kind of government which they desire."

And in his message to the Congress in January 1946, he said,

> "This Government is committed to the democratic principle that it is for the dependent peoples themselves to decide what their status shall be."

Each of the alternatives of independence, statehood, and association has been represented in Puerto Rico by a political party which favored it, and which actively campaigned for the support of the electorate and nominated candidates for the legislature and the governorship. In the 1948 elections the three alternatives were fully presented to the electorate by the three main political parties. The preference of the people, expressed in an election which was as democratic as any in the world, was unmistakably expressed in favor of the third alternative: a free Commonwealth associated with the United States on the basis of mutual consent. Their choice is aptly summed up in the Spanish name of the new body politic, "Estado Libre Asociado."

It was at the request of the officials of the Puerto Rican government acting pursuant to the mandate of the people that the Congress of the United States initiated the series of actions which resulted in the creation of the Commonwealth. On July 3, 1950, the 81st Congress enacted Public Law 600. This was, in effect, an offer by the Congress to the people of Puerto Rico, which we might accept or reject, to enter into a compact defining the status of Puerto Rico and the relationships between the respective communities. The compact offered the people of Puerto Rico an opportunity to establish our own government and to remain in association with the United States on defined terms. It was the precise formula that the people, through their elected representatives, had requested.

According to its terms, Public Law 600 was submitted to the qualified voters of Puerto Rico in a referendum held on June 4, 1951 after months of intensive debate. The Law was accepted by the people of Puerto Rico by a vote of 387,016 to 119,169. Sixty-five per cent of the eligible voters participated in the referendum. In this as in all elections in Puerto Rico, all citizens of at least 21 years of age, male or female, without property or literacy requirements, were entitled to vote.

After acceptance of Law 600, a Constitutional Convention was elected on August 27, 1951 in an election where all the qualified voters had the right to participate. The Convention met at San Juan on September 17, 1951 and proceeded to draft a Constitution. On February 6, 1952 it approved the Constitution of the Commonwealth of Puerto Rico which it had drafted, by a vote of 88 to 3. On March 3, 1952 the qualified voters of Puerto Rico again went to the polls to express approval or disapproval of the Constitution drafted by the Convention. The Constitution was ratified in this referendum by a vote of 373,594 in favor of approval and 82,877 against approval.

Pursuant to the Provisions of the Compact, the Congress of the United States on July 3, 1952, approved the Constitution of the Commonwealth of . Puerto Rico. On July 11, 1952, the Constitutional Convention of Puerto Rico by resolution accepted amendments proposed by the Congress and took the final step in ratifying the Constitution of the Commonwealth. The Commonwealth was duly installed on July 25, 1952, and the flag of Puerto Rico was raised beside the flag of the United States.

The Commonwealth of Puerto Rico, therefore, represents the government that the people of Puerto Rico have freely adopted. It reflects our own decision as to the type of institutions and the kind of relationship to the United States which we desire. There can be no doubt that in the full sense of the term, in form as well as in fact, the people of Puerto Rico are now self-governing. We have chosen our institutions and relationship with the United States. We have determined the nature and distribution of the powers of government. We have created our own Constitution under which we established our own government, the nature of which is described in Article I, Section 2 of the Constitution as follows:

> "The government of the Commonwealth of Puerto Rico shall be republican in form and its legislative, judicial and executive branches as established by this Constitution shall be equally subordinate to the sovereignty of the people of Puerto Rico."

Under this Constitution, of course, all of our officials are either elected by the people or are appointed by officials whom we elect. The legislative power of the Commonwealth under the compact and the Constitution essentially parallels that of the state governments. The laws enacted by the Government of the Commonwealth pursuant to the compact cannot be repealed or modified by external authority, and their effect and validity are subject to adjudication by the courts. Our status and the terms of our association with the United States cannot be changed without our full consent.

The people of Puerto Rico are firm supporters of the United Nations, and this great organization may confidently rely upon us for a continuation of that good will. The Government of the Commonwealth of Puerto Rico will be ready at all times to cooperate with the United States in seeking to advance the purposes and principles of the United Nations.

Sincerely yours,
LUIS MUÑOZ MARIN
Governor
Commonwealth of Puerto Rico

Notes

The following abbreviations are used in the citation of archival material:

DI/NA	Department of Interior/National Archives
FDRL	Franklin D. Roosevelt Library
HSTL	Harry S. Truman Library
LJDD/NA	Legislative, Judicial, and Diplomatic Division/ National Archives
MD,LC	Manuscript Division, Library of Congress
NSHS	Nebraska State Historical Society
OT/NA	Office of Territories/National Archives
OT/WNRC	Office of Territories/Washington National Record Center
WHMC,UMC	Western Historical Manuscript Collection, University of Missouri at Columbia

INTRODUCTION

1. Edward J. Berbusse, *The United States in Puerto Rico: 1898–1900* (Chapel Hill, N.C.: University of North Carolina Press, 1966), pp. 3–73, 56–57; Gordon K. Lewis, *Puerto Rico: Freedom and Power in the Caribbean* (New York: Harper & Row, 1963), pp. 24–27.

2. Berbusse, *The United States in Puerto Rico*, pp. 56–64.

3. The theme of changes in values and institutions is superbly treated in Henry Wells, *The Modernization of Puerto Rico: A Political Study of Changing Values and Institutions* (Cambridge, Mass.: Harvard University Press, 1969).

4. Gordon K. Lewis, *A Case*

Study in the Problems of Contemporary Federalism (Whitehall, Port-of-Spain, Trinidad, W.I.: Office of the Premier of Trinidad and Tobago, 1960), pp. 5–6.

5. *Documents on the Constitutional History of Puerto Rico* (Washington: Office of the Commonwealth of Puerto Rico, 1964), pp. 64–80, 81–112.

6. Lewis, *A Case Study*, p. 5.

7. Robert J. Hunter, "The Historical Development of the Relationship between the United States and Puerto Rico, 1898–1963" (Ph.D. diss., University of Pittsburgh, 1963), p. 406; Daniel Boorstin, "Self-discovery in Puerto Rico," *Yale Review* 45 (Dec. 1955): 229–45.

CHAPTER ONE

1. Robert W. Anderson, *Party Politics in Puerto Rico* (Stanford: Stanford University Press, 1965), p. 48.

2. Thomas Mathews, *Puerto Rican Politics and the New Deal* (Gainesville: University of Florida Press, 1960), p. 30.

3. Frank Otto Gatell, "Independence Rejected: Puerto Rico and the Tydings Bill of 1936," *Hispanic American Historical Review* 38 (Feb. 1958): 26.

4. Jerome Fischman, "The Rise and Development of the Political Party in Puerto Rico under Spanish and American Rule and the Historical Significance of the Subsequent Emergence and Growth of the Popular Party" (Ph.D. diss., New York University, 1962), see chart on p. 407.

5. The Union Republican party formed the nucleus of the *Partido Estadista Puertorriqueño* (1948, 1952) and the *Partido Estadista Republicano* (PER, in 1956 and after). In recent years the PER has become committed exclusively to statehood. In the 1968 elections, however, the PER polled less than 5 percent of the total vote for the governor, and thus lost its legal standing in terms of the Puerto Rican electoral law.

6. The Socialist party suffered a serious setback when Iglesias died in 1940. It managed to struggle on until Aug. 1, 1954, when it was formally dissolved. In the 1952 elections the party failed to poll the necessary percentage to justify continued existence in terms of the election law.

7. Anderson, *Party Politics*, pp. 34–35; Mathews, *Puerto Rican Politics*, p. 31.

8. Mathews, *Puerto Rican Politics*, pp. 16–17. Miguel A. García Méndez places the rupturing of the *Alianza* in 1930, and not 1928 as Mathews indicates. Correspondence with García Méndez, June 30, 1973.

9. Mathews, *Puerto Rican Politics*, pp. 27–28.

10. Ibid., pp. 40–41. The articles appeared in *La Democracia*, Mar. 5, 10, and 11, 1932.

11. Fischman, "The Rise and Development," p. 407.

12. *New York Times*, Mar. 1, 1936, IV, p. 5.

13. Earl Parker Hanson, *Transformation: The Story of Modern Puerto Rico* (New York: Simon & Schuster, 1955), p. 83.

14. Mathews, *Puerto Rican Politics*, pp. 32–34; *Cong. Record*, 75th Cong., 1st Sess., June 3, 1937, pp. 5275–79, a report submitted by Governor Blanton Winship on the Nationalists.

15. Mathews, *Puerto Rican Politics*, pp. 34–35, 38–39.

16. Ibid., pp. 35–44; Fischman, "The Rise and Development," p. 407. See also the previously cited re-

port by Governor Winship, *Cong. Record*, 75th Cong., 1st Sess., June 3, 1937, pp. 5275–79.

17. *Cong. Record*, 75th Cong., 1st Sess., June 3, 1937, pp. 5275–79; *New York Times*, Feb. 24, 1936, p. 1.

18. Mathews, *Puerto Rican Politics*, p. 250.

19. The Nationalist party generally boycotted elections because of its weakness at the polls. Its participation in the 1932 elections was the exception rather than the rule.

20. *Documents on the Constitutional History of Puerto Rico*, secs. 26–28, 36 of the Organic Act of 1917, pp. 95–97, 103. As a member of the United States House of Representatives, the resident commissioner can serve on Congressional committees and participate in debates on the floor, but he cannot vote.

21. Ibid., see secs. 12–24 of the Organic Act of 1917, pp. 89–95.

22. *Puerto Rico: Freedom and Power*, p. 53.

23. Pedro Muñoz Amato, "Executive Reorganization in the Government of Puerto Rico under the Elective Governor Act of 1947" (Ph.D. diss., Harvard University, 1950), chaps. 3 and 4.

24. Report by Dr. Ernest M. Hopkins to Secretary of War Dern, Jan. 18, 1934, Franklin D. Roosevelt Papers/Franklin D. Roosevelt Library (hereinafter referred to as Roosevelt Papers/FDRL), PR400, Box 46.

25. (Washington: Brookings Institution, 1930).

26. In the series *Studies in American Imperialism* (New York: Vanguard Press, 1931).

27. Samuel Rosenman (ed.), *The Public Papers and Addresses of Franklin D. Roosevelt*, vol. 2 (New York: Random House, 1938), p. 227.

28. Address by Oscar L. Chapman over NBC in Washington, Oct. 10, 1934, Oscar L. Chapman Papers/Harry S. Truman Library (hereinafter referred to as Chapman Papers/HSTL), Box 74.

29. Ibid.

30. The previously cited report by Dr. Hopkins to Dern, Jan. 18, 1934, Roosevelt Papers/FDRL, PR-400, Box 46.

31. Mathews, *Puerto Rican Politics*, pp. 104–6, 114.

32. Eleanor Roosevelt, *This I Remember* (New York: Harper & Brothers, 1949), pp. 138–39.

33. Mathews, *Puerto Rican Politics*, pp. 127–28.

34. Earl Parker Hanson, *Puerto Rico: Land of Wonders* (New York: Knopf, 1960), p. 79.

35. Mathews, *Puerto Rican Politics*, pp. 129–30.

36. Ibid., pp. 211–12.

37. Roosevelt, *This I Remember*, p. 138.

38. Mathews, *Puerto Rican Politics*, pp. 151–61.

39. Ibid., pp. 163–74.

40. Rosenman (ed.), *The Public Papers and Addresses of Franklin D. Roosevelt*, vol. 4 (New York: Random House, 1938), pp. 193–97.

41. Harold L. Ickes, *The Secret Diary of Harold Ickes, 1933–1936, the First Thousand Days*, vol. 1 (New York: Simon & Schuster, 1953), p. 594.

42. Mathews, *Puerto Rican Politics*, pp. 207–10.

43. Ibid., pp. 189–92.

44. Ibid., pp. 199–202.

45. Ibid., pp. 234–40.

46. Hanson, *Transformation*, pp. 136, 139.

47. Ibid., p. 140.

48. Ickes, *The Secret Diary*, vol. 1, p. 503.

49. Gatell, "Independence Rejected," p. 28.

50. Ickes, *The Secret Diary*, vol. 1, p. 503.

51. Ibid.

52. *New York Times*, Feb. 24, 1936, p. 1.

53. Ibid., Feb. 25, 1936, p. 1.

54. Ibid., Mar. 6, 1936, p. 12, Mar. 10, 1936, p. 14.

55. Ibid., Feb. 26, 1936, p. 9.

56. Gatell, "Independence Rejected," p. 29.

57. *Cong. Record*, 74th Cong., 2d Sess., Feb. 24, 1936, pp. 2716–17.

58. Gatell, "Independence Rejected," p. 29.

59. *New York Times*, Mar. 8, 1936, p. 29.

60. Ibid., Mar. 10, 1936, p. 11.

61. "Memorandum for Secretary Ickes," from Gruening, Mar. 13, 1936, Office of Territories/National Archives (hereinafter referred to as OT/NA), RG 126, 9-8-68.

62. Ickes, *The Secret Diary*, vol. 1, pp. 547–48.

63. Ickes to Gruening, Mar. 19, 1936, OT/NA, RG126, 9-8-68.

64. Gatell maintains that there was an earlier version predating the two of Mar. 21 and 27. He bases this observation on Ickes' reference to a draft bill in his letter to Gruening of Mar. 19, 1936. Gatell, "Independence Rejected," p. 32.

65. Gatell deals with the question of authorship of the Tydings bill. Ickes was "a passive but approving" spectator. He accepts Tydings' explanation to him in an interview that Gruening was "the motivating force of the issue." Ibid.

66. *Cong. Record*, 74th Cong., 2d Sess., Apr. 23, 1936, p. 5925.

67. *New York Times*, Apr. 24, 1936, p. 1.

68. Ibid.

69. "Memorandum for Secretary Ickes," from Muñoz Marín, Jan. 5, 1937, Office of Territories/Washington National Record Center (hereinafter referred to as OT/WNRC), 62-A-401.

70. *New York Times*, Apr. 24, 1936, p. 1.

71. "Memorandum for Gruening," from Muñoz Marín, Apr. 27, 1936, OT/NA, RG 126, 9-8-68.

72. Ibid.

73. *New York Times*, Apr. 26, 1936, IV, p. 6.

74. Ibid., Apr. 25, 1936, p. 2.

75. Ibid., Apr. 28, 1936, p. 8.

76. Ibid., Apr. 27, 1936, p. 8, May 3, 1936, IV, p. 6.

77. Ibid., Apr. 29, 1936, p. 9.

78. Ibid., Apr. 25, 1936, p. 2.

79. Mathews, *Puerto Rican Politics*, pp. 106–7.

80. "Preliminary Study by Planning Division, PRRA," May 2, 1936, OT/NA, RG 126, 9-8-68.

81. Hanson, *Transformation*, p. 160.

82. Gatell, "Independence Rejected," p. 36.

83. *Cong. Record*, 74th Cong., 2d Sess., May 7, 1936, p. 6764.

84. *New York Times*, May 18, 1936, p. 32.

85. *Cong. Record*, 74th Cong., 2d Sess., May 25, 1936, p. 7835, June 1, 1936, p. 8460.

CHAPTER TWO

1. Mathews, *Puerto Rican Politics*, pp. 290–92.

2. Ibid., pp. 258–62; *New York Times*, June 2, 1936, p. 10.

3. "Memorandum for Secretary Ickes," from Muñoz Marín, Jan. 5,

1937, OT/WNRC, RG 126, 62-A-401.

4. *New York Times*, June 2, 1936, p. 10.

5. Ibid., July 28, 1936, p. 4.

6. "Memorandum for Secretary Ickes," from Muñoz Marín, Jan. 5, 1937, OT/WNRC, RG 126, 62-A-401.

7. Ibid.

8. Mathews, *Puerto Rican Politics*, pp. 293–95.

9. Ibid., p. 295; *New York Times*, June 26, 1938, p. 8, June 28, 1936, p. 3.

10. *New York Times*, Aug. 18, 1936, p. 2; Mathews, *Puerto Rican Politics*, pp. 297–98.

11. Mathews, *Puerto Rican Politics*, p. 307.

12. Fischman, "The Rise and Development," pp. 160–62; *New York Times*, Nov. 5, 1936, p. 20.

13. "Memorandum for Secretary Ickes," from Muñoz Marín, Jan. 5, 1937, OT/WNRC, 62-A-401.

14. Mathews, *Puerto Rican Politics*, pp. 270–76, 323–24.

15. *New York Times*, Aug. 30, 1936, IV, p. 7; Hanson, *Transformation*, pp. 53–60.

16. Ickes, *The Secret Diary*, vol. 2, p. 6.

17. Mathews, *Puerto Rican Politics*, pp. 279–81.

18. Roosevelt to Gallardo, Apr. 17, 1937, in Rosenman (ed.), *The Public Papers and Addresses of Franklin D. Roosevelt*, vol. 6, pp. 160–61.

19. Mathews, *Puerto Rican Politics*, pp. 261, 267–69; *New York Times*, Mar. 2, 1931, p. 1; Thomas Aitkin, Jr., *Poet in Fortress: The Story of Luis Muñoz Marín* (New York: New American Library, 1964), pp. 113–114.

20. Mathews, *Puerto Rican Poli-*

tics, pp. 311–14; "Governor Winship's Report," *Cong. Record*, 75th Cong., 1st Sess., pp. 5275–79; Ickes, *The Secret Diary*, vol. 2, pp. 148–49, 329.

21. Muñoz Marín to Roosevelt, Apr. 19, 1939, Roosevelt Papers/FDRL, PR 400, Box 48.

22. Aitkin, *Poet in Fortress*, p. 114; Mathews, *Puerto Rican Politics*, pp. 320–21.

23. Mathews, *Puerto Rican Politics*, pp. 255–56; Hanson, *Transformation*, pp. 154–55; Gatell, "Independence Rejected," n. 30. In a letter to Gatell, Aug. 8, 1958, Muñoz Marín admitted that he had made a mistake in not issuing the statement.

24. Rexford G. Tugwell, *The Art of Politics As Practiced by Three Great Americans: Franklin Delano Roosevelt, Luis Muñoz Marin, and Fiorello H. La Guardia* (New York: Doubleday & Co., 1958), pp. 79–80, 146–48.

25. Ickes to Chapman, Feb. 5, 1937, Chapman Papers/HSTL, "General Correspondence File."

26. "Memorandum for Secretary Ickes," from Muñoz Marín, Jan. 5, 1937, OT/WNRC, RG 126, 62-A-401.

27. Muñoz Marín to Roosevelt, Apr. 19, 1937, Roosevelt Papers/FDRL, PR 400.

28. "Memorandum for Secretary Ickes," from Muñoz Marín, Jan. 5, 1937, OT/WNRC, RG 126, 62-A-401.

29. Ibid.

30. Ibid.

31. Ibid.

32. Ibid.

33. Ibid.

34. Ibid.

35. Fischman, "The Rise and Development," pp. 160–62.

36. Ibid., pp. 163–64; Tugwell, *The Art of Politics*, pp. 82–83.

37. Anderson, *Party Politics*, p. 52.

38. Fischman, "The Rise and Development," pp. 164–65; *New York Times*, June 29, 1937, p. 11.

39. Fischman, "The Rise and Development," pp. 165–74; Hanson, *Transformation*, pp. 174–76.

40. *New York Times*, July 22, 1940, p. 8.

41. Anderson, *Party Politics*, pp. 52–53.

42. Ibid., pp. 54–55.

43. Fischman, "The Rise and Development," pp. 186–87; Aitkin, *Poet in Fortress*, pp. 137–39.

44. Hanson, *Transformation*, pp. 174–76; Aitkin, *Poet in Fortress*, pp. 126–48.

45. Hanson, *Puerto Rico: Land of Wonders*, pp. 118–27; Aitkin, *Poet in Fortress*, pp. 126–48.

46. *New York Times*, July 16, 1940, p. 6.

47. *New York Times*, Nov. 7, 1940, p. 6, Nov. 9, 1940, p. 8, Feb. 10, 1941, p. 11; Fischman, "The Rise and Development," p. 407; Aitkin, *Poet in Fortress*, p. 144.

48. Fischman, "The Rise and Development," p. 91.

49. George A. Malcolm, *American Colonial Careerist: Half a Century of Official Life and Personal Experience in the Philippines and Puerto Rico* (Boston: Christopher Publishing House, 1953), pp. 238, 239.

50. "Brophy's Diary," Dec. 9, 1942, William Brophy Papers/Harry S. Truman Library (hereinafter referred to as Brophy Papers/HSTL).

51. Wells, *The Modernization of Puerto Rico*, pp. 301–4; Wells, "Ideology and Leadership in Puerto Rican Politics," *American Political Science Review* 49 (1959): 32–33.

52. *Cong. Record*, 75th Cong., 1st Sess., Feb. 18, 1937, p. 1389.

53. Gruening to Bailey W. Diffie, Feb. 27, 1937, OT/NA, RG 126, 9-8-68.

54. *Cong. Record*, 75th Cong., 1st Sess., Jan. 6, 1937, p. 101, 76th Cong., 1st Sess., Jan. 3, 1939, p. 26, June 26, 1939, p. 7931, and July 11, 1939, p. 8804.

55. *Cong. Record*, 76th Cong., 3d Sess., Apr. 12, 1940, p. 4464.

56. "Report on Political and Economic Conditions in Puerto Rico with Special reference to the Independence Question," by H. Murray-Jacoby, Mar. 11, 1937, OT/NA, RG 126, 9-8-68.

57. "The Political Status of Puerto Rico," by Benjamin Horton, Mar. 30, 1937, OT/NA, RG 126, 9-8-68.

58. "Survey of Conditions in Puerto Rico," by Walter F. McCaleb, Sept. 15, 1937, Department of Interior/National Archives (hereinafter referred to as DI/NA), RG 48, 9-8-2.

59. "Staff Report to the Interdepartmental Committee on Puerto Rico," by Dr. Eric W. Zimmerman, Sept. 9, 1940, DI/NA, RG 48, 9-8-2.

60. Harvey S. Perloff, *Puerto Rico's Economic Future: A Study in Planned Development* (Chicago: University of Chicago Press, 1950), p. 71.

61. Rexford G. Tugwell, *Puerto Rican Papers* (San Juan: Government of Puerto Rico, 1945), pp. 291–347.

CHAPTER THREE

1. See Roland Young, *Congressional Politics in the Second World*

War (New York: Columbia University Press, 1956), pp. 3–28, 218–37.

2. Fischman, "The Rise and Development," pp. 197–98.

3. Ibid.; Tugwell, *The Art of Politics*, pp. 78–79, 148.

4. *Hearings before the Senate Committee on Territories and Insular Affairs on the Nomination of Rexford G. Tugwell as Governor of Puerto Rico*, 78th Cong., 1st Sess., Aug. 6, 12, 13, and 18, 1941, pp. 1–91; *New York Times*, July 31, 1941, p. 36, Aug. 7, 1941, p. 14, Aug. 12, 1941, p. 14, Aug. 19, 1941, p. 4, Aug. 22, 1941, p. 14.

5. *New York Times*, Aug. 26, 1941, p. 2.

6. Ibid.

7. Ibid., Sept. 20, 1941, p. 7, Sept. 18, 1941, p. 4.

8. Rexford G. Tugwell, *Stricken Land: The Story of Puerto Rico* (Garden City: Doubleday & Co., 1947), p. XXIII.

9. Charles T. Goodsell, *Administration of a Revolution: Executive Reform in Puerto Rico Under Governor Tugwell, 1941–1946* (Cambridge, Mass.: Harvard University Press, 1967), pp. 16–17; *New York Times*, Sept. 14, 1941, II, p. 6.

10. Fischman, "The Rise and Development," pp. 198–201.

11. Tugwell, *Stricken Land*, pp. 172–74.

12. Fischman, "The Rise and Development," pp. 220–21.

13. Tugwell, *Stricken Land*, pp. 78, 228–29, 297; Goodsell, *Administration of a Revolution*, pp. 36–46.

14. Goodsell, *Administration of a Revolution*, pp. 45–50.

15. Ibid., pp. 50–52.

16. Tugwell, *Stricken Land*, p. 297.

17. Ibid., p. 417.

18. John C. Honey, "Public Personnel Administration in Puerto Rico" (Ph.D. diss., Syracuse University, 1950), pp. 97–98.

19. Amato, "Executive Reorganization," pp. 169–71.

20. Joseph M. Jones, "Let's Begin with Puerto Rico," *Fortune* 29 (May, 1944): 135.

21. Goodsell, *Administration of a Revolution*, pp. 61–89.

22. Enrique Lugo-Silva, *The Tugwell Administration in Puerto Rico, 1941–1946* (Rio Piedras: Editorial Cultura, 1955), p. 122.

23. "Report on the 'Five-Hundred-Acre Law,'" in Tugwell, *Puerto Rican Papers*, pp. 331–33, 339–43.

24. Lugo-Silva, *The Tugwell Administration*, pp. 126–27.

25. Ibid., pp. 122–23; Fischman, "The Rise and Development," p. 216; Perloff, *Puerto Rico's Economic Future*, pp. 76–77.

26. Lugo-Silva, *The Tugwell Administration*, p. 124. A *cuerda* is a Puerto Rican unit of land measure equal to 0.97 acre.

27. Ibid., pp. 82–85.

28. Goodsell, *Administration of a Revolution*, p. 167; Perloff, *Puerto Rico's Economic Future*, pp. 40, 380.

29. Lugo-Silva, *The Tugwell Administration*, pp. 85–87, 91–94.

30. Ibid., pp. 88–90; Goodsell, *Administration of a Revolution*, p. 174; H. C. Barton, "Puerto Rico's Industrial Development Program, 1942–1960" (Paper presented at Center for International Affairs, Cambridge, Harvard University, Oct. 29, 1959), pp. 8–10.

31. Lugo-Silva, *The Tugwell Administration*, p. 89.

32. Ibid., p. 90; Barton, "Puerto Rico's Industrial Development Program," p. 9.

33. Tugwell, *Stricken Land*, p. 255.

34. Goodsell, *Administration of a Revolution*, pp. 177–78; Barton, "Puerto Rico's Industrial Development Program," p. 10; Tugwell, *Stricken Land*, p. 683.

35. Perloff, *Puerto Rico's Economic Future*, pp. 39–40; Lugo-Silva, *The Tugwell Administration*, pp. 131–33.

36. Perloff, *Puerto Rico's Economic Future*, table 10, p. 58.

37. Barton, "Puerto Rico's Industrial Development Program," p. 11.

38. Fischman, "The Rise and Development," pp. 204–6.

39. *Cong. Record*, 77th Cong., 2d Sess., Feb. 17, 1942, p. A583.

40. Ibid., Feb. 18, 1942, p. A619.

41. Ibid., Feb. 18, 1942, p. A619, Feb. 23, 1942, p. A691.

42. Ibid., Feb. 23, 1942, p. A691, Feb. 24, 1942, p. A699, Feb. 25, 1942, p. A727, Mar. 9, 1942, p. A919, Mar. 30, 1942, p. A1277, Mar. 17, 1942, p. A1060, Apr. 2, 1942, p. A1309, Apr. 9, 1942, p. A1361.

43. Ibid., Mar. 6, 1942, p. A871, Mar. 23, 1942, p. A1139.

44. Pagán to Truman, Feb. 24, 1942, Harry S. Truman Papers/Harry S. Truman Library (hereinafter referred to as Truman Papers/HSTL), official file.

45. Tugwell, *Stricken Land*, pp. 387–88; *New York Times*, June 29, 1942, p. 17.

46. Muñoz Marín to Roosevelt, Jan. 19, 1942, Roosevelt Papers/FDRL, PR 400.

47. Muñoz Marín to Truman, Feb. 10, 1942, Truman Papers/HSTL, official file.

48. Puerto Rican House to Roosevelt, Feb. 10, 1942, Roosevelt Papers/FDRL, PR 400.

49. Puerto Rican Senate to Roosevelt, Feb. 13, 1942, Roosevelt Papers/FDRL, PR 400.

50. Tugwell, *Stricken Land*, p. 387.

51. Ickes to Tugwell, Jan. 27, 1942, DI/NA, RG 48, 9-8-1.

52. Tugwell to Ickes, Feb. 17, 1942, DI/NA, RG 48, 9-8-1.

53. Ickes to Hoover, Feb. 25, 1942, DI/NA, RG 48, 9-8-1.

54. Pagán to Ickes, Apr. 10, 1942, Ickes to Pagán, Apr. 13, 1942, DI/NA, RG 48, 9-8-1.

55. *New York Times*, Aug. 25, 1942, p. 10.

56. Ibid., Oct. 27, 1942, p. 11, Nov. 15, 1942, III, p. 1, Nov. 16, 1942, p. 10.

57. *Cong. Record*, 77th Cong., 2d Sess., Oct. 20, 1942, p. 8392.

58. Ibid., Nov. 27, 1942, pp. 9144–52.

59. Ibid., Nov. 19, 1942, p. 9002; *House Report 2641*, 77th Cong., 2d Sess.; *New York Times*, Nov. 28, 1942, p. 16.

60. *New York Times*, Nov. 19, 1942, p. 15.

61. *Hearings before a Subcommittee of the Senate Committee on Territories and Insular Affairs pursuant to S. Res. 309, a resolution authorizing an investigation of economic and social conditions in Puerto Rico*, 77th Cong., 2d Sess., Dec. 7, 8, 9, and 17, 1942. Report to be found in appendix in *Hearings before a Subcommittee of the Senate Committee on Territories and Insular Affairs pursuant to S. Res. 26 on economic and social conditions in Puerto Rico*, 77th Cong., 2d Sess., Feb. 10–19, 1943, pp. 299–322.

62. *Cong. Record*, 78th Cong., 1st Sess., Jan. 7, 1943, pp. 37, 49, 252; *New York Times*, Jan. 4, 1943, p. 10.

63. *Senate Report 15*, 78th

Cong., 1st Sess., Jan. 21, 1943; *New York Times*, Jan. 19, 1943, p. 17; *La Prensa* (New York), Jan. 19, 1943, p. 1.

64. Ickes to Tydings, Jan. 27, 1943, OT/NA, RG 126, 9-8-68.

65. Press Conference, Feb. 4, 1943, OT/NA, RG 126, 9-8-68; communications concerning recall of elected officials: Muñoz Marín to Ickes, Dec. 21, 1943, Ickes to Muñoz Marín, Jan. 9, 1943, OT/NA, RG 126, 9-8-68.

66. Ickes to Bell, Feb. 9, 1943, OT/NA, RG 126, 9-8-68.

67. Warner G. Gardner's memorandum to B. W. Thoron, Feb. 17, 1943, OT/NA, RG 126, 9-8-68.

68. *Hearings before the House Committee on Insular Affairs on HR 784, providing for the term of office of the Governor of Puerto Rico*, 78th Cong., 1st Sess., Feb. 16, 18, 24, 26, 1943, pp. 34, 35–41.

69. *Cong. Record*, 78th Cong., 2d Sess., Apr. 1, 1944, p. 3407, Dec. 4, 1944, pp. 8714, 9020; *House Report 2038*, 78th Cong., 2d Sess., Dec. 7, 1944.

70. *Cong. Record*, 78th Cong., 1st Sess., Jan. 11, 1943, p. 112.

71. Quoted in Fischman, "The Rise and Development," p. 238.

72. "Brophy's Diary," Dec. 1942, Brophy Papers/HSTL.

73. Tugwell, *Stricken Land*, pp. 463–64.

74. *Cong. Record*, 78th Cong., 1st Sess., Jan. 7, 1943, p. 42, Jan. 21, 1943, p. 252, Jan. 28, 1943, p. 415, Mar. 27, 1943, p. 2575, Mar. 29, 1943, p. 2610, Apr. 10, 1943, pp. 3630–33.

75. *Hearings before a Subcommittee of the Senate Committee on Territories and Insular Affairs pursuant to S. Res. 26 on economic and social conditions in Puerto Rico*,

77th Cong., 2d Sess., Feb. 10–19, 1943, pts. 1 and 2.

76. Tugwell, *Stricken Land*, p. 470.

77. *Senate Report 628*, 78th Cong., 1st Sess., Dec. 21, 1943, pp. 1–56; Lugo-Silva, *The Tugwell Administration*, p. 99.

78. *Hearings before a Subcommittee of the House Committee on Insular Affairs pursuant to H. Res. 159 for the investigation of political, economic, and social conditions in Puerto Rico*, 78th Cong., 1st Sess., Apr.–July, Nov.–Dec., 1943, Mar.–May, 1944, 14 pts.

79. Vernon E. Moore (clerk of the subcommittee) to Ohio Representative Robert F. Jones, Aug. 28, 1944, Jasper Bell Papers/Western Historical Manuscript Collection, University of Missouri at Columbia (hereinafter referred to as Bell Papers/WHMC, UMC), f. 7926.

80. *House Report 497*, 79th Cong., 1st Sess., May 1, 1945, p. 36.

81. Ibid., pp. 38–41.

82. Tugwell to Ickes, June 18, 1943, OT/NA, RG 126, 9-8-68.

83. Thoron to Bell, July 7, 1943, Brophy Papers/HSTL.

84. Ickes to Bell, Nov. 1, 1943, Bell to Ickes, Nov. 16, 1943, f. 8214, f. 8196, Bell Papers/WHMC, UMC; *House Report 810*, 78th Cong., 1st Sess., pt. I, Nov. 1, 1943, pt. II, Nov. 23, 1943.

CHAPTER FOUR

1. Tugwell, *The Art of Politics*, pp. 151–52.

2. Tugwell to Roosevelt, Mar. 11, 1942, OT/NA, RG 126, 9-8-68.

3. Tugwell, *Stricken Land*, p. 328.

4. *Cong. Record*, 77th Cong., 2d Sess., July 6, 1942, p. 6003.

5. Ickes to Pagán, Aug. 7, 1942, OT/NA, RG 126, 9-8-68.

6. Fortas to Leo Kocialkowlski, Aug. 26, 1942, OT/NA, RG 126, 9-8-68.

7. Ickes to Tugwell, Aug. 7, 1942, OT/NA, RG 126, 9-8-68.

8. Pagán to Roosevelt, Nov. 17, 1942, Roosevelt to Pagán, Nov. 30, 1942, OT/NA, RG 126, 9-8-68.

9. Tugwell, *Puerto Rican Public Papers*, p. 136.

10. Ibid., pp. 151–52, 153, 175.

11. *New York Times*, Feb. 5, 1943, p. 13.

12. Muñoz Marín, Iriarte, Ramírez Santibáñez to Ickes, Feb. 5, 1943, OT/NA, RG 126, 9-8-68.

13. *New York Times*, Feb. 11, 1943, p. 6.

14. Ickes to Roosevelt, Mar. 3, 1943, OT/NA, RG 126, 9-8-68.

15. *Cong. Record*, 78th Cong., 1st Sess., Mar. 9, 1943, p. 1686.

16. Roosevelt to Fortas et al., Mar. 8, 1943, Roosevelt Papers/ FDRL, PR 400.

17. Tugwell, *Stricken Land*, pp. 493–97.

18. Ibid.

19. Pagán to Roosevelt, Mar. 10, 1943, OT/NA, RG 126, 9-8-68.

20. Puerto Rican legislature to Ickes, Mar. 10, 1943, Mar. 11, 1943, OT/NA, RG 126, 9-8-68.

21. Newspaper clippings, Mar. 15, 1943, OT/NA, RG 126, 9-8-68.

22. *La Prensa*, Mar. 15, 1943, p. 1, Mar. 16, 1943, p. 2, Mar. 29, 1943, p. 2.

23. *Cong. Record*, 78th Cong., 1st Sess., Mar. 9, 1943, p. 1686.

24. Fortas to Ickes, Mar. 27, 1943, OT/NA, RG 126, 9-8-68.

25. *Cong. Record*, 78th Cong., 1st Sess., Apr. 2, 1943, p. 2835; *Hearings before the Senate Committee on Territories and Insular Affairs on S.952, a bill to provide for the withdrawal of sovereignty of the United States over the Island of Puerto Rico and for the Recognition of Its Independence* (hereinafter referred to as *Hearings before the Senate Committee on Territories and Insular Affairs on S.952*), 78th Cong., 1st Sess., May, 1943, pp. 1–6.

26. Ickes to Tydings, Apr. 23, 1943, OT/NA, RG 126, 9-8-68.

27. Concurrent Resolution, Apr. 24, 1943, OT/NA, RG 126, 9-8-68.

28. *Hearings before the Senate Committee on Territories and Insular Affairs on S.952*, 78th Cong., 1st Sess., May, 1943, pp. 9–11.

29. Ibid., pp. 20–21.

30. Ibid., passim.

31. Ickes to Tydings, May 13, 1943, OT/NA, RG 126, 9-8-68.

32. *La Prensa*, Apr. 13, 1943, p. 2, May 21, 1943, p. 2.

33. Ibid., May 26, 1943, p. 1.

34. *New York Times*, July 7, 1943, p. 10.

35. Morgenthau to Tydings, July 13, 1943, Legislative, Judicial and Diplomatic Division/National Archives (hereinafter referred to as LJDD/NA), RG 148, 14977, file on S.952.

36. "Memorandum for B. W. Thoron," from Jack Fahy, n.d., OT/ NA, RG 126, 9-8-68. See also "Memorandum for the Under-Secretary," from R. C. Durham, Apr. 12, 1943, OT/NA, RG 126, 9-8-68.

37. "Memorandum for the Secretary," from Fortas, Mar. 18, 1943, OT/NA, RG 126, 9-8-68.

38. News reports extracted from *El Mundo* (San Juan, Puerto Rico), OT/NA, RG 126, 9-8-68.

39. *New York Times*, July 20, 1943, p. 13.

40. *Meeting of the President's Committee to Revise the Organic*

Act of Puerto Rico (hereinafter referred to as the *Meeting of the President's Committee*), July 19–Aug. 7, 1943, in appendix of *Hearings before a Subcommittee of the Senate Committee on Territories and Insular Affairs on S.1407, a bill to amend the Organic Act of Puerto Rico*, 78th Cong., 1st Sess., pp. 491–97, passim.

41. Ibid.

42. Ibid., pp. 354–82.

43. Ibid., passim; Tugwell, *Stricken Land*, p. 555.

44. Ickes to Roosevelt, Aug. 31, 1943, Roosevelt Papers/FDRL, PR 400.

45. *Cong. Record*, 78th Cong., 1st Sess., Sept. 28, 1943, pp. 7841–42; *New York Times*, Sept. 29, 1943, p. 28.

46. *Cong. Record*, 78th Cong., 1st Sess., Oct. 1, 1943, p. 7959.

47. *New York Times*, Oct. 3, 1943, p. 17.

48. *Hearings before a Subcommittee of the Senate Committee on Territories and Insular Affairs on S.1407, a bill to amend the Organic Act of Puerto Rico*, 78th Cong., 1st Sess., Nov. 16, 17, 18, 24, 25, 26, Dec. 1, 1943, pp. 6–17, 33–136, passim.

49. Thoron to Tugwell, Nov. 18, 1943, Tugwell to Thoron, Dec. 6, 1943, Ickes to Chavez, Jan. 6, 1944, Thoron to Tugwell, Jan. 15, 1944, OT/NA, RG 126, 9-8-68.

50. *Senate Report 659*, 78th Cong., 2d Sess., Feb. 2, 1944, pp. 1–9.

51. Ibid.

52. Translated excerpts from *El Mundo*, Feb. 7, 1944, OT/NA, RG 126, 9-8-68.

53. Brophy to Fortas, Feb. 8, 1944, "Analysis of S.1407," by Tug-

well, Feb. 21, 1944, OT/NA, RG 126, 9-8-68.

54. *Cong. Record*, 78th Cong., 2d Sess., Feb. 15, 1944, pp. 1663–70, Feb. 18, 1944, p. 1870.

55. *House Report 810*, 78th Cong., 1st Sess., pt. I, Nov. 1, 1943; *Cong. Record*, 78th Cong., 2nd Sess., Feb. 7, 1944, p. 1311, Mar. 20, 1944, p. 2706.

56. "Memorandum for Under-Secretary Fortas," from Brophy, Apr. 14, 1944, OT/NA, RG 126, 9-8-68.

57. *La Prensa*, Mar. 16, 1944, p. 1, Mar. 17, 1944, p. 2.

58. *Cong. Record*, 78th Cong., 2d Sess., Apr. 1, 1944, p. 3407.

59. Henry A. Hirshberg to Thoron, May 4, 1944, OT/NA, RG 126, 9-8-68.

60. "Memorandum for Secretary Ickes," from Fortas, May 4, 1944, OT/NA, RG 126, 9-8-68.

61. Thoron to Tugwell, June 9, 1944, OT/NA, RG 126, 9-8-68.

62. *La Prensa*, Mar. 28, 1944, p. 1.

63. "Memorandum for Under-Secretary Fortas," from Brophy, Apr. 14, 1944, OT/NA, RG 126, 9-8-68.

64. Ickes to Bell, June 23, 1944, OT/NA, RG 126, 9-8-68.

65. Mr. Fortas explained his position to the author thus, "I was optimistic that if we could make an initial breakthrough, even though it was far short of the desirable reform, the people of Puerto Rico would demonstrate their capacity for self-government and Congress would be reassured that a relaxation of United States control would not lead to chaos and the anti-Americanism which some of the influential members of Congress feared." Correspondence with author, June 9, 1971.

66. *Hearing before the House Committee on Insular Affairs on*

S.1407, a bill to amend the Organic Act to provide a civil government for Puerto Rico and other purposes (hereinafter referred to as *Hearing before the House Committee on Insular Affairs on S.1407*), 78th Cong., 2d Sess., Aug. 26, 1944, pp. 23–27.

67. Tugwell to Muñoz Marín et al., Apr. 18, 1944, OT/NA, RG 126, 9-8-68.

68. Tugwell to Fortas, May 1, 1944, OT/NA, RG 126, 9-8-68.

69. *Hearing before the House Committee on Insular Affairs on S.1407*, 78th Cong., 2d Sess., Aug. 26, 1944, pp. 27–35, 35–38.

70. Fortas to Rosenman, Aug. 26, 1944, OT/NA, RG 126, 9-8-68.

71. Fortas to Welch, Aug. 28, 1944, OT/NA, RG 126, 9-8-68.

72. Roosevelt to Bell, Aug. 29, 1944, Roosevelt Papers/FDRL, PR 400.

73. Bell to Roosevelt, Sept. 5, 1944, Roosevelt Papers/FDRL, PR 400.

74. Bell to Woodruff (position?), Dec. 9, 1944, Bell Papers/WHMC, UMC, 2306, f. 8147.

75. Muñoz Marín to Ickes, Nov. 13, 1944, OT/NA, RG 126, 9-8-68.

76. Ickes to Muñoz Marín, Nov. 30, 1944, OT/NA, RG 126, 9-8-68.

77. *Cong. Record*, 78th Cong., 2d Sess., Dec. 4 and 7, 1944, pp. 8714, 9020; *House Report 2038*, 78th Cong., 2d Sess., Dec. 7, 1944, pp. 1–2.

78. Ickes to McCormack, Dec. 6, 1944, Dec. 11, 1944, OT/NA, RG 126, 9-8-68.

79. *New York Times*, Dec. 9, 1944, p. 7.

80. In contrast, the Elective Governor Act of 1947 was considerably the result of close cooperation and consultation between the Republican-dominated Eightieth Congress and the Democratic administration of Harry S. Truman. See chap. 6.

81. Joseph M. Jones, "Let's Begin with Puerto Rico," *Fortune* 29 (May, 1944): 135–36.

82. Ibid., pp. 135–36, 186.

CHAPTER FIVE

1. Emil J. Sady, *The United Nations and Dependent Peoples* (Washington: Brookings Institution, 1956), pp. 3–28; James N. Murray, Jr., *The United Nations Trusteeship System* (Urbana: University of Illinois Press, 1957), chaps. 1 and 2; Charmian E. Toussaint, *The Trusteeship System of the United Nations* (London: Stevens & Sons, 1956), chaps. 1 and 2.

2. Anderson, *Party Politics*, p. 56.

3. *Hearings before the Senate Committee on Territories and Insular Affairs on S.952, a bill to provide for the withdrawal of the sovereignty of the United States over the island of Puerto Rico, and for the recognition of its independence*, 78th Cong., 1st Sess., May, 1943, pp. 57–80.

4. *La Prensa*, July 27, 1943, p. 2.

5. Cited in Anderson, *Party Politics*, p. 97.

6. Ibid.

7. Ibid., pp. 97–98; *La Prensa*, Aug. 16, 1943, p. 2; *New York Times*, Aug. 16, 1943, p. 5.

8. Anderson, *Party Politics*, p. 98.

9. See chap. 4.

10. Anderson, *Party Politics*, pp. 98–99.

11. *La Prensa*, Oct. 22, 1943, p. 1.

12. Ibid., Jan. 24, 1944, p. 1,

May 27, 1944, p. 1, May 29, 1944, p. 1, July 29, 1944, p. 2.

13. Ibid., July 28, 1944, p. 2.
14. Ibid., July 31, 1944, p. 2.
15. Ibid., Aug. 9, 1944, p. 2.
16. Ibid., Aug. 1, 1944, p. 2, Aug. 2, 1944, p. 2, Aug. 3, 1944, p. 2, Aug. 7, 1944, p. 2, Aug. 8, 1944, p. 2, Aug. 10, 1944, p. 1, Aug. 11, 1944, p. 2, Aug. 14, 1944, p. 2, Aug. 15, 1944, p. 2, Aug. 18, 1944, p. 2.
17. Ibid., Aug. 28, 1944, p. 2.
18. Anderson, *Party Politics*, pp. 56–57.
19. Ibid., pp. 57–58.
20. Correspondence with Vicente Geigel Polanco, Mar., 1973. Mr. Geigel Polanco was the acting president of the *independentista* meeting.
21. *New York Times*, Dec. 11, 1944, p. 4; Fischman, "The Rise and Development," pp. 304–5.
22. *New York Times*, Dec. 26, 1944, p. 13.
23. Anderson, *Party Politics*, p. 100; Fischman, "The Rise and Development," p. 306.
24. Tugwell to Fortas, Dec. 11, 1944, DI/NA, RG 48, 9-8-2.
25. Ickes to Fortas, Dec. 19, 1944, DI/NA, RG 48, 9-8-2.
26. Fortas to Tugwell, Dec. 19, 1944, DI/NA, RG 48, 9-8-2.
27. *Cong. Record*, 79th Cong., 1st Sess., Jan. 10, 1945, p. 159.
28. *Hearings before the Senate Committee on Territories and Insular Affairs on S.227, a bill to provide for the withdrawal of the sovereignty of the United States over the Island of Puerto Rico and for the recognition of its independence* (hereinafter referred to as *Hearings before the Senate Committee on Territories and Insular Affairs on S.227*), 79th Cong., 1st Sess., Mar., Apr., May, 1945, pp. 1–8.

29. *La Prensa*, Mar. 19, 1945, p. 2.
30. *Cong. Record*, 79th Cong., 1st Sess., Mar. 26, 1945, p. 2795; Anderson, *Party Politics*, p. 100.
31. *New York Times*, May 4, 1945, p. 11. See also Leslie Highley, "Puerto Rico Pushes Independence," *Washington Post*, Apr. 1, 1945, II, p. 6.
32. Tugwell, *The Stricken Land*, p. 508.
33. *La Prensa*, Jan. 22, 1945, p. 2.
34. Tugwell, *Puerto Rican Public Papers*, p. 265.
35. Muñoz Marín to Ickes, Feb. 23, 1945, OT/NA, RG 126, 9-8-68.
36. *Cong. Record*, 79th Cong., 1st Sess., Mar. 6, 1945, p. 1752.
37. Lugo-Silva, *The Tugwell Administration*, p. 62.
38. *Hearings before the Senate Committee on Territories and Insular Affairs on S.227*, 79th Cong., 1st Sess., Mar. 5, 6, 7, 8, 1945, Apr. 23, 24, 26, 27, 1945, May 1, 8, 1945, passim.
39. Ickes to Tydings, Mar. 3, 1945, OT/NA, RG 126, 9-8-68.
40. Anderson, *Party Politics*, p. 58.
41. "Balance Sheet of Interests," from Fahy to B. W. Thoron, Apr. 4, 1945, OT/NA, RG 126, 9-8-68.
42. Ibid.
43. Ibid.
44. In Nov., 1945, Assistant Secretary of the Interior Oscar L. Chapman organized a debate among Interior's staff, and invited policy papers. Fahy submitted the memorandum he prepared in Apr., 1945. A critique was delivered by Brophy, who believed that Puerto Rico's answer lay in the dominion status. Brophy Papers/HSTL, Box 14.

45. Tugwell to Ickes, Apr. 23, 1945, OT/NA, RG 126, 9-8-68.

46. "Memorandum for the Secretary," from Thoron, May 5, 1945, OT/NA, RG 126, 9-8-68.

47. Ibid.

48. *Washington Post*, May 6, 1945, II, p. 2.

49. *Hearings before the Senate Committee on Territories and Insular Affairs on S.227*, 79th Cong., 1st Sess., May 7, 1945, pp. 373–75.

50. Ibid., p. 389.

51. *La Prensa*, May 14, 1945, p. 1.

52. *Cong. Record*, 79th Cong., 1st Sess., May 15, 1945, p. 4587, May 16, 1945, p. 4684.

53. Anderson, *Party Politics*, p. 58.

54. "Digest of S.1002," May, 1945, OT/NA, RG 126, 9-8-68.

55. *La Prensa*, June 2, 1945, p. 1.

56. Ibid., June 16, 1945, p. 2.

57. Muñoz Marín to Truman, July 25, 1945, Truman Papers/HSTL, PR 400.

58. *La Prensa*, July 16, 1945, p. 2.

59. Ibid., Aug. 2, 1945, p. 2.

60. Thomas L. Karsten (aide to Tugwell) to Rosenman, Aug. 29, 1945, Samuel Rosenman Papers/Harry S. Truman Library (hereinafter referred to as Rosenman Papers/HSTL), PR 400.

61. Rosenman to Tugwell, Sept. 29, 1945, Rosenman Papers/HSTL, PR 400.

62. Rosenman to Tugwell, Oct. 3, 1945, Tydings to Rosenman, Oct. 3, 1945, "Memorandum for President Truman," from Rosenman, Oct. 3, 1945, Rosenman Papers/HSTL, PR 400.

63. Muñoz Marín to Ickes, Oct.

8, 1945, Ickes to Muñoz Marín, Oct. 29, 1945, OT/NA, RG 126, 9-8-68.

64. Tugwell to Fortas, Oct. 10, 1945, Fortas to Tugwell, Oct. 26, 1945, OT/NA, RG 126, 9-8-68.

65. "Memorandum for President Truman," from Rosenman, Oct. 11, 1945, Rosenman Papers/HSTL, PR 400.

66. *Cong. Record*, 79th Cong., 1st Sess., Oct. 16, 1945, p. 9676.

67. *La Prensa*, Sept. 20, 1945, p. 1.

68. *New York Times*, Oct. 18, 1945, p. 2.

69. Tydings to Butler et al., Oct. 26, 1945, Hugh Butler Papers/Nebraska State Historical Society (hereinafter referred to as Butler Papers/NSHS), Folder on Territories and Insular Affairs Committee.

70. *La Prensa*, Nov. 28, 1945, p. 1.

71. Muñoz Marín to Tydings, Dec. 1, 1945, Tydings to Muñoz Marín, Dec. 3, 1945, Muñoz Marín to Tydings, Dec. 12, 1945, LJDD/NA, RG 148, 14977, File on S.227.

72. Muñoz Marín to Bell, Dec. 1, 1945, Bell to Muñoz Marín, Dec. 3, 1945, Bell Papers/WHMC,UMC, 2306, f. 8175.

73. *La Prensa*, Dec. 4, 1945, p. 1.

74. Ibid., Dec. 7, 1945, p. 1.

75. Ibid., Dec. 29, 1945, p. 1.

76. Muñoz Marín to Chapman, Feb. 27, 1946, OT/NA, RG 126, 9-8-98/104. The two bills are discussed in chap. 6 in a somewhat different context.

77. *La Prensa*, Dec. 15, 1945, p. 1.

78. *New York Times*, Mar. 3, 1946, p. 8.

79. Ibid., Mar. 5, 1946, p. 4.

80. Ibid., Mar. 3, 1946, p. 8.

81. Ibid., Apr. 22, 1946, p. 2.

82. *La Prensa*, Apr. 26, 1946, p. 1.

83. Ibid., May 23, 1946, p. 2.

84. Silverman to Day (full name and position unknown), Apr. 25, 1946, DI/NA, RG 48, 9-8-2.

85. Krug to Bailey, May 3, 1946, DI/NA, RG 48, 9-8-2.

86. Ibid.

87. Truman to Tugwell (draft letters probably not sent), May 3, 1946, DI/NA, RG 48, 9-8-2.

88. Truman to Tugwell, May 16, 1945, Truman Papers/HSTL, PR 400.

89. See chap. 2 for details of the "Memorandum for Secretary Ickes," from Muñoz Marín, Jan. 5, 1937, OT/NA, RG 126, 9-8-68.

90. "Memorandum for the Secretary," from Thoron, May 5, 1945, OT/NA, RG 126, 9-8-68.

91. *La Prensa*, Sept. 15, 1945, p. 2, Sept. 17, 1945, p. 2, Sept. 21, 1945, p. 1.

92. Ibid., Oct. 6, 1945, p. 2.

93. Anderson, *Party Politics*, p. 102.

94. Ibid.

95. *La Prensa*, Feb. 13, 1946, p. 2.

96. Ibid., Feb. 16, 1946, p. 2, Feb. 10, 1946, p. 2.

97. U.S. Tariff Commission Report, Mar. 1946, OT/NA, RG 126, 9-8-68; *New York Times*, Mar. 29, 1946, p. 13; *La Prensa*, Mar. 28, 1946, p. 2.

98. Anderson, *Party Politics*, p. 61.

99. Ibid., pp. 61–62.

100. Ibid.

101. Ibid., pp. 102–3.

CHAPTER SIX

1. *New York Times*, Dec. 21, 1945, p. 19. However, rumor of the resignation and speculation as to the successor circulated nearly six months before that date. See *La Prensa*, June 28, 1945, p. 1, Aug. 13, 1945, p. 2, Aug. 22, 1945, p. 2.

2. "Memorandum for the Secretary [Ickes]," from Arnold, Jan. 31, 1946, OT/NA, RG 126, 9-8-98/104.

3. "Memorandum for the Secretary [Ickes]," from Arnold, Jan. 31, 1946, OT/NA, RG 126, 9-8-98/104.

4. Ibid.

5. Ibid.

6. Arnold to Secretary Krug, Apr. 8, 1946, DI/NA, RG 48, 9-8-2.

7. "Memorandum for Secretary Krug," from Silverman, May 9, 1946, OT/NA, RG 126, 9-8-68.

8. Krug to Truman, June 5, 1946, DI/NA, RG 48, 9-8-2. Names of the continental members suggested by Krug were: former Justice Owen J. Roberts (chairman), Senators Tydings of Maryland and Taft of Ohio, and Representatives Bell of Missouri and Welch of California. The Puerto Rican members suggested were: Senators Muñoz Marín and Iriarte, Resident Commissioner Piñero, and Justice Cordova Diaz.

9. Truman to Krug, June 8, 1946, Arnold to Chapman, June 11, 1946, Chapman to Truman, June 13, 1946, OT/NA, RG 126, 9-8-68.

10. Muñoz Marín to Truman, Feb. 19, 1946, OT/NA, RG 126, 9-8-98/104.

11. *La Prensa*, June 28, 1945, p. 1, Aug. 13, 1945, p. 2, Aug. 22, 1945, p. 2; Tugwell, *Stricken Land*, p. 591.

12. News items on ticker, Feb. 19, 1946, OT/NA, RG 126, 9-8-98/104.

13. The two bills are discussed in a somewhat different context in chap. 5.

14. Muñoz Marín to Chapman, Feb. 27, 1946, OT/NA, RG 126, 9-8-98/104.

15. Ibid.

16. *New York Times*, Mar. 3, 1946, p. 8.

17. Chapman to Tugwell, Mar. 15, 1946, OT/NA, RG 126, 9-8-98/ 104.

18. Muñoz Marín to Krug, June 19, 1946, OT/NA, RG 126, 9-8-98/ 104.

19. Krug to Chapman (telephone, 11:15 A.M.), June 26, 1946, Julius A. Krug Papers/Manuscript Division, Library of Congress (hereinafter referred to as Krug Papers/ MD, LC), Box 48.

20. Chapman to Krug (telephone, 2:30 P.M.), June 28, 1946, Krug Papers/MD, LC, Box 48.

21. *New York Times*, July 10, 1946, p. 44.

22. Krug to Truman, July 16, 1946, OT/NA, RG 126, 9-8-104.

23. *La Prensa*, July 21, 1946, p. 1.

24. *New York Times*, July 26, 1946, p. 22; *La Prensa*, July 26, 1946, p. 1, July 30, 1946, p. 2, Aug. 1, 1946, p. 2, Aug. 3, 1946, p. 1.

25. *New York Times*, July 27, 1946, p. 16.

26. In *Cong. Record*, 79th Cong., 2d Sess., July 26, 1946, p. A4461.

27. In *Cong. Record*, 79th Cong., 2d Sess., Aug. 1, 1946, pp. A4731–32.

28. *La Prensa*, July 27, 1946, p. 4.

29. *New York Times*, Sept. 4, 1946, p. 8.

30. Congressional Quarterly Service, *Politics in America 1945– 1966: The Politics and Issues of the Postwar Years* (Washington, 1967), pp. 3–4.

31. *New York Times*, Aug. 13, 1946, p. 16.

32. Chapman joined the Roose-

velt administration in 1933 as Interior's assistant secretary. In May, 1946, he became undersecretary in place of Abe Fortas.

33. Krug to Truman, Aug. 5, 1946, Truman Papers/HSTL, PR 400; Truman to Piñero, Oct. 26, 1946, Truman Papers/HSTL, folder on "Territories and Possessions"; *New York Times*, Nov. 9, 1946, p. 6; *La Prensa*, Aug. 13, 1946, p. 1, Nov. 9, 1946, p. 1.

34. *La Prensa*, Jan. 17, 1947, p. 2, Jan. 30, 1947, p. 1.

35. Dr. Fernós-Isern states that he agreed to support the measure but did not wish to be identified as the sponsor because he had publicly committed himself a year before to a status formula not unlike the Commonwealth status of 1950. Correspondence with Fernós-Isern, Aug., 1972.

36. *La Prensa*, Feb. 3, 1947, p. 2.

37. Ibid., Feb. 10, 1947, p. 1.

38. From 1947 forward, all Puerto Rican matters were handled by the Public Lands Committee or its subcommittees. The House and the Senate Public Lands Committee incorporated the functions and duties of the old Territories and Insular Affairs Committee. See *Public Law 601*, 79th Cong., 2d Sess., Aug. 2, 1946, p. 819, 827.

39. *New York Times*, Feb. 12, 1947, p. 20.

40. *La Prensa*, Feb. 25, 1947, p. 1.

41. Article by Fernós-Isern, Ibid., Aug. 6, 1947, p. 1.

42. Ibid., Feb. 26, 1947, p. 1.

43. Ibid., Mar. 13, 1947, p. 1.

44. Krug to Fernós-Isern, Mar. 27, 1947, OT/NA, RG 126, 9-8-68; *La Prensa*, Apr. 16, 1947, p. 1.

45. *Cong. Record*, 80th Cong.,

1st Sess., Jan. 7, 1945, p. 125; *New York Times*, Jan. 15, 1947, p. 18, Jan. 24, 1947, p. 3, Feb. 3, 1947, p. 22, Mar. 8, 1947, p. 1.

46. *Cong. Record*, 80th Cong., 1st Sess., Apr. 24, 1947, p. 3897; *New York Times*, Apr. 25, 1947, p. 13.

47. Chapman to Butler, July 22, 1947, Chapman Papers/HSTL, Box 107.

48. Fernós-Isern p e r s u a d e d Crawford to introduce the bill in the House. He did not wish to sponsor it, for the reason already stated in note 35.

49. *Cong. Record*, 80th Cong., 1st Sess., Apr. 29, 1947, p. 4183, May 2, 1947, p. 4478.

50. *Hearing before the House Subcommittee on Territories and Insular Possessions of the Committee on Public Lands on HR 3309, a bill to amend the Organic Act of Puerto Rico*, 80th Cong., 1st Sess., May 19, 1947, pp. 2–15.

51. Ibid., pp. 15–46.

52. Ibid., p. 1.

53. Article by Fernós-Isern, *La Prensa*, Aug. 6, 1947, p. 1.

54. *House Report 455*, 80th Cong., 1st Sess., May 26, 1947, pp. 1–6; *Cong. Record*, 80th Cong., 1st Sess., May 26, 1947, p. 5815.

55. Correspondence with Fernós-Isern, Aug. and Nov., 1972.

56. *Cong. Record*, 80th Cong., 1st Sess., June 16, 1947, pp. 7076–79.

57. Chapman to Muñoz Marín, June 20, 1947, OT/NA, RG 126, 9-8-68.

58. *Cong. Record*, 80th Cong., 1st Sess., June 17, 1947, p. 7120.

59. Chapman to Muñoz Marín, OT/NA, RG 126, 9-8-68.

60. Krug to Butler, June 23, 1947, OT/NA, RG 126, 9-8-68.

61. Silverman to Orville Watkins of the Senate Committee on Public Lands, June 25, 1947, Silverman to Watkins and Crawford, June 27, 1947, July 1, 1947, July 2, 1947, OT/NA, RG 126, 9-8-68.

62. *Senate Report 422*, 80th Cong., 1st Sess., July 2, 1947, pp. 1–2.

63. *La Prensa*, July 4, 1947, p. 1, July 7, 1947, p. 1.

64. Fernós-Isern writes further, "At Secretary Chapman's office, the officials expressed their views. So did Governor Piñero. Rather abandon the bill than have a Coordinator. Commissioner Fernós-Isern expressed a contrary view. At this moment a cable from Puerto Rico arrived and was brought in and handed over to the Secretary. It was Muñoz Marín's cable as requested by the Commissioner. Secretary Chapman allowed everyone present to read it. He said: 'There is nothing else to do.' " Correspondence with Fernós-Isern, Aug., 1972.

65. Chapman to Muñoz Marín, July 8, 1947, Chapman Papers/HSTL, Box 107; Muñoz Marín to Chapman, July 3, 1947, Silverman to H. J. Slaughter, July 8, 1947, OT/NA, RG 126, 9-8-68.

66. Fernós-Isern was worried about the bill being repeatedly passed over. He enlisted the help of Senator Chavez of New Mexico, who objected to an important military bill. This quickly brought Taft to Chavez, who was assured by the first that the Butler-Crawford bill would pass. Correspondence with Fernós-Isern, Aug., 1972.

67. Lee to Piñero, July 28, 1947, OT/NA, RG 126, 9-8-68.

68. Fernós-Isern relates, "That Mr. Rex Lee may have consulted Crawford and Butler in order to elicit their approval to the amend-

ment is news to me. At no time did Senator Butler during the day and night session of July the 26 intimate any such thing to Commissioner Fernós-Isern. Crawford did not seem to know of Taft's purpose until Fernós-Isern told him of his hunch about it. Senator Taft could not know of Crawford's acceptance of amendment until he read Crawford's note." The note was to the effect that Taft should make the amendment immediately if he wanted to do so. To this Taft agreed. Correspondence with Fernós-Isern, Aug., 1972.

69. Recalled later by Fernós-Isern to Butler, Aug. 1, 1969, Butler Papers/NSHS, Box 153; "Statements of Senator Butler on HR 3309," July 27, 1947, Butler Papers/ NSHS; articles by Fernós-Isern in *La Prensa*, Aug. 6, 1947, p. 1, Aug. 7, 1947, p. 1, Aug. 9, 1947, p. 1; *Cong. Record*, 80th Cong., 1st Sess., July 26, 1947, pp. 10389, 10402.

70. No coordinator was ever appointed by the DTIP or the Department of the Interior after the bill's passage, so matters continued as before. The 1950 Constitution Act (Public Law 600) eliminated the post. Correspondence with Fernós-Isern, Aug., 1972.

71. Truman to Piñero, Aug. 5, 1947, OT/NA, RG 126, 9-8-68; *Cong. Record*, 80th Cong., 1st Sess., Aug. 5, 1947, p. 10584.

72. "Work of the Senate Committee on Interior and Insular Affairs," anon., n.d., Butler Papers/ NSHS, Box 126.

73. "Need for a Study of Land Holdings of Armed Forces in Puerto Rico," by Puerto Rico Planning Board, Krug Papers/MD, LC, Box 74. For some disputes over land transfer see Krug to Forrestal, May

3, 1947, Forrestal to Krug, May 27, 1947, Silverman to Piñero, Aug. 8, 1947, W. John Kenney to Krug, Sept. 17, 1947, Chapman to Piñero, Nov. 18, 1947, OT/WNRC, RG 126, 62-A-401.

74. Forrestal to Krug, May 27, 1947, OT/WNRC, RG 126, 62-A-401.

75. Lewis, *Puerto Rico: Freedom and Power*, pp. 72, 346.

CHAPTER SEVEN

1. A translation of a report in *El Mundo*, 1922, Bureau of Indian Affairs, Department of War/National Archives, 26429-A/158.

2. Miguel A. García Méndez disclosed to the author that the Union party leader, Antonio Barceló, and his counterpart in the Republican party, José Tous Soto, were returning on the same ship to Puerto Rico in 1924 after a fruitless meeting with officials in Washington over the status question. The two leaders used the good offices of a well-known Puerto Rican lawyer, José A. Poventud, to agree on an alliance after accepting "a middle road status under the slogan of 'sovereignty within the American sovereignty.'" Correspondence with García Méndez, June 30, 1973.

3. Mathews, *Puerto Rican Politics*, pp. 16–17.

4. See chap. 4.

5. Campos del Toro et al. to President's Committee, OT/NA, RG 126, 9-8-68.

6. Moscoso to Fortas, June 24, 1943, "Memorandum for Benjamin Thoron," from Gilbert Ramírez, July 19, 1943, OT/NA, RG 126, 9-8-68; *New York Times*, July 24, 1943, p. 12.

7. See chap. 4.

8. See chap. 5.

9. Tugwell, *The Stricken Land*, p. 492.

10. Anderson, *Party Politics*, pp. 60–62.

11. Correspondence with Dr. Fernós-Isern, Sept. 14, 1973.

12. "The Mind of Puerto Rico: Address by Resident Commissioner Antonio Fernós-Isern," delivered on Feb. 27, 1947, at Rollins College, Florida, in *Mind of America* series, p. 18 passim. (Xerox copy supplied by Rollins College.)

13. *New York Times*, Feb. 22, 1948, p. 1.

14. *La Prensa*, May 6, 1948, p. 2.

15. Dr. Fernós-Isern argues that the Commonwealth idea originated with him. He writes, "The proposal was first made in an article published in the newspaper El Mundo of San Juan, Puerto Rico, on July 4, 1946. This formula was adopted two years later by Mr. Muñoz Marín in his speech of July 4, 1948. The Popular Democratic Party adopted it two months later." Correspondence with Fernós-Isern, Sept. 14, 1973.

16. "Muñoz Marín's Address," July 4, 1948, OT/NA, RG 126, 9-8-68.

17. Ibid.

18. Dr. Fernós-Isern states that the plan adopted by the PPD was really the proposal he made in his July 4, 1946, article in *El Mundo*. See also note 15. Correspondence with Fernós-Isern, Sept. 14, 1973.

19. Fischman, "The Rise and Development," pp. 348–49; *La Prensa*, Aug. 16, 1948, p. 1, Oct. 26, 1948, p. 1; *New York Times*, Aug. 16, 1948, p. 6.

20. *New York Times*, July 15, 1948, p. 8.

21. The PEP was formerly the Union Republican party. In 1956 it changed its name to *Partido Estadista Republicano* (PER), at which time it more strongly adopted statehood as an official party goal. See Anderson, *Party Politics*, p. 43.

22. Fischman, "The Rise and Development," pp. 344–45; *La Prensa*, Aug. 16, 1948, p. 1, Oct. 26, 1948, p. 1; *New York Times*, Aug. 16, 1948, p. 6.

23. *New York Times*, June 23, 1948, p. 6.

24. *La Prensa*, Aug. 16, 1948, p. 1, Oct. 26, 1948, p. 1.

25. *New York Times*, July 25, 1948, p. 29.

26. *La Prensa*, Oct. 26, 1948, p. 1. There were also two minority parties. One was an independent party in Caguas, and the other was the Communist party. The Nationalist party did not participate in the elections.

27. Whenever reference is made specifically to members of the PIP, *independentistas* will be capitalized *Independentistas*. The same rule will apply in the case of *estadistas* and *Estadistas*, the second being specifically members of PEP.

28. Fischman, "The Rise and Development," p. 347; Anderson, *Party Politics*, p. 63; Hunter, "The Historical Development," p. 302.

29. Reprinted in *Hearings before the House Committee on Public Lands on HR 7674 and S.3336 to provide for the organization of a Constitutional Government by the People of Puerto Rico* (hereinafter referred to as *Hearings before the House Committee on Public Lands on HR 7674 and S.3336*), 81st Cong., 1st and 2nd Sessions, July 12, 1949, Mar. 14, May 16, June 8, 1950, pp. 121–31.

30. Fischman, "The Rise and

Development," pp. 345–46; *La Pren-sa*, Nov. 1, 1948, p. 1.

31. Fischman, "The Rise and Development," table on p. 407; Anderson, *Party Politics*, table on p. 43; *La Prensa*, Nov. 4, 1948, p. 1, Nov. 9, 1948, p. 1; *New York Times*, Nov. 4, 1948, p. 32.

32. *New York Times*, Nov. 4, 1948, p. 32.

33. *New York Times*, Jan. 3, 1949, p. 1; *La Prensa*, Jan. 3, 1949, p. 1; *Cong. Record*, 81st Cong., 1st Sess., Jan. 17, 1949, pp. 308–11.

34. "Chapman's Address," Jan. 2, 1949, Chapman Papers/HSTL, Box 75.

35. *Cong. Record*, 81st Cong., 1st Sess., Jan. 17, 1949, p. 300.

36. Butler to Muñoz Marín, Jan. 18, 1949, Muñoz Marín to Butler, Jan. 21, 1949, Butler Papers/NSHS, Box 153.

37. Chapman to O'Mahoney, Apr. 1, 1949, Chapman Papers/HSTL, Box 111.

38. *Cong. Record*, 81st Cong., 1st Sess., Mar. 28, 1949, p. 3321.

39. Fernós-Isern to Davis, June 3, 1949, OT/NA, RG 126, 9-8-68.

40. *New York Times*, July 5, 1949, pp. 10, 12.

41. Memorandum by Secretary Krug, July 5, 1949, OT/NA, RG 126, 9-8-68; *New York Times*, July 6, 1949, p. 10.

42. Krug to Truman, July 18, 1949, OT/NA, RG 126, 9-8-68. The Puerto Rican legislature approved in April, 1950, $50,000 for the island's role in the Point Four program. *New York Times*, Apr. 17, 1950, p. 2.

43. *La Prensa*, July 9, 1949, p. 1; *New York Times*, July 19, 1949, p. 6.

44. "Report of the Governor of Puerto Rico," incorporated in *Hear-ings before the House Committee on Public Lands on HR 7674 and S.3336*, 81st Cong., 1st Sess., July 12, 1949, pp. 1–16.

45. Krug to Truman, July 18, 1949, Krug Papers/MD,LC, Box 18.

46. *La Prensa*, July 13, 1949, p. 1.

47. Krug to Truman, July 18, 1949, Krug Papers/MD, LC, Box 18.

48. *La Prensa*, July 18, 1949, p. 1.

49. Ibid., July 19, 1949, p. 1, Aug. 2, 1949, p. 1.

50. Ibid., July 15, 1949, p. 2. See also *El Mundo*, July 16, 1949, p. 6.

51. *La Prensa*, July 16, 1949, p. 1.

52. Ibid., July 25, 1949, p. 1.

53. Nash to Spingarn, Dec. 27, 1949, Philleo Nash Papers/Harry S. Truman Library (hereinafter referred to as Nash Papers/HSTL), Folder "WH-Puerto Rican Constitution, 1949–1952."

54. Dr. Fernós-Isern states it was natural for Barr to be "pessimistic with respect to Congress agreeing to an unprecedented political concept" because he was a "regular bureaucrat," but he "was proved wrong." Correspondence with Dr. Fernós-Isern, Sept. 14, 1973.

55. Barr to Nash, Dec. 28, 1949, OT/NA, RG 126, 9-8-68.

56. *The Public Papers of Harry S. Truman Containing the Public Messages, Speeches and Statements of the President, January 1 to December 31, 1950*. In the series *Public Papers of the President of the United States* (Washington: U.S. Government Printing Office, 1965), p. 9.

57. *La Prensa*, Jan. 12, 1950, p. 1, Jan. 14, 1950, p. 1.

58. "Muñoz Marín's Statement

on Political Status," Jan. 16, 1950, OT/NA, RG 126, 9-8-68.

59. Ibid.

60. Correspondence with Dr. Fernós-Isern, Sept. 14, 1973.

61. *La Prensa*, Jan. 29, 1950, p. 1.

62. Ibid., Feb. 14, 1950, p. 1.

63. Ibid., Feb. 2, 1950, p. 2, Feb. 10, 1950, p. 1.

64. Silverman to Fernós-Isern, Feb. 21, 1950, OT/WNRC, RG 126, 62-A-401.

65. *La Prensa*, Feb. 28, 1950, p. 1; *New York Times*, Feb. 28, 1950, p. 22.

66. "Memorandum for Secretary Chapman," from Davis, Mar. 3, 1950, OT/WNRC, RG 126, 62-A-401.

67. Ibid.

68. *La Prensa*, Mar. 1, 1950, p. 1.

69. Ibid., Mar. 3, 1950, p. 1.

70. Ibid., Mar. 6, 1950, p. 1.

71. Ibid., Mar. 7, 1950, p. 1.

72. Dr. Fernós-Isern writes, "The Governor consulted in Puerto Rico with attorneys [José] Trias [Monge] and A[be] Fortas. He arrived in Washington in January [it was at the end of February] 1950 and again conferred with Dr. Fernós. Changes of style as recommended by Mr. Fortas and Mr. Trias were agreed to." Correspondence with Dr. Fernós-Isern, Sept. 14, 1973.

73. *La Prensa*, Mar. 8, 1950, p. 1, Mar. 10, 1950, p. 1.

74. "Memorandum for Senator O'Mahoney," from French, Mar. 12, 1950, Butler Papers/NSHS, Folder on S.3336, Box 182.

75. Ibid.

76. "Memorandum for Senator Butler," from Lynn (second name unknown), Mar. 13, 1950, Butler Papers/NSHS, Folder on S.3336, Box 182.

77. The governor's statement in *Hearing before the Senate Committee on Interior and Insular Affairs*, 81st Cong., 2d Sess., Mar. 13, 1950, pp. 7–9.

78. Ibid., pp. 11–12; *La Prensa*, Mar. 14, 1950, p. 1.

79. *Cong. Record*, 81st Cong., 2d Sess., Mar. 13, 1950, p. 3260.

80. See *Hearings before House Committee on Public Lands on HR 7674 and S.3336*, 81st Cong., 2d Sess., May 16, 1950, pp. 37–38.

81. Ibid.

82. *Hearings before the House Committee on Public Lands on HR 7674 and S.3336*, 81st Cong., 2d Sess., Mar. 14, 1950, pp. 17–34, 30.

83. Davis to Miles, Mar. 16, 1950, Stephen J. Spingarn Papers/Harry S. Truman Library (hereinafter referred to as Spingarn Papers/HSTL), PR 400, Folder on International Affairs.

84. *La Prensa*, Mar. 27, 1950, p. 1.

85. "Memorandum for Senators O'Mahoney and Butler," from French, Mar. 20, 1950, Butler Papers/NSHS, Folder on S.3336, Box 182.

86. Ibid.

87. *New York Times*, Mar. 31, 1950, p. 11.

88. *Cong. Record*, 81st Cong., 2d Sess., Mar. 31, 1950, p. 4446.

89. See *Hearings before a Senate Subcommittee of the Committee on Interior and Insular Affairs on S.3336, a bill to provide for the organization of a constitutional government by the people of Puerto Rico* (hereinafter referred to as *Hearings before a Senate Subcommittee of the Committee on Interior and Insular Affairs on S.3336*), 81st

Cong., 2d Sess., May 17, 1950, pp. 1-2.

90. "Memorandum for Senator O'Mahoney," Mar. 12, 1950, "Memorandum for Senators O'Mahoney and Butler," from French, Mar. 20, 1950, Butler Papers/NSHS, Folder on S. 3336, Box 182.

91. "Statement by Senators O'Mahoney and Butler," Mar. 31, 1950, Butler Papers/NSHS, Box 182.

92. Spingarn to Roger Jones (of the Budget Bureau), Apr. 17, 1950, Nash Papers/HSTL, Folder marked "WH-Puerto Rican Constitution, 1949–1952."

93. Chapman to Peterson, Apr. 28, 1950, OT/WNRC, RG 126, 62-A-401.

94. *Hearings before the House Public Lands Committee on HR 7674 and S.3336*, 81st Cong., 2d Sess., May 16, 1950, pp. 38–47.

95. Ibid., pp. 38–47, 48–51.

96. Ibid., pp. 51–59, 59–62, 62–65.

97. Ibid., pp. 72–77.

98. Ibid., p. 72, passim; *La Prensa*, May 18, 1950, p. 1.

99. *Hearings before a Senate Subcommittee of the Committee on Interior and Insular Affairs on S.3336*, 81st Cong., 2d Sess., May 17, 1950, pp. 1–34.

100. Butler to O'Mahoney, May 20, 1950, Butler Papers/NSHS, Box 153.

101. Chapman to O'Mahoney, May 19, 1950, Butler Papers/NSHS, Folder on S.3336, Box 182.

102. Davis to Muñoz Marín (radiogram), May 26, 1950, OT/WNRC, RG 126, 62-A-401; *La Prensa*, May 27, 1950, p. 1.

103. *Senate Report 1779*, 81st Cong., 2d Sess., June 6, 1950, pp. 1–6; *La Prensa*, May 27, 1950, p. 1.

104. Ibid.

105. *La Prensa*, May 29, 1950, p. 1.

106. *Cong. Record*, 81st Cong., 2d Sess., June 8, 1950, pp. 8321–22.

107. *Cong. Record*, 81st Cong., 2d Sess., Mar. 16, 1950, p. 3555; *Hearings before the House Committee on Public Lands on HR 7674 and S.3336*, 81st Cong., 2d Sess., June 8, 1950, pp. 79–87; Vito Marcantonio, *I Vote My Conscience: Debates, Speeches, and Writings* (New York: Book Craftsmen Associates, 1956), pp. 416–27.

108. *Hearings before the House Committee on Public Lands on HR 7674 and S.3336*, 81st Cong., 2d Sess., June 8, 1950, pp. 87–113.

109. Ibid., pp. 132, 151–60, passim.

110. *La Prensa*, June 12, 1950, p. 1.

111. Ibid., June 15, 1950, p. 1.

112. *House Report 2275*, 81st Cong., 2d Sess., June 19, 1950.

113. *Cong. Record*, 81st Cong., 2d Sess., June 19, 1950, p. 8857.

114. *La Prensa*, June 22, 1950, p. 1.

115. Muñoz Marín to Chapman and Davis, June 27, 1950, OT/WNRC, RG 126, 62-A-401; Muñoz Marín to Truman, June 27, 1950, Truman Papers/HSTL, White House Bill File.

116. *La Prensa*, June 29, 1950, p. 1; *New York Times*, June 29, 1950, p. 24; Davis to Muñoz Marín (cablegram), June 28, 1950, OT/WNRC, RG 126, 62-A-401.

117. Silverman to Muñoz Marín, June 30, 1950, OT/WNRC, RG 126, 62-A-401.

118. *Cong. Record*, 81st Cong., 2d Sess., June 30, 1950, pp. 9584–9602.

119. Ibid., pp. 9585–86, 9586–91, 9601–2.

120. William E. Warne (acting secretary of Interior) to Frederick J. Lawton (director of the Budget Bureau), June 30, 1950, Truman Papers/HSTL, White House Bill File.

121. *La Prensa*, July 4, 1950, p. 1; *New York Times*, July 2, 1950, p. 2, July 4, 1950, p. 30; *Cong. Record*, 2d Sess., July 3, 1950, p. 9634.

122. *Public Law 600*, 81st Cong., 2d Sess., July 3, 1950, p. 319.

123. *New York Times*, July 5, 1950, p. 24; *Cong. Record*, 81st Cong., 2d Sess., Aug. 24, 1950, pp. A6047–50.

124. In *Cong. Record*, 81st Cong., 2d Sess., July 10, 1950, p. A4981, July 11, 1950, p. A5039.

125. *New York Times*, July 7, 1950, p. 18.

CHAPTER EIGHT

1. *La Prensa*, Aug. 4, 1950, p. 2, Sept. 1, 1950, p. 1, Oct. 4, 1950, p. 2; *New York Times*, Sept. 1, 1950, p. 16.

2. *New York Times*, Sept. 28, 1950, p. 28.

3. Muñoz Marín to Chapman (cablegram), Aug. 3, 1950, OT/NA, RG 126, 9-8-62.

4. Davis to Muñoz Marín, Aug. 18, 1950, Muñoz Marín to Davis, Aug. 22, 1950, OT/NA, RG 126, 9-8-82.

5. Davis to Muñoz Marín, Sept. 18, 1950, Muñoz Marín to Davis, Aug. 22, 1950, OT/NA, RG 126, 9-8-82.

6. "Nationalist Party of Puerto Rico," by Charles B. Peck, Oct. 12, 1950, OT/WNRC, RG 126, 62-A-401.

7. *La Prensa*, Oct. 2, 1950, p. 2.

8. Ibid., Oct. 22, 1950, p. 2.

9. Ibid., Oct. 30, 1950, p. 2.

10. *New York Times*, Oct. 31, 1950, p. 1; *La Prensa*, Oct. 31, 1950, p. 1; Fischman, "The Rise and Development," pp. 364–66.

11. *New York Times*, Nov. 2, 1950, p. 1; *La Prensa*, Nov. 2, 1950, p. 1.

12. *New York Times*, Nov. 1, 1950, p. 26.

13. Ibid., Nov. 3, 1950, p. 1; *La Prensa*, Nov. 4, 1950, p. 1.

14. *New York Times*, Nov. 1, 1950, p. 26.

15. Muñoz Marín to Truman, Nov. 2, 1950, DI/NA, RG 48, 9-8-2.

16. *New York Times*, Nov. 1, 1950, p. 26.

17. *The Public Papers of Harry S. Truman, Containing the Public Messages, Speeches and Statements of the President, January 1 to December 31, 1950* in the series *Public Papers of the President* (Washington: U.S. Government Printing Office, 1965), pp. 9, 695–96.

18. "Radio Interview: Chapman and Bert Andrews," Nov. 4, 1950, Chapman Papers/HSTL, "Public Addresses and Statements."

19. *New York Times*, Nov. 5, 1950, III, p. 1.

20. Ibid., May 22, 1951, p. 14.

21. Ibid., Aug. 30, 1951, p. 3.

22. Ibid., Dec. 23, 1950, p. 30, Dec. 28, 1950, p. 18, Mar. 8, 1951, p. 1, Apr. 7, 1951, p. 1.

23. *La Prensa*, Nov. 5, 1950, p. 1.

24. *New York Times*, Nov. 7, 1950, p. 16.

25. *La Prensa*, Nov. 20, 1950, p. 1.

26. Ibid., Dec. 8, 1950, p. 1.

27. Ibid., Dec. 11, 1950, p. 2.

28. *El Mundo*, Jan. 27, 1951, p. 21.

29. Muñoz Marín, "A New Idea of Statehood," *United Nations World* (Feb., 1951): 57.

30. Fernós-Isern to Silverman, Feb. 27, 1951, OT/WNRC, RG 126, 62-A-401.

31. Correspondence with García Méndez, June 30, 1973.

32. *El Mundo*, Feb. 24, 1951, p. 1, Feb. 27, 1951, p. 1; Anderson, *Party Politics*, pp. 85–86.

33. *El Mundo*, Mar. 31, 1951, p. 4; Anderson, *Party Politics*, p. 109.

34. *El Mundo*, Apr. 7, 1951, p. 4.

35. Anderson, *Party Politics*, p. 109.

36. *El Mundo*, Apr. 24, 1951, p. 6, Apr. 25, 1951, p. 6, Apr. 26, 1951, p. 6, Apr. 27, 1951, p. 6, Apr. 28, 1951, p. 6, Apr. 30, 1951, p. 6, May 1, 1951, p. 6, May 2, 1951, p. 6, May 3, 1951, p. 6.

37. Ibid., May 12, 1951, p. 6, May 14, 1951, p. 6, May 15, 1951, p. 6, May 16, 1951, p. 6, May 17, 1951, p. 6.

38. Ibid., May 19, 1951, p. 6, May 20, 1951, p. 6, May 21, 1951, p. 6, May 22, 1951, p. 6, June 4, 1951, p. 6.

39. Ibid., May 26, 1951, p. 6, May 28, 1951, p. 6, May 29, 1951, p. 6, May 30, 1951, p. 6.

40. Ibid., June 1, 1951, p. 7.

41. Ibid., June 1, 1951, p. 7.

42. Ibid., May 31, 1951, p. 6, June 1, 1951, p. 6, June 2, 1951, p. 2.

43. *New York Times*, May 31, 1951, p. 19.

44. Muñoz Marín to Chapman, June 6, 1951, Chapman to Muñoz Marín, June 7, 1951, OT/WNRC, RG 126, 62-A-401; *New York Times*, June 5, 1951, p. 9, June 6, 1951, p. 12, June 27, 1951, p. 10.

45. Chapman to Muñoz Marín, June 27, 1951, DI/NA, RG 48, 9-8-2.

46. *New York Times*, June 9, 1951, p. 4.

47. Ibid., June 12, 1951, p. 15.

48. Ibid., June 20, 1951, p. 25; Anderson, *Party Politics*, pp. 35, 38.

49. Anderson, *Party Politics*, pp. 35, 87; Fischman, "The Rise and Development," pp. 376–77.

50. Fischman, "The Rise and Development," p. 377.

51. Anderson, *Party Politics*, pp. 105–7.

52. *New York Times*, Aug. 29, 1951, p. 8.

53. Ibid., Sept. 17, 1951, p. 2.

54. Truman to Constitutional Convention, Sept. 14, 1951, Chapman to Constitutional Convention, Sept. 18, 1951, OT/WNRC, RG 126, 62-A-401.

55. *New York Times*, Feb. 5, 1952, p. 21.

56. *Cong. Record*, 82nd Cong., 2d Sess., May 23, 1952, p. 6166.

57. Ibid., Mar. 31, 1952, pp. A2051–52.

58. Davis to Muñoz Marín, Feb. 14, 1952, OT/WNRC, RG 126, 62-A-401.

59. Silverman to Barth, Feb. 19, 1952, OT/WNRC, RG 126, 62-A-401.

60. Chester M. Wright, "Report on Puerto Rico," Nov. 9, 1951, Truman Papers/HSTL, PR 400, Official File; concerning the Long affair: Muñoz Marín to Lee Hills, Sept. 10, 1951, Muñoz Marín to Davis, Sept. 10, 1951, Feb. 27, 1952, OT/WNRC, RG 126, 62-A-401; *Cong. Record*, 82nd Cong., 1st Sess., Sept. 13, 1951, p. A5562.

61. *New York Times*, Feb. 12, 1952, p. 9.

62. "Chapman's Press Conference," Feb. 13, 1952, Chapman Papers/HSTL, Box 73.

63. *New York Times*, Jan. 21, 1952, p. 17, Feb. 18, 1952, p. 8.

64. Ibid., Mar. 3, 1952, p. 5.

65. Silverman to Muñoz Marín, Feb. 19, 1952, OT/WNRC, RG 126, 62-A-401.

66. *New York Times*, Mar. 4, 1952, p. 14; Muñoz Marín to Davis et al., Mar. 3, 1952, OT/WNRC, RG 126, 62-A-401.

67. *New York Times*, Mar. 4, 1952, p. 14.

68. Ibid., Mar. 5, 1952, p. 28.

69. *Cong. Record*, 82nd Cong., 2d Sess., Mar. 3, 1952, p. A1300.

70. Muñoz Marín to Truman, Mar. 12, 1952, Truman Papers/ HSTL, PR 400, Box 1092.

71. Muñoz Marín to Chapman, Mar. 12, 1952 and Apr. 4, 1952, OT/ WNRC, RG 126, 62-A-401.

72. Chapman to Truman, Mar. 12, 1952, OT/WNRC, RG 126, 62-A-401.

73. "President Truman's Message to Congress," Apr. 22, 1952, Nash Papers/HSTL, Folder marked "WH-Puerto Rico Constitution, 1949–1952."

74. Appendix in *Hearings before the Senate Committee on Interior and Insular Affairs on S.J. Res. 151, A Joint Resolution Approving the Constitution of the Commonwealth of Puerto Rico which was adopted by the People of Puerto Rico on March 3, 1952* (hereinafter referred to as *Hearings before the Senate Committee on Interior and Insular Affairs on S.J. Res. 151*), 82nd Cong., 2d Sess., Apr. 29, May 6, 1952, pp. 66–78. Appendix in *Hearing before the House Committee on Interior and Insular Affairs on H.J. Res. 430, A Joint Resolution Approving the Constitution of the Commonwealth of Puerto Rico which was adopted by the People of Puerto Rico on March 3, 1952* (hereinafter referred to as *Hearing before the House Committee on Interior and Insular Affairs on H.J. Res. 430*), 82nd Cong., 2d Sess., Apr. 25, 1952, pp. 38–39.

75. Appendix in *Hearings before the Senate Committee on Interior and Insular Affairs on S.J. Res. 151*, 82nd Cong., 2d Sess., Apr. 29, May 6, 1952, pp. 67–69.

76. Ibid.

77. Ibid., pp. 69–74.

78. Ibid., pp. 74–78.

79. Ibid.

80. *New York Times*, Apr. 23, 1952, p. 10.

81. *Cong. Record*, 82nd Cong., 2d Sess., Apr. 22, 1952, p. 4178.

82. *Hearing before the House Committee on Interior and Insular Affairs on S.J. Res. 430*, 82nd Cong., 2d Sess., Apr. 25, 1952, pp. 1–2.

83. Ibid., pp. 1–7, passim.

84. Ibid., pp. 8–13, 13–16.

85. Ibid., pp. 16–17.

86. *New York Times*, Apr. 26, 1952, p. 42.

87. *Hearings before the Senate Committee on Interior and Insular Affairs on S.J. Res. 151*, 82nd Cong., 2d Sess., Apr. 29, 1952, pp. 12–13.

88. Ibid., pp. 13–15.

89. Ibid., pp. 15–17.

90. Ibid., pp. 18–20.

91. Ibid., pp. 3–11, 21–23, 29–31.

92. Ibid., pp. 2–11, 25–26, passim.

93. "Chapman's Press Conference," Apr. 29, 1952, Chapman Papers/HSTL, Box 73.

94. *Hearings before the Senate Committee on Interior and Insular Affairs on S.J. Res. 151*, 82nd Cong., 2d Sess., May 6, 1952, pp. 33–38, 24–25, 39.

95. Ibid., pp. 40–47.

96. Ibid., pp. 47–48.

97. Ibid., pp. 48–49.

98. Ibid., pp. 50–54.

99. Ibid., pp. 97–108, 111–13, passim.
100. *Cong. Record*, 82nd Cong., 2d Sess., May 13, 1952, pp. 5119–28, 5126–27.
101. Ibid.
102. *New York Times*, May 14, 1952, p. 12.
103. Although the report was officially published on June 10, 1952, the Senate committee's action was reported by the *New York Times*, May 28, 1952, p. 9; *Senate Report 1720*, 82nd Cong., 2d Sess., June 10, 1952, pp. 1–2.
104. *Senate Report 1720*, 82nd Cong., 2d Sess., June 10, 1952, pp. 3–7; *New York Times*, May 28, 1952, p. 9.
105. *Cong. Record*, 82nd Cong., 2d Sess., May 28, 1952, pp. 6166–70.
106. Ibid., pp. 6166–81, 6177, 6175.
107. Ibid., pp. 6181–82, 6183.
108. Dr. Fernós-Isern argues that the Meader amendment would have been a contradiction in terms. Congress could not recognize Puerto Rico's sovereignty in its internal matters while at the same time claiming "plenary sovereignty under the Territorial clause." He says further, "The status of Puerto Rico, once the Commonwealth was created, ceased to be that of a 'possession' under the territorial clause and became that stemming from a compact. Verily as of now the Treaty of Paris of 1899 is obsolete." Correspondence with Fernós-Isern, Sept. 14, 1973.
109. *Cong. Record*, 82nd Cong., 2d Sess., May 28, 1952, pp. 6184–86; *New York Times*, May 29, 1952, p. 28.
110. *Cong. Record*, 82nd Cong., 2d Sess., Mar. 10, 1952, pp. 2003–11, May 15, 1952, p. A2979, May 29, 1952, pp. A3360–61.

111. Ibid., June 23, 1952, pp. 7840–46.
112. Ibid., pp. 7844, 7846–48.
113. Ibid., pp. 7848–50.
114. Ibid., *New York Times*, June 24, 1952, p. 25.
115. *Cong. Record*, 82nd Cong., 2d Sess., June 25, 1952, p. 8079.
116. Muñoz Marín to Davis, June 24, 1952, Wheeler to Muñoz Marín, June 24, 1952, OT/WNRC, RG 126, 62-A-401.
117. *Conference Report (House Report) 2350*, 82nd Cong., 2d Sess., June 28, 1952, pp. 1–3.
118. *Cong. Record*, 82nd Cong., 2d Sess., July 1, 1952, p. 8715.
119. R. D. Searles (acting secretary of Interior) to Frederick J. Lawton (director of the Budget Bureau), July 2, 1952, OT/WNRC, RG 126, 62-A-401.
120. McFall to Lawton, July 3, 1952, OT/WNRC, RG 126, 62-A-401.
121. *New York Times*, July 4, 1952, p. 30; "Press Statement by Harry S. Truman," July 3, 1952, Truman Papers/HSTL; *Cong. Record*, 82nd Cong., 2d Sess., July 7, 1952, p. 9752.
122. *New York Times*, July 5, 1952, p. 3, July 12, 1952, p. 10, July 30, 1952, p. 3.
123. Ibid., July 26, 1952, p. 11.

CHAPTER NINE

1. Sady, *The United Nations*, pp. 33–44.
2. Silverman to Davis, Aug. 25, 1952, OT/WNRC, RG 126, 62-A-401.
3. Correspondence with Fernós-Isern, Sept. 14, 1973.
4. Davis to Muñoz Marín, Sept. 25, 1952, OT/WNRC, RG 126, 62-A-401.

5. Ibid.

6. DTIP assistant director Wheeler to Muñoz Marín, Sept. 26, 1952, OT/WNRC, RG 126, 62-A-401.

7. Davis to Chapman, Sept. 26, 1952, OT/WNRC, RG 126, 62-A-401.

8. Muñoz Marín to Davis, Sept. 27, 1952, Davis to Muñoz Marín, Sept. 29, 1952, OT/WNRC, RG 126, 62-A-401.

9. Northrop to Dean Acheson, Oct. 9, 1952, OT/WNRC, RG 126, 62-A-401.

10. Muñoz Marín to Chapman, Jan. 17, 1953, OT/WNRC, RG 126, 62-A-401.

11. Chapman to Acheson, Jan. 19, 1953, OT/WNRC, RG 126, 62-A-401.

12. Muñoz Marín to Davis, Jan. 17, 1953, OT/WNRC, RG 126, 62-A-401.

13. Muñoz Marín to Truman, Jan. 17, 1953, OT/WNRC, RG 126, 62-A-401.

14. Ibid.

15. "Analysis of Proposed Revisions in U.S. Memorandum to U.N. concerning Puerto Rico," by Mrs. Fleming to Mr. Tate (full names unknown), Feb. 5, 1953, OT/WNRC, RG 126, 62-A-401.

16. Ibid.

17. Fernós-Isern to Tate, Feb. 24, 1954, OT/WNRC, RG 126, 62-A-401.

18. *U.S. Department of State Bulletin*, Apr. 20, 1953, pp. 584–88; Henry Cabot Lodge, Jr., to Trygve Lie, Mar. 20, 1953, OT/WNRC, RG 126, 62-A-401.

19. Ibid.

20. Ibid.

21. "Summary Report of Meeting with Governor Muñoz Marín Regarding Manner in which Puerto Rico's New Self-Governing status might be presented to and defended in the United Nations," by Gerig, June 30, 1953, OT/WNRC, RG 126, 62-A-401.

22. Ibid.

23. *U.S. Department of State Bulletin*, Sept. 21, 1953, pp. 392–93; Oct. 30, 1953, pp. 798–802; *Official Records of the General Assembly, 8th Sess., Fourth Committee, Trusteeship*, Nov., 1953, pp. 219–64.

24. Copies of the memoranda supplied to author by one of their writers, Vicente Geigel Polanco, March, 1973.

25. *Official Records of the General Assembly, 8th Sess., Fourth Committee, Trusteeship*, Sept. 30, 1953, pp. 29–34, Nov. 2–5, 1953, p. 256.

26. García Méndez explains that the Eisenhower administration agreed to independence only because as a group the *independentistas* "composed of part of the not yet mature idealistic universatarian youth and a few intellectual snobists[sic]." Correspondence with Miguel A. García Méndez, June 30, 1973.

27. *Official Records of the General Assembly, 8th Sess., 459th Plenary Meeting*, Nov. 27, 1953, pp. 309–21.

28. *Resolutions Adopted by the General Assembly, 8th Sess., Res. 748, Supplement No. 17(A/2630)*, Nov. 27, 1953, pp. 25–26.

29. Wells, *The Modernization of Puerto Rico*, p. 251.

30. *Cong. Record*, 86th Cong., 1st Sess., Mar. 24, 1959, p. 5022.

31. Ibid., Mar. 23, 1959, p. 4998, May 21, 1959, p. 8733.

32. Appendix in *Hearing before the Senate Committee on Interior and Insular Affairs on S.2023, a bill to provide for amendments to*

the compact between the people of Puerto Rico and the United States (hereinafter referred to as *Hearing before the Senate Committee on Interior and Insular Affairs on S.2023*), 86th Cong., 1st Sess., June 9, 1959, pp. 57–65, 25–55; correspondence with Fernós-Isern, Sept. 14, 1973.

33. *Hearing before the Senate Committee on Interior and Insular Affairs on S.2023*, 86th Cong., 1st Sess., June 9, 1959, pp. 57–65, 25–55.

34. "Puerto Rican Development during 1959," from Olson, Nov. 4, 1959, OT/WNRC, RG 126, 62-A-401.

35. *Hearing before the Senate Committee on Interior and Insular Affairs on S.2023*, 86th Cong., 1st Sess., June 9, 1959, pp. 44–42, passim; Lewis, *Puerto Rico: Freedom and Power*, p. 359.

36. Lewis, *Puerto Rico: A Case Study*, pp. 63–65, 100–107.

37. Says Fernós-Isern, "The Commissioner decided to introduce a clean bill, instead of modifying the original bill, in order to meet the objections made by the departments, even though certain amendments consisted of mere changes in language; others were more meaningful modifications. . . . There was absolutely no connection between the fact that the Commissioner decided to introduce a clean bill and the Cidra declaration." Correspondence with Fernós-Isern, Sept. 14, 1973.

38. *Cong. Record*, 86th Cong., 1st Sess., Sept. 12, 1959, p. 19392, Sept. 14, 1959, p. 19409; *Hearing before the Senate Committee on Interior and Insular Affairs on S.2023*, 86th Cong., 1st Sess., June 9, 1959, pp. 72–73.

39. *Hearings before a Special Subcommittee of the Senate Committee on Interior and Insular Affairs on HR 9234*, 86th Cong., 1st Sess., Dec. 3–10, 1959, pp. 26–47, 217–37, 237–48, 267–68, passim; "Puerto Rican Development during 1959," memorandum by Sylvester I. Olson, Nov. 1959, OT/WNRC, RG 126, 62-A-401.

40. *Hearing before the Senate Committee on Interior and Insular Affairs on S.2023*, 86th Cong., 1st Sess., June 9, 1959, pp. 90–111.

41. Ibid., pp. 111–23.

42. *Hearings before a Special Subcommittee of the Committee on Interior and Insular Affairs on HR 5926*, 86th Cong., 1st Sess., Dec. 3–10, 1959, pp. 733–44.

43. Correspondence with Fernós-Isern, Sept. 14, 1973.

44. Ibid.

45. *New York Times*, July 26, 1962, pp. 1, 8.

46. "Legislative History of the United States—Puerto Rican Commission on the Status of Puerto Rico," by Leibowitz, Feb. 1, 1965, LJDD/NA, RG 148, Records on US–PR Commission on the Status of Puerto Rico; García Méndez explains the opposition thus, "The strongest argument was that such a plebiscite without the previous express or implicit approval of Congress was tantamount to a beauty contest without any sound political results." Correspondence with García Méndez, June 30, 1973.

47. "Legislative History of the United States—Puerto Rican Commission on the Status of Puerto Rico," by Leibowitz, Feb. 1, 1965, LJDD/NA, RG 148, Records on US–PR Commission on the Status of Puerto Rico.

48. *Hearings before the Subcommittee on Territorial and Insular*

Affairs of the House Committee on Interior and Insular Affairs on HR 5945 and other bills to establish a procedure for the prompt settlement in a democratic manner of the political status of Puerto Rico (hereinafter referred to as *Hearings before the Subcommittee on Territorial and Insular Affairs of the House Committee on Interior and Insular Affairs on HR 5945*), 88th Cong., 1st Sess., May 16–17, 1963, pp. 1–2; *Cong. Record*, 88th Cong., 1st Sess., Apr. 30, 1963, p. 7474.

49. *Hearings before the Subcommittee on Territorial and Insular Affairs of the Committee on Interior and Insular Affairs on HR 5945*, 88th Cong., 1st Sess., May 16-17, 1963, passim.

50. García Méndez was approached by Fernós-Isern for approval of the new bill. The PER leader agreed because, as he explains, ". . . the new bill operated as a safe face [face-saving] for Muñoz Marín and Fernós and partly as a safe face [face-saving] for García Méndez and his party, as they all wanted to keep open the possibilities of joint action as long as both parties would be fighting for permanent union with the United States." Correspondence with García Méndez, June 30, 1973.

51. "Legislative History of the United States–Puerto Rican Commission on the Status of Puerto Rico," by Leibowitz, Feb. 1, 1965, LJDD/NA, RG 148, Records on US–PR Commission on the Status of Puerto Rico.

52. *Hearings before the United States–Puerto Rico Commission on the Status of Puerto Rico*, 89th Cong., 2d Sess., May–Dec. 1965, 3 volumes; *Report of the United States–Puerto Rico Commission on the Status of Puerto Rico* (Washington: Government Press, Aug., 1966).

53. *Report of the United States–Puerto Rico Commission*, pp. 3–18.

54. Ibid., pp. 44, 31–48.

55. Ibid., pp. 3–18.

56. Wells, *The Modernization of Puerto Rico*, pp. 258–59.

57. Ibid., pp. 259–60.

58. Ibid., pp. 260–61; *New York Times*, July 24, 1967, pp. 1, 18.

59. See the suggested areas of improvement in Carl Friedrich, *Puerto Rico: Middle Road to Freedom* (New York: Rinehart & Co., 1959), pp. 64–73, passim.

60. Correspondence with Fernós-Isern, Sept. 14, 1973.

CHAPTER TEN

1. See chap. 5.

2. Muñoz Marín, "Development Through Democracy," in Millard Hansen and Henry Wells (eds.), *Puerto Rico: A Study in Democratic Development*, Vol. 285, *The Annals of the American Academy of Political and Social Science* series (Philadelphia, 1953), pp. 3, 5.

3. David F. Ross, *The Long Uphill Path: A Historical Study of Puerto Rico's Program of Economic Development* (San Juan: Editorial Edil, 1969), pp. 78–81.

4. Ibid., pp. 64–66, 66–70.

5. Ibid., pp. 70–74.

6. Perloff, *Puerto Ricos Economic Future*, p. 180.

7. Teodoro Moscoso, "Industrial Development in Puerto Rico," in Hansen and Wells (eds.), *Puerto Rico: A Study in Democratic Development*, pp. 60–61.

8. Ibid.

9. Ross, *The Long Uphill Path*, p. 82.

10. Ibid., p. 83.

11. Moscoso in Hansen and

Wells (eds.), *Puerto Rico: A Study in Democratic Development,* p. 62.

12. Perloff, *Puerto Rico's Economic Future,* see tables on pp. 146, 147.

13. Moscoso in Hansen and Wells (eds.), *Puerto Rico: A Study in Democratic Development,* p. 61; Ross, *The Long Uphill Path,* p. 81.

14. Perloff, *Puerto Rico's Economic Future,* pp. 102–5, 184.

15. Ibid., pp. 109, 377.

16. Ross, *The Long Uphill Path,* p. 85.

17. Ibid., pp. 85–95; *Fortune* 33 (Feb., 1946): 229.

18. See *Fortune* 33 (Feb., 1946): 229.

19. Ross, *The Long Uphill Path,* pp. 85–95; Moscoso in Hansen and Wells (eds.), *Puerto Rico: A Study in Democratic Development,* p. 62.

20. Milton C. Taylor, *Industrial Tax-Exemption in Puerto Rico: A Case Study in the Use of Tax Subsidies for Industrializing Underdeveloped Areas* (Madison: University of Wisconsin Press, 1957), pp. 22–23.

21. Ibid., pp. 23, 31.

22. Ross, *The Long Uphill Path,* pp. 103–4; *New York Times,* Nov. 10, 1950, p. 49.

23. Ross, *The Long Uphill Path,* pp. 107–16.

24. Ibid.; *New York Times,* Nov. 10, 1950, p. 49.

25. Wells, *The Modernization of Puerto Rico,* p. 151.

26. *New York Times,* Feb. 17, 1948, p. 40. Some other news releases and reports appeared in *New York Times,* Mar. 6, 1948, p. 8, Mar. 24, 1948, p. 47, Apr. 4, 1948, p. 21. Full-page articles and ads appears in *New York Times,* Jan. 3, 1949, p. 68, *La Prensa,* June 18, 1950, II, p. 1.

27. *New York Times,* Feb. 18, 1951, p. 21.

28. Ibid., Jan. 2, 1949, p. 12.

29. *La Prensa,* July 15, 1948, p. 1; *New York Times,* Aug. 3, 1948, p. 29.

30. *New York Times,* Feb. 4, 1949, p. 36.

31. Ibid., July 9, 1949, p. 6.

32. Ibid., July 25, 1949, p. 25.

33. Ross, *The Long Uphill Path,* pp. 117–22; Taylor, *Industrial Tax-Exemption in Puerto Rico,* p. 14.

34. *New York Times,* Sept. 24, 1948, p. 12.

35. Ibid., Feb. 24, 1949, p. 18.

36. *Cong. Record,* 81st Cong., 1st Sess., Apr. 28, 1949, p. A2527.

37. Ross, *The Long Uphill Path,* pp. 122–23.

38. H. C. Barton, "Puerto Rico's Industrial Development Program, 1942–1960," (Paper presented at the Center for International Affairs, Cambridge, Harvard University, Oct. 29, 1959), see table on p. 23.

39. Lewis, *Puerto Rico: Freedom and Power,* pp. 120–21; Ross, *The Long Uphill Path,* pp. 126–28.

40. Ibid.

41. Barton, "Puerto Rico's Industrial Development Program, 1942–1960," pp. 18–19; Ross, *The Long Uphill Path,* pp. 126–28; Muñoz Amato, "Executive Reorganization," chap. 7; Honey, "Public Personnel Administration," pp. 100–5; Wells, "Administrative Reorganization in Puerto Rico," *Western Political Quarterly* (June 1956): 470–90.

42. Taylor, *Industrial Tax-Exemption in Puerto Rico,* p. 65.

43. Barton, "Puerto Rico's Industrial Development Program, 1942–1960," p. 23.

44. Taylor, *Industrial Tax-*

Exemption in Puerto Rico, p. 118.

45. Ibid., p. 15; Moscoso in Hansen and Wells (eds.), *Puerto Rico: A Study in Democratic Development*, p. 65.

46. Werner Baer, *The Puerto Rican Economy and United States Economic Fluctuations* (Rio Piedras, San Juan: University of Puerto Rico, 1965), p. 15.

47. Taylor, *Industrial Tax-Exemption in Puerto Rico*, tables 4 and 5, p. 126.

48. Ibid., p. 24.

49. Ibid., p. 118.

50. Baer, *The Puerto Rican Economy*, p. 17.

51. James C. Ingram, *Regional Payments Mechanisms: The Case of Puerto Rico* (Chapel Hill: University of North Carolina Press, 1962), p. 70.

52. Wells, *The Modernization of Puerto Rico*, pp. 153, 156.

53. Tables supplied by the Office of Economic and Financial Research, Department of the Treasury, Puerto Rico, Dec., 1972.

54. Ibid.

55. Taylor, *Industrial Tax-Exemption in Puerto Rico*, p. 114.

56. Baer, *The Puerto Rican Economy*, p. 21, 23, 24; Ross, *The Long Uphill Path*, pp. 157–58.

57. Perloff, *Puerto Rico's Economic Future*, p. 110; see also William McIntosh, "The Development of Political Democracy in Puerto Rico" (Ph.D. diss., University of Minnesota, 1953), pp. 254–55.

58. Baer, *The Puerto Rican Economy*, table 4, p. 18.

59. "Memorandum on Economic Conditions in Puerto Rico," by Fernós-Isern, *Cong. Record*, 82d Cong., 2d Sess., Feb. 26, 1952, pp. 1404–5.

60. Barton, "Puerto Rico's Industrial Development Program, 1942–1960," pp. 48–49.

61. Baer, *The Puerto Rican Economy*, p. 60.

62. Hy Sang Lee, "The Entrepreneurial Activities of the Government in the Economic Development of Puerto Rico" (Ph.D. diss., University of Wisconsin, 1965), table 15, p. 170.

63. "Memorandum on Economic Conditions in Puerto Rico," by Fernós-Isern, *Cong. Record*, 82d Cong., 2d Sess., Feb. 26, 1952, pp. 1404–5; *New York Times*, April 28, 1950, p. 19.

64. Percentages calculated from tables supplied by the Office of Economic and Financial Research, Department of the Treasury, Puerto Rico, Dec., 1972.

65. Frank Sanchez-Aran, "Financial Aspects of Economic Development in Puerto Rico" (Ph.D. diss., New York University, 1963), pp. 44, 112.

66. From table supplied by the Office of Economic and Financial Research, Department of the Treasury, Puerto Rico, Dec., 1972.

67. Frank K. Haszard, director of the Office of Economic and Financial Research of the insular Treasury Department writes further, "These same figures also show the precarious nature of the relationship. Suppose the alcoholic beverage interests in the United States were able to persuade Congress to reduce the tax on alcoholic beverages from $10.50 to, say, $5.00 a gallon. By this supposedly isolated act of the U.S. Government, we would suddenly find our own revenues reduced by $50 million in a single year. Even though this example is strictly hypothetical (at the moment), in my judgment we can't ever live in a

tranquil state of mind until we eliminate at least those revenues from
tobacco shipped to the United
States. But how does a political
party, that wants to stay in power,
propose that we do away with 10
per cent of our income?" Correspondence with Dr. Haszard, Dec.,
1972.

68. From tables supplied by the
Office of Economic and Financial
Research, Department of the Treas-
ury, Puerto Rico, Dec., 1972.

69. Armando Díaz-Rojas, "Financing Economic Development in
Puerto Rico, 1942 to date" (Ph.D.
diss., New York University, 1964),
table on p. 308.

70. Perloff, *Puerto Rico's Economic Future*, p. 115.

71. Muñoz Marín, "Development Through Democracy," in Hansen and Wells (eds.), *Puerto Rico: A
Study in Democratic Development*,
p. 7.

72. Baer, *The Puerto Rican
Economy*, p. 17.

73. *Economist*, Aug. 17, 1957, p.
546.

74. Baer, *The Puerto Rican
Economy*, pp. 4, 45–46, 72, 101.

75. Kingsley Davis, "Puerto
Rico: A Crowded Island," in Hansen and Wells (eds.), *Puerto Rico: A
Study in Democratic Development*,
p. 116.

76. Perloff, "Unfinished Business in Puerto Rico," *Caribbean
Commission: Monthly Information
Bulletin* (Nov., 1951): 127; Clar-
ence Senior, "Migration and Puerto
Rico's Population Problem," in Hansen and Wells (eds.), *Puerto Rico: A
Study in Democratic Development*,
pp. 130–36; Ross, *The Long Uphill
Path*, p. 130; Anderson, *Party Politics*, pp. 8–9.

77. Lee, "Entrepreneurial Activities," p. 151.

78. Information supplied by Dr.
Haszard.

79. Davis in Hansen and Wells
(eds.), *Puerto Rico: A Study in
Democratic Development*, p. 119.

80. Barton, "Puerto Rico's Industrial Development Program,
1942–1960," p. 28.

81. *La Prensa*, Jan. 5, 1949, p.
1.

82. Lewis, *Puerto Rico: Freedom and Power*, pp. 135–36; see also
Cong. Record, 81st Cong., 2d Sess.,
June 20, 1950, p. A4560, June 12,
1950, p. A4615.

83. Ross, *The Long Uphill
Path*, p. 172.

84. Lewis, *Puerto Rico: Freedom and Power*, pp. 124–25; Moscoso in Hansen and Wells (eds.),
*Puerto Rico: A Study in Democratic
Development*, p. 68.

85. Ross, *The Long Uphill
Path*, p. 148–50, 135–55.

86. *La Prensa*, Sept. 10, 1948, p.
2. The letter was made public by
PIP leader Concepción de Gracia,
and was verified by a representative
of the firm. The *independentista*
was presumably trying to make political capital out of it for the November 1948 elections.

87. Ibid., Jan. 6, 1949, p. 1.

88. Ibid., Jan. 12, 1950, p. 1,
Oct. 25, 1950, p. 2.

89. *Report of the Governor of
Puerto Rico*, incorporated in the
*Hearings before the House Commit-
tee on Public Lands on HR 7674
and S. 3336*, 81st Cong., 1st Sess.,
July 12, 1949, pp. 1–12.

90. Muñoz Marín in Hansen
and Wells (eds.), *Puerto Rico: A
Study in Democratic Development*,
p. 5; see also Muñoz Marín, "Puerto

Rico and the U.S.: Their Future Together," *Foreign Affairs* 32 (July,
1954): 541–51.

CHAPTER ELEVEN

1. Correspondence with Abe
Fortas, June 9, 1971.
2. Correspondence with Fernós-
Isern, Sept. 14, 1973.
3. Correspondence with García
Méndez, June 30, 1973.
4. Gavan Daws, *Shoal of Time:
A History of the Hawaiian Islands*
(New York: Macmillan Co., 1968),
pp. 381–91; Ernest H. Gruening,
The State of Alaska (New York:
Random House, 1968), pp. 460–508.
For some other territories see: Earl
S. Pomeroy, *Pacific Outposts: Amer-
ican Strategy in Guam and Micro-
nesia* (Stanford: Stanford University
Press, 1951); Charles Beardsley,
Guam: Past and Present (Rutland,

Vermont: Charles E. Tuttle Co.,
1964).
5. García Méndez argues that
Congress could maintain "equal
conditions as now maintained" for
at least ten to fifteen years to help
in the transition to statehood economy as Congress had helped in the
Philippines' adjustment to independence and Alaskas' to statehood. He
further maintains that Puerto Rico
need not necessarily pay federal
taxation under statehood because
the "uniformity provision" of article
I of the United States Constitution
covers duties, imposts, and excises,
but not income tax. Correspondence
with García Méndez, June 30, 1973.
6. Correspondence with Geigel
Polanco, Mar. 27, 1973.
7. Correspondence with García
Méndez, June 30, 1973.
8. Correspondence with Fernós-
Isern, Sept. 14, 1973.

Bibliography

A. ARCHIVES

Records of the Bureau of Insular Affairs of the Department of War, National Archives, RG 126.

Records of the Legislative, Judicial, and Diplomatic Division in the National Archives, RG 148.

Records of the Office of Secretary of the Department of Interior, National Archives, RG 48.

Records of the Office of Territories of the Department of Interior, National Archives, Washington and the Washington National Records Center, Suitland, Maryland, RG 126.

B. PERSONAL PAPERS

The Papers of Edwin G. Arnold, 1933–1952, Harry S. Truman Library, Independence, Missouri.

The Papers of C. Jasper Bell, 1935–1949, Western Historical Manuscript Collection, University of Missouri at Columbia.

The Papers of Hugh A. Butler, 1945–1954, Nebraska State Historical Society, Lincoln, Nebraska.

The Papers of William A. Brophy, 1930–1952, Harry S. Truman Library, Independence, Missouri.

The Papers of Oscar L. Chapman, 1933–1953, Harry S. Truman Library, Independence, Missouri.

The Papers of Clark M. Clifford, 1945–1952, Harry S. Truman Library, Independence, Missouri.

The Papers of Warner W. Gardner, 1937–1947, Harry S. Truman Library, Independence, Missouri.

The Papers of Julius A. Krug, 1946–1952, Library of Congress, Manuscript Division, Washington, D.C.

The Papers of William D. Leahy, 1893–1952, Library of Congress, Manuscript Division, Washington, D.C.

The Papers of Philleo Nash, 1946–1952, Harry S. Truman Library, Independence, Missouri.

The Papers of William C. Rigby, 1935–1942, Library of Congress, Manuscript Division, Washington, D.C.

The Papers of Franklin D. Roosevelt, 1933–1945, Franklin D. Roosevelt Library, Hyde Park, New York.

The Papers of Samuel I. Rosenman, 1944–1952, Harry S. Truman Library, Independence, Missouri.

The Papers of Stephen J. Spingarn, 1933–1952, Harry S. Truman Library, Independence, Missouri.

The Papers of Charles W. Taussig, 1928–1948, Franklin D. Roosevelt Library, Hyde Park, New York.

The Papers of Harry S. Truman, 1940–1953, Harry S. Truman Library, Independence, Missouri.

The Papers of Rexford G. Tugwell up to 1936, Franklin D. Roosevelt Library, Hyde Park, New York.

C. PRINTED SOURCES: OFFICIAL DOCUMENTS

1. *Anglo-American Caribbean Commission*

Caribbean Commission Monthly Bulletin (Port-of-Spain, Trinidad: Caribbean Commission, 1947–1951), vols. 1–5.

The Caribbean Islands and the War: A Record of Progress Facing Stern Realities (Washington: Anglo-American Commission, 1943).

Report of the Anglo-American Caribbean Commission to the Governments of the United States and Great Britain for the year 1945 (Washington: Anglo-American Commission, 1946).

2. *Puerto Rican*

Documents on the Constitutional History of Puerto Rico (Washington: Office of the Commonwealth of Puerto Rico, 1964).

Memorandum of the Puerto Rican Independence Party to the United Nations, San Juan, Puerto Rico, 1953. (Copy supplied by Vicente Geigel Polanco.)

Naciones Unidas: Sesion Plenaria de la Asamblea General: Memorial del Partido Independentista Puertorriqueño, San Juan, Puerto Rico, Nov., 1953. (Copy supplied by Vicente Geigel Polanco.)

Notes and Comments on the Constitution of the Commonwealth of Puerto Rico (Washington, 1952).

Tugwell, Rexford G., *Changing the Colonial Climate* (San Juan, Bureau of Supplies, Printing and Transportation, 1942).

————, *Puerto Rican Public Papers* (San Juan: Service Office of the Government of Puerto Rico, 1945).

United Nations: Fourth Committee General Assembly: Supplementary Memorandum of the Puerto Rico Independence Party, New York, Oct. 26, 1953. (Copy supplied by Vicente Geigel Polanco.)

3. *United Nations*

Official Records of the General Assembly, 8th Sess., Fourth Committee, Trusteeship (Oct.–Nov.), 215–62.

Official Records of the General Assembly, 8th Sess., 459th Plenary Meeting (Nov., 1959), 305–21.

Resolutions Adopted by the General Assembly, 8th Sess., Res. 748, Supplement No. 17 (A/2630) (Nov., 1953), 747 (VIII), 25.

4. *United States*

Congressional Record, 74th to 82nd Congress, 1935–1952.

Fernós-Isern, Antonio, "Statement of Puerto Rico's New Political Status," *U.S. Department of State Bulletin*, 29 (Sept. 21, 1953): 392–98.

Hacket, William H., *The Nationalist Party* (For the Committee on Interior and Insular Affairs, Washington: U.S. Government Printing Office, 1951).

Hearings before the Senate Committee on Territories and Insular Affairs on the Nomination of Rexford G. Tugwell as Governor of Puerto Rico, 77th Cong., 1st Sess., Aug., 1941.

Hearings before the Subcommittee of the Senate Committee on Territories and Insular Affairs pursuant to S.Res.309, a resolution authorizing an investigation of economic and social conditions in Puerto Rico, 77th Cong., 2d Sess., Dec., 1942.

Hearings before the House Committee on Insular Affairs on HR 784, a bill to provide for the term of office of the Governor of Puerto Rico, 78th Cong., 1st Sess., Feb., 1943.

Hearings before the Subcommittee of the Committee on Territories and Insular Affairs pursuant to S.Res.26 authorizing investigation of economic and social conditions in Puerto Rico, 78th Cong., 1st Sess., Feb., 1943.

Hearings before the Subcommittee of the House Committee on Insular Affairs pursuant to H.Res.159 authorizing investigation of political, economic and social conditions in Puerto Rico, 78th Cong., 1st Sess., Apr.–Dec., 1943, Mar.–Apr., 1944.

Hearings before the Senate Committee on Territories and Insular Affairs pursuant to S.981, a bill to assist in relieving economic distress in Puerto Rico and the Virgin Islands, 78th Cong., 1st Sess., May 19–25, 1943.

Hearings before the Senate Committee on Territories and Insular Affairs on S.952, a bill to provide for the withdrawal of the sovereignty of the United States over Puerto Rico, 78th Cong., 1st Sess., May, 1943.

Hearings before the Subcommittee of the Senate Committee on Territories and Insular Affairs on S.1407, a bill to amend the Organic Act of Puerto Rico, 78th Cong., 1st Sess., Nov.–Dec., 1943.

Hearing before the House Committee on Insular Affairs on S.1407, a bill to amend the Organic Act of Puerto Rico, 78th Cong., 2d Sess., Aug. 26, 1944.

Hearings before the Senate Committee on Territories and Insular Affairs on S.227, a bill to provide for the withdrawal of the sovereignty of the United States over Puerto Rico, 79th Cong., 1st Sess., Mar., Apr., May, 1945.

Hearing before the Subcommittee on Territorial and Insular Possessions of the House Committee on Public Lands on HR 3309, a bill to amend the Organic Act of Puerto Rico, 80th Cong., 1st Sess., May 19, 1947.

Hearings before the House Committee on Public Lands on HR 7674 and S.3336, a bill to provide for the organization of a constitutional government by the people of Puerto Rico, 81st Cong., 1st Sess., July, 1949, Mar., May, June, 1950.

Hearing before the Subcommittee of the Senate Committee on Interior and Insular Affairs on S.3336, a bill to provide for the organization of a constitutional government by the people of Puerto Rico, 81st Cong., 2d Sess., May, 1950.

Hearings before the Senate Committee on Interior and Insular Affairs on S.J.Res.151, a joint resolution approving the constitution of the Commonwealth of Puerto Rico, 82d Cong., 2d Sess., Apr. and May, 1952.

Hearing before the House Committee on Interior and Insular Affairs on H.J.Res.430, a joint resolution approving the constitution of the Commonwealth of Puerto Rico, 82d Cong., 2d Sess., Apr. 25, 1952.

Hearing before the Senate Committee on Interior and Insular Affairs on S.2023, a bill to provide for amendments to the compact between the people of Puerto Rico and the United States, 86th Cong., 1st Sess., June 9, 1959.

Hearings before a Special Subcommittee of the Senate Committee on Interior and Insular Affairs on HR 9234, a bill to provide for amendments to the compact between the people of Puerto Rico and the United States, 86th Cong., 1st Sess., Dec., 1959.

Hearings before the Subcommittee on Territorial and Insular Affairs of the Committee on Interior and Insular Affairs on HR 5945 and other bills to establish a procedure for the prompt settlement in a democratic manner of the political status of Puerto Rico, 88th Cong., 1st Sess., May, 1963.

Hearings before the United States–Puerto Rico Commission on the Status of Puerto Rico, 89th Cong., 2d Sess., May–Dec., 1965.

House Document 304, 78th Cong., 1st Sess., Sept. 23, 1943.

House Reports Nos. 1399, 1467 and 1676, on hearings pursuant to H. Res. 159 authorizing the investigation of economic, social, and political conditions in Puerto Rico, 78th Cong., 2d Sess., Apr. 27, May 18, June 17, 1944.

House Report No. 2038 on HR 5570, a bill providing for the amendment of the Organic Act, 78th Cong., 2d Sess., Dec. 7, 1944.

House Report No. 497 on hearings pursuant to H.Res.159 authorizing the investigation of the political, social, and economic conditions in Puerto Rico, 79th Cong., 1st Sess., May, 1945.

House Report No. 455 on HR 3309, a bill to amend the Organic Act of Puerto Rico, 80th Cong., 1st Sess., May 26, 1947.

House Report No. 2035 on HR 6502, a bill to provide for the amending of the Organic Act of Puerto Rico, 80th Cong., 2d Sess., May 25, 1948.

House Report No. 2275 on S.3336, a bill to provide for the organization of constitutional government by the people of Puerto Rico, 81st Cong., 2d Sess., June 19, 1950.

House Report No. 1832 on H.J.Res.430, a joint resolution approving the constitution of the Commonwealth of Puerto Rico, 82d Cong., 2d Sess., Apr. 30, 1952.

House Report No. 1844 on H.J.Res.430, a joint resolution approving the constitution of the Commonwealth of Puerto Rico, 82d Cong., 2d Sess., May 6, 1952.

House Report No. 2350 on H.J.Res.430, a joint resolution approving the constitution of the Commonwealth of Puerto Rico, 82nd Cong., 2d Sess., June 28, 1952.

Meeting of the President's Committee to Revise the Organic Act of Puerto Rico, July 19, 1943–August 7, 1943 in the appendix of *Hearings before the Subcommittee of the Senate Committee of Territories and Insular Affairs on S.1407,* 78th Cong., 1st Sess., Nov.–Dec., 1943.

Public Law 600, 81st Cong., 2d Sess., July 3, 1950.

Public Law 447, 82d Cong., 2d Sess., July 3, 1952.

Public Papers of Harry S. Truman: Containing the Public Messages, Speeches, and Statements of the President in the series *Public Papers of the Presidents of the United States* (Washington: Government Printing Office, 1961), vols. 1–8.

Report of the United States–Puerto Rico Commission on the Status of Puerto Rico (Washington: Government Press, 1966).

Samuel I. Rosenman (ed.), *The Public Papers of Franklin D. Roosevelt*, vols. 2–13 (New York: Random House, 1938, Macmillan, 1941, and Harper and Brothers, 1950).

Senate Report No. 15 on S.40, a bill to amend the Organic Act of Puerto Rico, 78th Cong., 1st Sess., Jan. 21, 1943.

Senate Report No. 16 on hearings pursuant to S.Res.26 authorizing the investigation of economic and social conditions in Puerto Rico, 78th Cong., 1st Sess., Jan. 21, 1943.

Senate Report No. 628 on hearings pursuant to S.Res.26 authorizing investigation of economic and social conditions in Puerto Rico, 78th Cong., 1st Sess., Dec. 21, 1943.

Senate Report No. 659 on S.1407, a bill to amend the Organic Act of Puerto Rico, 78th Cong., 2d Sess., Feb. 2, 1944.

Senate Report No. 422 on HR 3309, a bill to amend the Organic Act of Puerto Rico, 80th Cong., 1st Sess., July, 1947.

Senate Report No. 1779 on S.3336, a bill to provide for the organization of a constitutional government by the people of Puerto Rico, 81st Cong., 2d Sess., June 6, 1950.

Senate Report No. 2365 on S.3336, a bill to provide for the organization of a constitutional government by the people of Puerto Rico, 81st Cong., 2d Sess., June 28, 1950.

Senate Report No. 1720 on H.J.Res.430, a joint resolution approving the constitution of the Commonwealth of Puerto Rico, 82d Cong., 2d Sess., June 10, 1952.

Status of Puerto Rico: Selected Background Studies Prepared for the United States–Puerto Rico Commission on the Status of Puerto Rico (Washington: U.S. Government Printing Office, 1966).

U.S. Tariff Commission (Washington: Government Printing Office, 1946).

D. BOOKS

Aitkin, Thomas, Jr., *Poet in the Fortress: The Story of Luis Muñoz Marin* (New York: New American Library, 1964).

Anderson, Robert W., *Party Politics in Puerto Rico* (Stanford: Stanford University Press, 1965).

Baer, Werner, *The Puerto Rican Economy and United States Economic Fluctuations* (Rio Piedras, San Juan: Social Science Research Center, University of Puerto Rico, 1962).

Benítez, José A., *Puerto Rico and the Political Destiny of America* (Birmingham, Ala.: Southwestern University Press, 1958).

Berbusse, Edward J., *The United States in Puerto Rico, 1898–1900* (Chapel Hill: University of North Carolina Press, 1966).

Bernstein, Barton J. (ed.), *Politics and Policies of the Truman Administration* (Chicago: Quadrangle Books, 1970).

Blanshard, Paul, *Democracy and Empire in the Caribbean* (New York: Macmillan and Company, 1947).

Brown, Wenzell, *Dynamite on Our Doorstep* (New York: Greenberg, 1945).

Calcott, Wilfred H., *The Caribbean Policy of the United States, 1890–1920* (New York: Octagon Books, 1942).

Clark, Victor S., et al., *Porto Rico and Its Progress* (Washington: Brookings Institution, 1930).

Cordova, Lieban, *Siete (7) años con Muñoz Marín; diario íntimo de un taquigrafo* (San Juan: Editorial Esther, 1945).

Creamer, Daniel and Henrietta, *Gross Product of Puerto Rico* (Rio Piedras, San Juan: University of Puerto Rico, 1949).

Creamer, Daniel, *The Net Income of the Puerto Rican Economy, 1940–1944* (Rio Piedras, San Juan: University of Puerto Rico Press, 1947).

Diffie, Bailey and Justine, *Puerto Rico: A Broken Pledge* (New York: Vanguard Press, 1931).

Dorvillier, William, *Workshop U.S.A.: The Challenge of Puerto Rico* (New York: Coward–McCann, 1962).

Eastman, Samuel E., and Daniel Marx, Jr., *Ships and Sugar: An Evaluation of Puerto Rican Offshore Shipping* (Rio Piedras, San Juan: Social Research Center, University of Puerto Rico Press, 1953).

Fernós-Isern, Antonio, *Puerto Rico: libre y federado* (San Juan: Imprenta Venezuela, 1951).

Friedrich, Carl J., *Puerto Rico: Middle Road to Freedom* (New York: Rinehart and Co., 1959).

Garver, Earl S., and Ernest B. Fincher, *Puerto Rico: Unresolved Problem* (Elgin, Ill.: Brethren Publishing House, 1945).

Goodsell, Charles T., *Administration of a Revolution: Executive Reform in Puerto Rico under Governor Tugwell, 1941–1946* (Cambridge: Harvard University Press, 1965).

Greene, Theodore P., *American Imperialism in 1898* (Boston: Heath and Co., 1955).

Hancock, Ralph, *Puerto Rico: A Success Story* (New York: D. Van Nostrand Co., 1960).

Hansen, Millard, and Henry Wells (eds.), *Puerto Rico: A Study in Democratic Development* in the series *Annals of the American Academy of Political and Social Science*, vol. 285 (Philadelphia, 1953).

Hanson, Earl Parker, *Puerto Rico, Ally for Progress* (Princeton: Van Nostrand, 1962).

————, *Puerto Rico: Land of Wonders* (New York: Alfred A. Knopf, 1960).

————, *Transformation: The Story of Modern Puerto Rico* (New York: Simon and Schuster, 1955).

Hibben, Thomas, and Rafael Picó, *Industrial Development of Puerto Rico and the Virgin Islands of the United States* (Port-of-Spain, Trinidad: Caribbean Commission, 1948).

Huebener, Theodore, *Puerto Rico Today* (New York: Holt, Rinehart and Winston, 1960).

Ickes, Harold, *The Secret Diary of Harold Ickes, The First Thousand Days*, vol. 1 (New York: Simon and Schuster, 1953).

————, *The Secret Diary of Harold Ickes, The Inside Triangle*, vol. 2 (New York: Simon and Schuster, 1953).

Ingram, James C., *Regional Payments Mechanisms: The Case of Puerto Rico* (Chapel Hill: University of North Carolina Press, 1962).

Lewis, Gordon K., *Puerto Rico: A Case Study in the Problems of Contemporary American Federalism* (Port-of-Spain, Trinidad: Office of the Premier of Trinidad and Tobago, 1960).

————, *The Growth of the Modern West Indies* (New York: MR Press, 1968).

————, *Puerto Rico: Freedom and Power in the Caribbean* (New York: Monthly Review Press, 1963).

Lockett, Edward B., *The Puerto Rico Problem* (New York: Exposition Press, 1964).

Lugo-Silva, Enrique, *The Tugwell Administration, 1941–1946* (Rio Piedras: Editorial Cultura, 1955).

McGuire, Edna, *Puerto Rico: Bridge to Freedom* (New York: Macmillan, 1963).

Malcolm, George A., *American Colonial Careerist: Half a Century of Official Life and Personal Experience in the Philippines and Puerto Rico* (Boston: Christopher Publishing House, 1957).

Marcantonio, Vito, *I Vote My Conscience: Debates, Speeches and Writings of Vito Marcantonio, 1935–1950* (New York: Book Craftsmen Associates, 1956).

Mathews, Thomas, *Luis Muñoz Marin: A Concise Biography* (New York: American R.D.M. Corp., 1967).

————, *Puerto Rican Politics and the New Deal* (Gainesville: University of Florida Press, 1960).

Mayhew, David R., *Party Loyalty Among Congressmen: The Difference between Democrats and Republicans, 1947–1962* (Cambridge: Harvard University Press, 1966).

Norris, Marianna, *Father and Son for Freedom: the Story of Puerto Rico's Luis Muñoz Rivera and Luis Muñoz Marin* (New York: Dodd, Mead and Co., 1968).

Packard, Walter E., *The Land Authority and Democratic Processes in Puerto Rico* (Rio Piedras, San Juan: University of Puerto Rico Press, 1948).

Pagán, Bolivar, *Historia de los partidos politicos puertorriqueños, 1898–1956* (San Juan: Libreria Campos, 1959).

Page, Homer, *Puerto Rico: The Quiet Revolution* (New York: Viking Press, 1963).

Perkins, Dexter, *The United States and the Caribbean* (Cambridge: Harvard University Press, 1966).

Perloff, Harvey S. (ed.), *Economic Development of Puerto Rico, 1940–50 and 1951–1960* (Santurce: Puerto Rico Planning Board, 1951).

————, *Puerto Rico's Economic Future* (Chicago: University of Chicago Press, 1950).

Petrullo, Vicenzo, *Puerto Rican Paradox* (Philadelphia: University of Philadelphia Press, 1947).

Phillips, Cabell, *The Truman Presidency: The History of a Triumphant Succession* (Baltimore: Penguin Books, 1966).

Polanco, Vicente Geigel, *La farsa del Estado Libre Asociado* (Rio Piedras: Editorial Edil, 1972).

Proudfoot, Mary, *Britain and the United States in the Caribbean: A Comparative Study in Methods of Development* (London: Faber and Faber, 1954).

Roosevelt, Theodore, Jr., *Colonial Policies of the United States* (New York: Doubleday and Co., 1937).

Ross, David F., *The Long Uphill Path: A Historical Study of Puerto Rico's Program of Economic Development* (San Juan: Talleres Gráficos Interamericanos, 1966).

Rowe, L. S., *The Supreme Court and the Insular Cases*, in the series *Annals of American Academy of Political and Social Change*, vol. 18 (Philadelphia, 1901).

Sady, Emil J., *The United Nations and Dependent Peoples* (Washington: Brookings Institution, 1956).

Sammons, Robert L., and Belen H. Cestero, *Balance of Expenditure Payments of Puerto Rico: 1942–1946* (Rio Piedras, San Juan: Editorial Universitaria, 1948).

Shuckman, Roy, *Puerto Rican Neighbor* (Pendle Hill, Pennsylvania, 1954).

Stead, William H., *Fomento—the Economic Development of Puerto Rico* (Washington: National Planning Association, 1958).

Sterling, Philip, and Maria Brau, *The Quiet Rebels, Four Puerto Rican Leaders: José Celsó Barbosa, Luis Muñoz Rivera, José de Diego, Luis Muñoz Marín* (Garden City: Doubleday and Company, 1968).

Taylor, Milton C., *Industrial Tax Exemption in Puerto Rico* (Madison: University of Wisconsin Press, 1957).

Torregrosa Liceaga, Angel M., *Luis Muñoz Marín, su vida y su patriotica obra* (San Juan: Editorial Esther, 1944).

Tugwell, Rexford Guy, *The Art of Politics as Practiced by Three Great*

Americans: Franklin Delano Roosevelt, Luis Muñoz Marin, and Fiorello H. La Guardia (Garden City: Doubleday and Co., 1958).

——, *The Stricken Land: The Story of Puerto Rico* (Garden City: Doubleday and Co., 1947).

Wells, Henry, *Government Financing of Political Parties in Puerto Rico* (Princeton: Cititzens' Research Foundation, 1961).

——, *The Modernization of Puerto Rico: A Political Study of Changing Values and Institution* (Cambridge: Harvard University Press, 1969).

E. ARTICLES

Arnold, Edwin G., "Self-Government in U.S. Territories," *Foreign Affairs*, 25 (July, 1947): 655–66.

Benner, Thomas E., "American Difficulties in Puerto Rico," *Foreign Affairs*, 8 (July, 1930): 609–19.

Boorstin, Daniel, "Self Discovery in Puerto Rico," *Yale Review*, 45 (Winter, 1956): 229–45.

Clark, Charles E., and William D. Rogers, "The New Judiciary Act of Puerto Rico: A Definite Court Reorganization," *Yale Law Journal*, 61 (Nov., 1952): 1147–71.

Durand, Rafael, "Building an Industrial Base: Puerto Rico and Moscoso," *Vital Speeches of the Day*, 25 (Aug. 15, 1959): 647–50.

Fischman, Jerome, "The Church in Politics: The 1960 Election in Puerto Rico," *Western Political Quarterly*, 18 (Dec., 1965): 821–39.

Fliess, Peter, "Puerto Rico's Political Status under the New Constitution," *Western Political Quarterly*, 5 (Dec., 1952): 635–56.

García-Passalacqua, J. M., "The Alternative: A Federal Solution to the Colonial Problem," *Documentos Básicos-Primer Instituto de Verano de Relaciones Internacionales* (University of Puerto Rico, 1959), 69–79.

——, "The Judicial Process and the Status of Puerto Rico," *Revista Juridica de la Universidad de Puerto Rico*, 30 (1961).

——, "The Legality of the Associated Statehood of Puerto Rico," *Inter-American Law Review*, 4 (July–Dec., 1962): 287–315.

Gatell, Frank Otto, "Independence Rejected: Puerto Rico and the Tydings Bill of 1936," *Hispanic American Historical Review*, 38 (Feb., 1958): 25–44.

Helfeld, David M., "Congressional Intent and Attitude toward Public Law 600 and the Constitution of the Commonwealth of Puerto Rico," *Revista Juridica de la Universidad de Puerto Rico*, 21 (May–June, 1952): 225–315.

Holmes, Olive, "Puerto Rico: An American Responsibility," *Foreign Policy Reports*, 22 (Mar., 1947): 282–91.

Jones, Joseph M., "Caribbean Laboratory: There We Can Learn the Potentials of the U.S. Influence on World Colonial Policy," *Fortune*, 29 (Feb., 1944): 121.

————, "Let's Begin with Puerto Rico," *Fortune*, 29 (May, 1944): 133–200.

Leibowitz, Arnold H., "The Applicability of Federal Law to the Commonwealth of Puerto Rico," *Georgetown Law Journal*, 56 (1967).

Lewis, W. Arthur, "Industrial Development in Puerto Rico," *The Caribbean Economic Review*, 1 (Dec., 1949): 153–76.

Lewis, Gordon K., "Puerto Rico: A Case-study of Change in an Underdeveloped Area," *Journal of Politics*, 17 (Nov., 1955): 614–50.

————, "Puerto Rico: A New Constitution in American Government," *Journal of Politics*, 15 (Feb., 1953): 42–66.

Magruder, Calvert, "The Commonwealth Status of Puerto Rico," *University of Pittsburgh Law Review*, 15 (1953–1954): 1–33.

Massolo, Arthur, "Puerto Rico's Muñoz Marín," *New York Post* (March 9, 1959–March 15, 1959).

Morales, Carríon Arturo, "The Historical Roots and Political Significance of Puerto Rico," in A. Curtis Wilgus (ed.), *The Caribbean: British, Dutch, French, United States* (Gainesville: University of Florida Press, 1958), 154–61.

Morales-Yordán, Jorge, "The Constitutional and International Status of the Commonwealth of Puerto Rico," *Revista del Colegio de Abogados de Puerto Rico*, 5 (1957).

Muñoz Marín, Luis, "A New Idea in Statehood," *United Nations World*, 5 (Feb., 1951): 57–58.

————, "Americanization: Three Cases," *American Mercury*, 21 (Sept., 1930): 84–96.

————, "Crisis in Latin America—Operation Seeing Is Believing," *Vital Speeches of the Day*, 28 (Jan. 1, 1962): 175–79.

————, "The 'Ninety-Eight Percent American' in Puerto Rico," *New Republic*, 29 (Jan. 4, 1962): 151–53.

————, "Plight of Puerto Rico," *New Republic*, 108 (Jan. 11, 1943): 51–52.

————, "Plight of Puerto Rico," *Political Science Quarterly*, 57 (Dec., 1942): 481–503.

————, "Porto Rico: The American Colony," *The Nation*, 120 (Apr. 8, 1925): 379–82.

————, "Porto Rico: The American Colony," in Ernest Gruening (ed.), *These United States* (New York: Boni and Liveright, 1924).

————, "Puerto Rico and the United States: Their Future Together," *Foreign Affairs*, 32 (1954): 541–51.

————, "Puerto Rico Does Not Want to be a State," *New York Times Magazine* (Aug. 16, 1945): 35–40.

————, "The Sad Case of Porto Rico," *American Mercury*, 16 (1929): 136–41.

————, "Song-maker of a Continent," *American Mercury*, 4 (Mar., 1925): 337–41.

————, "We've Come a Long Way in a Peaceful Revolution," *U.S. News and World Report* (Mar. 28, 1960): 58–59.

————, "What Next in Puerto Rico?" *The Nation*, 129 (Nov. 20, 1929): 608–9.

Nader, Ralph, "The Commonwealth Status in Puerto Rico," *Harvard Law Review*, 33 (Dec. 13, 1956): 1–8.

Pomeroy, Earl S., "Election of the Governor of Puerto Rico," *Southwestern Social Science Quarterly*, 23 (Mar., 1943): 355–60.

"Puerto Rico's Bootstraps," *The Economist* (London), 184 (1957): 546.

Robinson, Donald, "Muñoz Marín—Puerto Rico's 'Poet Leader,'" *Reader's Digest*, 69 (Nov., 1956): 113–17.

Rosenn, Keith S., "Puerto Rican Land Reform: The History of an Instructive Experiment," *Yale Law Journal*, 73 (1963): 334–56.

Segal, Stanley R., "Puerto Rico's Constitution," *Mercer Law Review*, 8 (1957): 361–63.

Tugwell, Rexford Guy, "The Fuel of Magnificence: The Case of Puerto Rico," *Confluence*, 4 (Oct., 1955): 266–91.

————, "Rebirth of an Underdeveloped Island," *Saturday Review*, 38 (Feb. 12, 1955): 16–17.

Wells, Henry, "Administrative Reorganization in Puerto Rico," *Western Political Quarterly*, 9 (1956): 470–90.

————, "Constitutional Conventions in Hawaii, Puerto Rico, and Alaska," in W. Brooke Graves (ed.), *Major Problems in State Constitutional Revision* (Chicago: Public Administration Service, 1960).

————, "Ideology and Leadership in Puerto Rican Politics," *American Political Science Review*, 49 (1955): 22–38.

————, "Puerto Rico," in Paul T. David, et al. (eds.), *Presidential Nominating Politics* (Baltimore: Johns Hopkins Press, 1954).

————, "Puerto Rico's Association with the United States," *Caribbean Studies*, 5 (Apr., 1965): 6–22.

F. NEWSPAPERS

El Mundo (San Juan), Nov., 1948–Dec., 1951.
La Prensa (New York), 1940–1950.
New York Times, 1936–1952.
Washington Post, 1940–1942, 1946–1947.

G. UNPUBLISHED MATERIAL

Barbosa, Pilar, "The Political Status of Porto Rico in relation to the United States" (M.A. thesis, Clark University, 1925).

Barton, H. C., Jr., "Puerto Rico's Industrial Development Program, 1942–1960," (Paper presented at Center for International Affairs, Cambridge, Harvard University, Oct. 29, 1959).

Brownback, Annadrue H., "Congressional and Insular Opposition to Puerto Rican Autonomy" (Ph.D. diss., University of Alabama, 1964).

Carpenter, Bruce Rogers, "Puerto Rico's Planned Development of Tourism" (Ph.D. diss., American University, 1964).

Díaz-Rojas, Armando, "Financing Economic Development in Puerto Rico, 1942 to Date" (Ph.D. diss., New York University, 1964).

Fischman, Jerome T., "The Rise and Development of the Political Party in Puerto Rico under Spanish and American Rule and the Historical Significance of the Subsequent Emergence and Growth of the Popular Party" (Ph.D. diss., New York University, 1962).

Freyre, Jorge Fabio Serra, "External and Domestic Financing in the Economic Development of Puerto Rico: Analysis and Projections" (Ph.D. diss., Yale University, 1966).

Gonzales, Luis Manuel, "The Economic Development of Puerto Rico from 1898–1940" (Ph.D. diss., University of Florida, 1964).

Gould, Lyman Jay, "The Foraker Act: The Roots of American Colonial Policy" (Ph.D. diss., University of Michigan, 1958).

Gray, Lois Spier, "Economic Incentives to Labor Mobility: The Puerto Rican Case" (Ph.D. diss., Columbia University, 1966).

Haddad, Donald Francis M., "The Political Development of the Puerto Rican Government under United States Jurisdiction" (M.S. thesis, Georgetown University, Washington, 1956).

Hernandez, Joseph William, "The Sociological Implications of Return Migration in Puerto Rico: An Exploratory Study" (Ph.D. diss., University of Minnesota, 1964).

Hines, Calvin Warner, "United States Diplomacy in the Caribbean during World War II" (Ph.D. diss., University of Texas, 1968).

Honey, John C., "Public Personnel Administration in Puerto Rico" (Ph.D. diss., Sryacuse University, 1950).

Hunter, Robert J., "The Historical Development of the Relationship Between the United States and Puerto Rico, 1898–1963" (Ph.D. diss., University of Pittsburgh, 1963).

Kidder, Frederick E., "The Political Concepts of Luis Muñoz Rivera (1859–1916) of Puerto Rico" (Ph.D. diss., University of Florida, 1965).

Larrieux Suárez, J., "National Policy Toward the Political Status of Puerto Rico," A Paper submitted in a Department of Political Science Seminar, University of Wisconsin, Madison.

Lee, Hy Sang, "The Entrepreneurial Activities of the Government in the Economic Development of Puerto Rico" (Ph.D. diss., University of Wisconsin, 1965).

Le Veness, Frank Paul, "The Commonwealth of Puerto Rico: Democracy Thrives in the Caribbean" (Ph.D. diss., St. John's University, 1968).

"Luis Muñoz Marín: Collected Speeches, July 25, 1952–August 28, 1957," An unpublished collection located at University of Florida, Gainesville.

McIntosh, William, "The Development of Political Democracy in Puerto Rico" (Ph.D. diss., University of Minnesota, 1953).

Molinea, James Harold, "The Concept of the Caribbean in the Latin American Policy of the United States" (Ph.D. diss., American University, 1968).

Morales-Yordán, Jorge, "The Status of Puerto Rico in International Law" (M.A. thesis, American University, Washington, 1957).

Muñiz, Dolores, "Puerto Rico under the Administration of Governor Yager, 1913–1921" (Ph.D. diss., University of Michigan, 1945).

Muñoz Amato, Pedro, "Executive Reorganization in the Government of Puerto Rico under the Elective Governor Act of 1947" (Ph.D. diss., Harvard University, 1950).

"The Mind of Puerto Rico: Address by Resident Commissioner Antonio Fernós-Isern," delivered on Feb. 27, 1947, at Rollins College, Florida, in *Mind of America* series (Xerox copy of the address supplied by Rollins College).

O'Leary, Daniel, "The Development of Political Parties in Puerto Rico under American Occupation" (Ph.D. diss., Boston College, 1936).

Perkins, Ernest R., "The Development of the Colonial Policy of the United States to the Passage of the Jones Act for the Philippines and Puerto Rico, 1916–1917" (Ph.D. diss., Clark University, 1930).

Sanchez-Aran, Frank, "Financial Aspects of Economic Development in Puerto Rico" (Ph.D. diss., New York University, 1963).

Senff, Earl K., "Puerto Rico under American Rule" (Ph.D. diss., University of Kentucky, 1948).

Stahl, John Emery, "Economic Development through Land Reform in Puerto Rico" (Ph.D. diss., Iowa State University, 1966).

Vázquez, J. L., "The Demographic Evolution of Puerto Rico" (Ph.D. diss., University of Chicago, 1964).

Vélez, Luis Antonio Aquino, "Puerto Rican Press Reaction to the Shift from Spanish to United States Sovereignty, 1898–1917" (Ph.D. diss., Columbia University, 1968).

H. PRIVATE CORRESPONDENCE

Correspondence with Antonio Fernós-Isern, June 24, Aug. 15, Aug., 1972, June 22, Sept. 14, Oct. 16, 1973.

Correspondence with Abe Fortas, May 17, June 9, 1971.

Correspondence with Miguel A. García Méndez, Feb. 3, May 29, June 28, June 30, Sept. 14, 1973.

Correspondence with Vicente Geigel Polanco, Jan. 31, Mar. 27, July 11, 1973.
Correspondence with Frank K. Haszard, Dec. 12, 1972.
Correspondence with Luis Muñoz Marín, Jan. 10, 1973.

Index